Taxation of Business Entities

STEVEN A. BANK

Paul Hastings Professor of Business Law
University of California, Los Angeles

Fifteenth Edition

GILBERT

Gilbert Law Summaries is a trademark registered in the U.S. Patent and Trademark Office

© 2011 Thomson/West
© 2016 LEG, Inc. d/b/a West Academic
    444 Cedar Street, Suite 700
    St. Paul, MN 55101
    1-877-888-1330

West, West Academic Publishing, and West Academic are trademarks of West Publishing Corporation, used under license.

Printed in the United States of America

ISBN: 978-1-63459-930-6

Summary of Contents

Capsule Summary

I. PARTNERSHIP TAXATION

A. INTRODUCTION

Income of a partnership is taxed to the partners, but the partnership files an information return.

B. CLASSIFICATION OF ENTITY AS PARTNERSHIP OR CORPORATION

1. Introduction

Traditionally, the courts and the Internal Revenue Service ("IRS") classified organizations as corporations (separate entities subject to corporate tax) or as partnerships (pass-through entities not subject to corporate tax) based on a four-factor test. This approach was difficult to apply, particularly to limited partnerships and newer forms of unincorporated business entities, such as limited liability companies ("LLCs") and limited liability partnerships ("LLPs"). In 1997, the Treasury abandoned the four-factor test and substituted a "check-the-box" system under which taxpayers can elect how their unincorporated business entities should be taxed.

2. Check-the-Box System for Unincorporated Business Entities

The check-the-box system applies to *all unincorporated business entities*, including entities with a single owner. Whether a business organization is an entity for federal tax purposes is determined by federal tax law rather than by state law.

a. Multiple-Owner Entities

Under the "check-the-box" system, an unincorporated business entity with two or more owners, such as a partnership, limited partnership, LLC, or LLP, generally is taxed as a partnership unless it elects to be taxed as a corporation. There is an exception for publicly traded partnerships, which are taxed as corporations.

b. Single-Owner Entities

Certain single-owner unincorporated business organizations may be treated as entities under the federal tax laws. Under the "check-the-box" system, an unincorporated business entity with a single owner can elect to be taxed as a corporation or to be treated as a sole proprietorship (essentially disregarded for tax purposes).

c. Strategy

Because the partnership tax scheme is more flexible than the corporate tax scheme and avoids double taxation of profits, it is usually more advantageous for an unincorporated entity to be taxed as a partnership.

3. Corporations

An entity that is incorporated under a federal or state statute (or certain foreign statutes) *must be taxed as a corporation.* However, corporations can elect under Subchapter S to be taxed in a manner similar to partnerships. (*See infra*, p. 165 *et seq.*)

4. Trusts

Normally, trusts created by a will or inter vivos declaration are subject to tax under the trust rules. However, business trusts normally are taxed as corporations.

C. ANTI-ABUSE REGULATIONS

1. Introduction

The partnership tax provisions in subchapter K are quite flexible, and taxpayers have often taken advantage of them to avoid or defer tax or shift tax burdens. To curb such activity, the Treasury adopted a set of anti-abuse regulations intending to permit taxpayers to conduct joint business activities through the flexible partnership form without an entity-level tax only if the partnership is bona fide and only for partnership transactions entered into for a substantial business purpose. When such is not the case, the regulations empower the Commissioner to recast the transactions. For example, the purported *partnership may be disregarded* and its assets and activities considered to be owned and conducted by one or more of the purported partners; *one or more of the purported partners may not be treated as a partner*; a claimed *tax treatment may be otherwise adjusted or modified*; etc.

2. When Remedies Applicable

The anti-abuse remedies may be applied once it is determined that a partnership was formed or used for the principal purpose of reducing substantially the present value of the partners' aggregate federal tax liability in a manner inconsistent with the intent of subchapter K, considering *all of the facts and circumstances* surrounding the case.

D. DEFINITION OF PARTNERSHIP

1. What Is a Partnership

A partnership is any business venture that is not a trust, estate, or corporation.

a. Investment Partnerships

A partnership used solely for investment (nonbusiness) purposes can elect not to be taxed as a partnership. Each partner accounts separately for his own share of the income and expenses.

b. Joint Ventures

A joint venture is a partnership created to carry out a single business venture. It is subject to the same tax rules as other partnerships. Whether there is a joint venture depends on whether the parties *intended* to go into business together, sharing profits and control.

2. Family Partnerships

a. Capital-Intensive Partnerships

A family partnership can effectively split income if capital is a *material income-producing factor*, the interests were in fact transferred to the donees, and the donor receives reasonable compensation for services from the partnership.

b. Non-Capital-Intensive Partnerships

A family partnership can effectively split income even though capital is not a material income-producing factor, as long as each donee contributed capital or services.

E. CURRENT PARTNERSHIP INCOME

1. General Rule

Allocation of partnership income and deductions is determined by the partnership agreement.

a. Partners Taxed as Individuals

The partnership itself pays no tax. Instead, partners reflect the partnership net income or loss on their own returns.

b. Certain Items Treated Separately

Some items, such as charitable contributions, must be stated separately from net gain or loss because they will have a *different effect on each partner* depending on her tax position.

c. Character of Items

An item of partnership income or a deduction has the same character on a partner's individual return as if it had been realized by the partner directly.

d. Deduction of Losses

If the partnership suffers a loss, the partners deduct the loss on their personal returns.

(1) Limitation

However, such losses are deductible by a partner only to the extent of her basis in her partnership interest. Losses are not deductible by a partner who has no basis, or by a partner who already has deducted her basis in full.

e. Effect on Basis

The basis of a partner's interest in the partnership is increased by his distributive share of income and decreased by partnership distributions and the partner's share of losses and nondeductible partnership expenditures.

f. Partnership Tax Return

A partnership files a return for information purposes, stating items of income and certain deductions.

g. Special Allocations

The partnership agreement may provide that specific items, such as depreciation, shall be allocated among the partners in a ratio different from the general profit-sharing formula in the agreement so long as the special allocation has *substantial economic effect* (*i.e.*, there must be an economic benefit or burden to the partner to match the tax allocation, both in the year of allocation and over the life of the partnership). A *minimum gain chargeback* or deficit restoration provision is needed in the case of *nonrecourse deductions*.

h. Year in Which Taxable

Partnership income is taxable to (or partnership loss is deductible by) partners on the *last day* of the *partnership's taxable year*.

(1) Limitation

The partnership must use the calendar year unless its majority partner uses a different year. It may use yet a different taxable year if it can show a business purpose for doing so.

(2) Closing of Partnership Year

(a) Termination of Partnership

If the partnership terminates, the taxable year closes as to all partners.

(b) Events That Do Not Close the Taxable Year

The death of a partner, entry of a new partner, liquidation of a partner's interest, or the sale or exchange of a partner's interest does *not* close the taxable year.

1) Sale of Individual Partner's Interest

If the partnership year closes as to a particular partner (*e.g.*, due to the sale of his entire partnership interest), then that partner's tax return for the year in which this event occurred must reflect his share of all partnership activities that preceded the date of closing.

2) Death of Partner

Formerly, a partner's death was not like other terminations, but now it is: On a partner's death, the partner's year closes on that date and profits and losses are reported on his final return. Profits and losses occurring after the partner's death are reported on his estate tax returns if the estate remains a partner.

3) Admission of New Partners

When there is a change in partnership interests during the year (*e.g.*, by admission of a new partner), the various items of income and deduction must be allocated between the partners for the periods before and after the change.

i. Cancellation of Debt Income

A taxpayer must recognize cancellation of debt ("COD") income when a debt is canceled for less than its full amount. However, the Code provides for numerous exceptions to COD income, including an exception that applies when a taxpayer is insolvent. When a partnership debt is canceled, the partnership has COD income but the various exceptions are applied at the partner level. Note that the IRS recently announced that a partner's basis is now increased by his share of the partnership's cancellation of debt income regardless of the income exclusion because of his *insolvency.*

2. Transactions Between Partner and Partnership

a. Treating Partner as Stranger

When a partner is not acting in his capacity as "partner," he can deal with his partnership as if he were a stranger. Thus, if he loans money to his partnership, the interest is taxable to him and deductible by the partnership.

b. Guaranteed Payments

Guaranteed payments are payments to partners made *without regard to the net income* of the partnership, such as salary, a management bonus based on *gross returns*, or a preferred return on capital invested in the partnership. They are taxed as *ordinary income* to the recipient (not when received, but when the partnership's *taxable year closes*), and are deductible by the partnership.

(1) Capitalization

If the services confer a long-term benefit (in excess of one year) on the partnership, they must be capitalized.

(2) Other Cash Distributions

The treatment of salaries received by partners is quite different from other cash distributions to partners, which are not taxed to the partners, but rather only reduce their basis.

c. Certain Losses Disallowed

A partner cannot deduct a loss on his sale of property to the partnership if he directly or indirectly owns *more than 50%* of the interest in the partnership.

d. Sales at Gain

Similarly, if assets are sold by a partner to the partnership at a gain, the gain is ordinary income if the partner owns *more than 50%* of the partnership and the asset is not a capital asset in the partnership's hands.

F. CONTRIBUTIONS OF PROPERTY TO THE PARTNERSHIP

1. Contributions of Property—Nonrecognition Rule

Neither a partner nor the partnership recognizes income when the partner contributes property to the partnership, and the partnership takes over his adjusted basis. The partnership's basis is known as *"inside basis."*

a. Subsequent Partnership Disposition

When the partnership sells the property, the gain or loss is recognized and divided among the partners in proportion to their partnership interest, except for gain or loss built in at the time of the contribution, which are allocated to the contributing partner.

2. Contribution of Services

a. Capital Interest

A partner has a capital interest in her partnership if she has a right to a pro rata share of partnership assets if the partnership is dissolved. A partner's *receipt of a capital interest for services* is immediately taxable on the value of that interest.

b. Profits Interest

A profits interest allows a partner to share in future profits of the partnership, but not in its assets. The IRS generally does not treat *receipt of a profits interest* as income; generally the partner is treated as having income only when the profits themselves are received.

c. Assignment of Income

If upon becoming a partner, a partner assigns all future fees earned from a particular client, and fees are later collected from that client based on the partner's services, the IRS contended that under traditional assignment of income principles, the fee should be taxed to the partner. The Tax Court, however, has held that under partnership principles (*e.g.*, partnership is a separate entity), fees earned by the partner after becoming a partner should be taxed to partnership.

3. Basis of Partnership Interest

Generally, a partner's interest in the partnership (called *"outside basis"*) initially is equal to the adjusted basis of what the partner contributes for the interest. Outside basis then rises when the partner's share of partnership liabilities increases and falls when the partner's share of the partnership's liabilities decreases. Liabilities are allocated as follows:

a. **Recourse Liabilities**

Recourse liabilities (*i.e.*, debts that one or more partners are personally liable to repay) are allocated among partners in accordance with the economic risk that each bears with respect to the liability, under a worst-case scenario.

b. **Limited Partnerships**

In a limited partnership, generally all recourse liabilities are allocated to the general partner(s) (because generally only they are liable on recourse liabilities) *except in unusual cases* where the partnership agreement requires a limited partner to repay any deficit in the partner's capital account or to reimburse the general partner(s) for any loss.

c. **Nonrecourse Liabilities**

Nonrecourse liabilities are debts that the debtor has no personal obligation to repay. In general, nonrecourse liabilities are shared between the partners based on their share of partnership *profits*. As a result, both limited and general partners increase outside basis by reason of nonrecourse liabilities.

4. **Limits on Deduction of Partnership Losses**

a. **At Risk Rules**

A partner can deduct partnership losses only to the extent of his basis. Moreover, such deductions are not permitted beyond the amount he has placed "at risk" in the partnership (*i.e.*, his actual contributions and those partnership liabilities for which he can be held personally responsible).

b. **Passive Loss**

Partners *cannot* deduct losses from passive activities (*e.g.*, real estate rental) in excess of income from such sources. A passive activity is a trade or business in which the partner does not *materially participate*, which requires involvement on a regular, continuous, and substantial basis. Passive losses in excess of passive gains, however, may be carried forward to be used against passive gains in future years. A disallowed loss can also be deducted upon a taxable disposition of the property.

(1) **Exception—Real Estate Professionals**

A real estate professional can deduct passive losses from rental real estate without limit. A real estate professional is a taxpayer who performs more than 750 hours of service in real property trades or businesses in which the taxpayer materially participates.

G. **SALES OF PARTNERSHIP INTERESTS**

1. **General Rule**

A partnership interest is a capital asset. When it is sold, the transferor-partner recognizes capital gain or loss.

2. **Exception—Hot Assets**

To the extent the amount realized is attributable to the partner's interests in *unrealized receivables and inventory items*, the gain is *ordinary income* to the selling partner. *Depreciation recapture* is treated as an unrealized receivable.

3. **Liabilities**

If a partner sells a partnership interest, his amount realized includes his share of partnership liabilities.

4. **Basis of Partnership Assets After Transfer of Interest**

   a. **General Rule**

   Ordinarily, the basis of assets in a partnership is not changed merely because a partnership interest has been sold.

   b. **Special Basis Adjustment**

   The partnership can *elect to increase* the basis of partnership assets for the benefit of the buyer of a partnership interest.

   c. **Required Basis Adjustment**

   The partnership **must** adjust the inside basis of partnership property downward with respect to the transferee partner's interest if there is a built-in loss excess of $250,000 immediately following a transfer of a partnership interest.

5. **Termination of Partnerships**

   a. **Consequence**

   If a partnership terminates, all income or loss to the date of the termination must be reflected on the returns of the partners for the *year in which the termination occurs*. On termination, the partnership's assets are deemed distributed to the partners; if they continue the business, this would be treated as a contribution of assets to a new partnership.

   b. **Events That Terminate Partnership**

   (1) **Discontinuance of Business**

   If no part of the business of the partnership continues to be carried on by any of its partners, the partnership is terminated.

   (2) **Sale of Interest**

   A sale of *50% or more* of partnership interests terminates the partnership and requires that income earned up to the date of termination be taxed to the partners.

H. PARTNERSHIP DISTRIBUTIONS AND BASIS ADJUSTMENTS

1. **General Rule**

   Generally, the *distribution* of cash or property by a partnership to a partner is *not* a taxable event, either to the partnership or to the partner. Instead, the basis of the interest is reduced, both by any money distributed and by the partnership's basis in distributed assets.

   a. **Distribution of Cash or Marketable Securities**

   If a partnership distributes cash or marketable securities (*e.g.*, stocks and bonds) to a partner, the partner recognizes gain *if* the cash plus the fair market value of the marketable securities *exceeds the partner's outside basis*.

   b. **Exception—Guaranteed Payments**

   Receipt of a guaranteed payment is taxable to the partner as ordinary income. (*See supra*, p. 19.)

   c. **Exception—Hot Assets**

   A distribution of cash or other assets in exchange for a partner's interest in unrealized receivables or inventory items may be taxed to that partner. Similarly, a distribution of hot assets to a partner by a partnership is taxable to the partnership.

d. Caution—Partnership Liabilities

Recall that a reduction in a partner's share of partnership liabilities is treated as a distribution of money and can, if it exceeds outside basis, trigger gain recognition. (*See* p. 28 in text.)

e. Draws

A "draw" is an advance payment of a partner's expected year-end distribution. A draw is treated as a loan to the partner that is not taxable until the end of the partnership's taxable year.

f. Loss Recognition

Loss can be recognized only in connection with a liquidation of the partner's interest. (*See infra.*)

2. Distributions of Property

If a partnership distributes property other than money, generally the partnership's inside basis becomes the distributee partner's basis for the property.

3. Disproportionate Distributions of Receivables or Inventory

Partnership distributions of hot assets in exchange for a partner's interest in other partnership assets may be treated as if the partnership sold the assets to an outsider; *i.e.*, such distributions may generate ordinary income to the partnership.

a. Substantially Appreciated Inventory Items

For purposes of the disproportionate distribution rules, inventory items must be "substantially appreciated" (*i.e.*, fair market value must exceed the partnership's basis in the item by at least 120%).

b. Roles Reversed

Similarly, partnership distributions of cash or other assets in exchange for a partner's interest in hot assets may be treated as if the partner had sold her interest in those assets to the other partners; *i.e.*, such distributions are taxable as ordinary income to the distributee-partner to the extent of her transfer of an interest in the assets.

4. Mixing Bowl Transactions

While most partnership distributions are tax-free, Congress became concerned with strategies to avoid tax on precontribution gains, or to shift or defer tax on those gains, through the device of contributions to and distributions of appreciated property from a partnership (*i.e.*, "mixing bowl transactions"). The Code sections relating to mixing bowl transactions (taxing precontribution gain) apply only if the related contribution and distribution occur within *seven* years of each other.

I. PARTNERSHIP LIQUIDATIONS

1. Flexible Treatment

The Code provides for flexible treatment when the interest of one partner is bought *by the partnership*.

a. Section 736(a)—Payments Not in Exchange for Assets

A payment made by a partnership to a retiring or deceased partner that is not in exchange for the latter's interest in partnership assets (*e.g.*, *a guaranteed payment or distributive share*) is *ordinary income*, taxable to the partner and deductible by the partnership.

b.   Section 736(b)—Payments in Exchange for Assets

A cash payment made by a partnership in exchange for a retiring or deceased partner's interest in partnership assets is a *distribution*, and thus gives rise to capital gain or loss to the partner.

(1) Unrealized Receivables Distinguished

A payment made in exchange for unrealized receivables must be treated as ordinary income in cases where capital was not a material income-producing factor for the partnership *and* the retiring or deceased partner was a general partner.

(2) Substantially Appreciated Inventory Items

A payment in exchange for a partner's interest in substantially appreciated inventory items (hot assets) is dealt with under section 736(b), but it produces ordinary income rather than capital gain (*supra*).

(3) Payments in Exchange for Goodwill

In most cases, these are taxed as capital gain if the partnership agreement provides for a payment for goodwill; otherwise, such payments are taxed as ordinary income.

2.   Distributions of Property in Liquidation

a.   Distributions of Money

If a partner receives *only money* in a liquidating distribution, he recognizes gain if the money distributed exceeds his outside basis in the partnership; if the distribution is less than the partner's outside basis, he has a loss.

b.   Distributions of Property

Generally, if a partner receives property in a liquidating distribution, he usually recognizes *no gain or loss*. The partner's outside basis (less cash received) becomes the basis of the assets.

(1) Distributions of Unrealized Receivables and Inventory

A partner who acquires hot assets in a liquidating distribution takes *the same basis* the assets had when they were held by the partnership.

3.   Loss on Liquidation

A partner recognizes loss on a liquidation if the partner receives no consideration except cash, marketable securities, or hot assets. Normally the loss is a *capital loss.*

a.   Exception—Abandonment Loss

However, if a partner receives nothing at all in exchange for a partnership interest that has become worthless, the partner has an ordinary loss rather than a capital loss because this transaction does not satisfy the "sale or exchange" requirement for capital gain or loss.

b.   Caution—Decrease in Liabilities

Assume partnership liabilities are allocated to a partner. When that partner abandons his partnership interest, he is treated as having received money on the abandonment owing to a decrease in the liabilities to which he is subject. As a result, that partner's loss is capital rather than ordinary. If no partnership liabilities are allocated to the partner, he receives no money on the abandonment and has ordinary loss.

II. CORPORATE TAXATION—PROBLEMS OF ENTITY, PENALTY TAXES, AND FORMATION

A. CORPORATION AS TAXABLE ENTITY

1. Introduction

A corporation is taxed as a separate entity. Dividends are taxable to the shareholders (albeit at capital gains rates) but are not deductible by the corporation. Double taxation of dividends is responsible for most of the complexity of corporate tax.

2. Tax Rates

There are four rate brackets. Multiple corporations that are members of either a brother-sister or a parent-subsidiary controlled group must share the lower tax brackets.

a. Capital Gains

Corporations receive no benefit from capital gains because they are taxed to corporations at or above the top marginal corporate tax rate. Corporate capital loss is deductible only to the extent of corporate capital gains. If capital loss exceeds capital gains, the excess can be carried back three years and forward five years.

b. Charitable Donations

A corporation can deduct charitable contributions up to 10% of taxable income.

3. Consolidated Returns

If one corporation owns at least 80% of the stock of another, the two corporations can file consolidated returns. Thus, intercorporate sales of goods or services are not taxed, and losses of one member can be offset against the profits of another.

4. Allocation Between Corporations

a. Reallocation Between Corporations

The IRS can reallocate income or deductions between corporations belonging to a single controlled group if the related entities have failed to deal at arm's length. There are five categories of transactions between commonly controlled entities that are most likely to trigger reallocation:

(1) *Loans and advances*;

(2) *Performance of services*;

(3) *Use of tangible property,* such as a lease of business premises;

(4) *Sale of tangible property*; and

(5) *Sale or use of intangible property.*

5. When Will Corporate Entity Be Ignored

The corporate entity will be ignored for tax purposes if the corporation neither performs any business nor serves any business purpose.

6. Transactions Between Shareholder and Corporation

Generally, sales of property between the corporation and shareholder, or between related corporations, are treated as if the parties were independent entities. But there are a number of exceptions.

a. **Sales of Depreciable Property at a Gain Are Recognized**

If an individual owns more than 50% (in value) of a corporation's stock, any gain on sales of depreciable property between the shareholder and corporation is ordinary income, not capital gain.

b. **Sales at a Loss Are Not Recognized**

The loss produced by the sale of property between a shareholder and a corporation in which he owns more than 50% (in value) of the stock is not recognized.

7. **Alternative Minimum Tax**

The Code imposes a minimum tax on corporations similar to that imposed on individuals. There is an exception for small corporations.

a. **Tax Rate**

The corporate minimum tax is 20% of the alternative minimum taxable income ("AMTI") in excess of $40,000 to the extent the minimum tax exceeds the regular tax.

b. **Computation of AMTI**

AMTI is computed by starting with corporate taxable income. Tax preferences are added. Then taxable income is "adjusted."

B. **PENALTY TAXES ON CORPORATIONS THAT DO NOT PAY DIVIDENDS**

1. **Accumulated Earnings Tax**

a. **Basic Standard**

The tax is levied on a corporation that has retained an unreasonable accumulation of assets for the purpose of avoiding the taxation of dividends.

b. **Reasonable Needs Test**

The test is whether the accumulation exceeds the reasonable needs of the business.

c. **Calculation**

The tax is based on taxable income, less taxes and dividends paid, less either the amounts retained to meet the reasonable needs of the business *or* a minimum deduction if earnings and profits were less than $250,000 at the beginning of the year.

2. **Personal Holding Company ("PHC") Tax**

a. **Purpose and Ownership Requirement**

A PHC is a corporation that receives passive income on behalf of its shareholders. The purpose of the PHC tax is to encourage distribution of the PHC's income to the shareholders so that it can be taxed at their rates (although, now that dividends are taxed at low capital gains rates, there is less incentive for shareholders to accumulate income in a PHC). The tax is levied on a corporation of which at least 60% of the ordinary income is passive income, and of which at least 50% of the outstanding stock is owned by five or fewer shareholders.

(1) **PHC Income**

PHC income includes rents (unless rents comprise 50% or more of ordinary income), dividends, interest, etc. It also includes amounts for personal services performed by a 25% shareholder provided that an outsider had the right to designate that shareholder as the one to render the services.

b. Computation of Tax

The tax is imposed at the rate of 15% of undistributed personal holding company income.

C. CREATING THE CORPORATION

1. Nonrecognition

Under I.R.C. section 351, ordinarily when stock is issued in exchange for property *upon the formation of a corporation*, no gain or loss is recognized.

2. Summary of Requirements for Nonrecognition

As a group the transferors of the assets to the corporation must have 80% control immediately after the transfer, must not lose control as a result of contractually required transfers, and must receive only stock in exchange for their assets.

3. Exceptions to Nonrecognition Rule

a. Stock for Services

The person who receives stock for services has ordinary income on the exchange and the stockholders who transfer property do not get 80% control, the conditions for section 351's nonrecognition rule do not apply, and they must recognize gain or loss on the exchange.

b. Stock for Debt

Stock issued in cancellation of a debt owed by the corporation is not treated as issued in exchange for property. Thus, if the debt has a basis less than its value, the recipient would recognize gain on receipt of stock for the debt.

4. Recognition of Gain

a. Distribution of Other Property

If the corporation distributes property other than stock (*i.e.*, "boot") to the transferor, *gain* is recognized up to the value of the other property, but loss is not recognized.

b. Preferred Stock as Boot

Nonqualified preferred stock is more like debt than stock and so is not treated as stock, but rather as boot (*infra*).

c. Liabilities as Boot

Although a corporation ordinarily can assume a transferor's liabilities without imposition of tax, gain is recognized in the following two situations.

(1) Exception for Tax Avoidance

Gain is recognized if the transaction resulted from a tax avoidance purpose.

(2) Liabilities in Excess of Basis

Gain is recognized if the liabilities exceeded the basis of the assets transferred. For this purpose, however, a cash basis transferor's liabilities are ignored if they are accounts payable.

d. Allocation of Gain

If the transferor transfers several assets and receives boot, it must be allocated among the assets transferred by prorating the boot according to the *fair market value* (not the bases) of the assets transferred. Gain is then computed.

e. Recapture of Depreciation

If gain is recognized because boot is received, depreciation on the assets is recaptured as ordinary income to the extent of the recognized gain.

f. Sale of Assets to Corporation

When assets are sold to a corporation by a taxpayer who seeks a stepped-up basis at the corporate level, the sale is frequently reclassified as a section 351 exchange if the sale appears to be part of the overall transaction in which the corporation is formed and capitalized.

(1) Consequences

If the transaction is treated as sale, the seller recognizes gain or loss in its entirety, but if the transaction is treated as a section 351 exchange, the section 351 rules apply (*i.e.*, gain or loss generally is not recognized except as discussed above).

5. Basis Adjustments Under Section 351

a. Corporation's Basis

In section 351 exchanges, the corporation's basis is the same as the shareholder's—but increased by any gain recognized by the transferor on the exchange.

(1) Built-In Loss Property

If the transferred properties have a net built-in loss, the transferee corporation's aggregated adjusted basis in the transferred properties shall be reduced to the fair market value of the properties at the time of the transfer unless the parties elect to reduce the transferor shareholder's basis instead.

b. Shareholder's Basis

Unless the parties elect to reduce the transferor shareholder's basis to fair market value in the case of a contribution of built-in loss property, the shareholder's basis in stock received in a section 351 exchange is the same as the basis of the assets she transferred, less liabilities assumed and less boot received, plus gain recognized.

c. Holding Period

For purposes of determining whether there is gain or loss when a stockholder sells stock obtained in a section 351 exchange, the stockholder generally includes the time he held the property that he exchanged for the stock.

d. Corporation's Gain

The corporation has no gain or loss from issuing its own stock in exchange for property. This is so even if it issued treasury stock.

6. Corporate Tax Shelters and Economic Substance Doctrine

A new corporation is sometimes established to facilitate corporate tax shelter transactions. Such transactions must not violate the economic substance doctrine, which is a judicial doctrine that inquires whether a transaction has any economic benefits apart from the tax benefits.

a. Codification of Economic Substance Doctrine

Under I.R.C. section 7710(o), a transaction is treated as having economic substance if (i) the transaction changes the taxpayer's pre-tax economic position in a meaningful way, and (ii) the taxpayer has a substantial non-tax business purpose for entering into the transaction.

D. CORPORATION'S CAPITAL STRUCTURE—DEBT OR EQUITY?

1. Why the Dispute

a. Advantages of Using Debt

The corporation can deduct interest that it pays; the repayment of principal is tax-free to the recipient; the corporation can accumulate assets reasonably for the repayment of debt; and debtholders can collect prior to shareholders if the corporation becomes insolvent.

b. Disadvantages of Using Debt

(1) Corporate Shareholder

If a corporation is the shareholder of another corporation, stock might be better than debt because income on debt is fully taxable as ordinary income, while a corporate shareholder can deduct from income 70% of dividends received (in some cases 80% or 100%).

(2) Higher Rate

Although interest payments and dividends both represent claims to the corporation's stream of income, interest is taxable at ordinary income rates as high as 35%, while dividends are taxable at capital gains rates, which only reach as high as 20%.

(3) Losses on Debts

Ordinarily there is no difference between holding stock or debt when a loss occurs: in either case the loss generally is a capital loss, except in the case of section 1244 stock (*infra*).

(4) Losses on Section 1244 Stock

If stock is section 1244 stock, losses on its sale or worthlessness are treated as ordinary rather than capital; thus, debt is not as advantageous as section 1244 stock.

(a) Requirements

Section 1244 stock must be in a domestic corporation and have been issued for money or other property. In addition, the corporation must have active income and must not have more than $1 million in paid-in capital.

(5) Gains on Small Business Stock

A taxpayer other than a corporation can exclude from income 100% of the gain on the sale of qualified small business stock issued after September 27, 2010 and held for at least five years.

2. Statutory and Case Law Guidelines

Some courts hold that an instrument's classification as debt or equity depends on the ratio of debt to equity, the proportionality of holdings, the risks assumed by the purported creditor, whether there is subordination to other debts, and the form of the instrument. Other courts look to whether an outside lender would lend money on similar terms. If not, the instrument will be considered equity rather than debt.

III. CORPORATE TAXATION—DISTRIBUTIONS

A. CONSEQUENCES TO SHAREHOLDERS OF CORPORATE DISTRIBUTIONS OF CASH AND PROPERTY

1. Distributions by the Going Concern

a. Earnings and Profits

A distribution is taxed as a dividend to the shareholder to the extent of either the corporation's current or accumulated earnings and profits ("E & P").

b. Effect of Distribution

(1) Individual Shareholders

Dividends are fully includible in a shareholder's income (if they constitute "qualified dividend income"), but are taxed only at capital gains rates.

(2) Corporate Shareholder

A corporate shareholder can deduct from income **70%** of the dividends (80% if it owns 20% or more of the stock of the dividend-paying corporation). If it is an electing parent owning at least 80% of its subsidiary's stock, the dividend exclusion is 100%.

(3) Distributions in Excess of E & P

If the distribution exceeds E & P, the excess reduces the shareholder's basis. After basis is reduced to zero, the distribution is taxable as capital gain.

c. Distributions of Property

If a corporation distributes property other than money as a dividend, the shareholder includes the fair market value of the property (less any liability to which the property is subject) in income. The value of the property becomes its basis in the hands of the shareholder.

(1) Effect on E & P

When appreciated property is distributed, the corporation increases E & P by the amount of recognized gain, and reduces E & P by the fair market value of the property. If the distributed property has decreased in value but the loss is not recognized, E & P are reduced by the adjusted basis of the property.

d. Disguised Dividends

Any transaction that benefits a shareholder (such as the corporation's sale of property to him for less than its value) will likely be treated as a dividend.

2. Distributions in Complete Liquidation

a. General Rule—Section 331

Ordinarily, a complete liquidation is taxed under I.R.C. section 331, and shareholders have capital gain or loss depending on whether the amount of money plus the value of property received in the liquidation is less than or greater than the basis of the stock. The basis of assets received is their fair market value. E & P is destroyed. Shareholders have successfully used the installment method to defer tax by selling the stock to a family trust before the liquidation was completed. Once the liquidation period has begun, it is too late to shift income by giving away the stock.

b. Section 332 Liquidations of Subsidiaries

If one corporation owns at least 80% of another corporation, liquidation of the latter produces no gain or loss to the parent. Distributions by subsidiary to parent must be completed within a single taxable year of the parent (or three years after the first distribution if a series of distributions is made).

(1) Basis After a Section 332 Liquidation

The basis of property received by the parent corporation is the same as the basis the assets had in the hands of the subsidiary.

3. Stock Redemptions

a. Overview

A corporate repurchase of stock from shareholders is treated as a dividend (which is taxable to the shareholder at capital gains rates, but which does not allow the shareholder any recovery of basis), unless the repurchase qualifies as a redemption under I.R.C. section 302(b)(1), (2), (3), or (4), or I.R.C. section 303. If the transaction qualifies as a redemption under the latter sections, it is treated as a sale giving rise to capital gain (to the extent that it exceeds basis) or loss.

b. Redemptions Are Not Treated as Dividends

(1) Complete Termination

According to I.R.C. section 302(b)(3), a transaction qualifies as a redemption, not a dividend, if it completely terminates the shareholder's interest (*i.e.*, the corporation purchases all the stock owned by the shareholder).

(a) Attribution Rules

These rules render complete termination difficult in the context of a close corporation. These rules attribute to the distributee stock owned by *family* (spouse, children, grandchildren, and parents); stock owned by *entities in which the distributee is interested* (estates, trusts, partnerships, and corporations); and *stock the distributee has an option to purchase*. In addition, stock is attributed to entities (estates, trusts, partnerships, and corporations) from their beneficiaries, partners, or shareholders.

(b) Relief from Family Attribution

Family attribution will not occur if the distributee retains no interest (other than as a creditor or independent contractor) in the entity; promises the IRS that he will not obtain any such interest within the *next 10 years*; and neither has acquired any stock from, nor has transferred any stock to, another family member within 10 years (unless such acquisition or transfer was not for tax avoidance purposes, in which case the waiver of attribution will not be disqualified).

(2) Substantially Disproportionate Redemptions

According to I.R.C. section 302(b)(2), a distribution is a redemption and not a dividend if the shareholder's interest in voting stock after the transaction is both *less than 80%* of what it was before the redemption, and *less than 50% of all voting stock*. *Attribution rules* once again play a part in quantifying the shareholder's interests.

(3) Nonequivalence to a Dividend

According to I.R.C. section 302(b)(1), a distribution is not a dividend if it is not "essentially equivalent to a dividend." Such nonequivalence requires a *meaningful reduction* in voting control. It is particularly important that the distributee *not* have control of the corporation after the distribution has occurred. *Attribution rules* apply, but might be relaxed if there is family dissension.

(4) Partial Liquidations

A distribution that "contracts" the corporation's business is a partial liquidation under section 302(b)(4) and is not taxed as a dividend to a shareholder-distributee. Only a *noncorporate shareholder* can take advantage of partial liquidation treatment.

(a) Code Test

An alternative, mechanical test provides that if both the liquidated and the retained businesses had been operated actively for five years by the corporation, the distribution qualifies as a partial liquidation.

(5) Section 303 Redemptions

A redemption in the amount of a decedent's *death taxes* and *funeral and administration expenses* is not a dividend. However, the shares must have exceeded 35% of the decedent's estate.

(6) Collateral Consequences of Redemptions

(a) Effect upon basis

If the redemption is treated as a dividend, the recipient must treat the entire amount received as capital gain and no recovery of basis is allowed. If the recipient has any shares remaining, the basis of the redeemed shares is added to the basis of the remaining shares. If all of the distributee's shares are redeemed, the basis of the redeemed shares is added to the basis of the shares owned by the shareholder from whom stock was attributed to the distributee.

(b) Effect upon E & P

If a distribution is treated as a redemption and not a dividend, corporate E & P is reduced by a ratable amount.

(c) Deductibility of Redemption Costs

Generally, no deduction is allowed for any amount paid or incurred by a corporation in connection with redemption of its stock. However, a corporation can deduct interest on debt incurred to repurchase its stock.

(7) Tax planning in Redemptions

(a) Bootstrap Redemptions

A taxpayer can acquire a corporation through its own cash by first purchasing some of the shares from existing shareholders and next causing the corporation to redeem the balance.

(b) Redemptions and Divorce

If divorcing spouses own a closely held corporation, they can structure a transaction similar to the bootstrap purchase, above, to occur after the divorce. Because of the attribution rules, a waiver would be required if the transaction occurred before the divorce.

(c) Gift and Redemption

A taxpayer might be able to avoid the capital gain on a redemption and get a charitable deduction by giving his stock to a charity and having the corporation redeem the stock from the charity. Such schemes have been upheld where no binding agreement existed at the time of the gift requiring the corporation to redeem.

c. Multicorporate Redemptions

(1) Brother-Sister Redemptions

If shareholder A controls both X Corp. and Y Corp., and Y Corp. buys some of A's stock in X Corp., the transaction is treated as a redemption by Y Corp. of its own stock. Unless the change in A's position in X Corp. satisfies either I.R.C. section 302(b) or section 303, the "sale" is a dividend to the extent of X Corp.'s and Y Corp.'s E & P. "Control" in multicorporate redemptions means 50% of the stock.

(2) Parent-Subsidiary Redemptions

If shareholder A controls P Corp., which in turn controls S Corp., and S Corp. buys some of A's stock in P Corp., the transaction is treated as a redemption by P Corp. of its own stock, and, depending on the change in A's voting stock position in P Corp., may be treated as a dividend from P Corp. (to the extent of P Corp.'s E & P).

B. DISTRIBUTIONS OF PROPERTY IN KIND—IMPACT ON THE CORPORATION

1. General Rule—Gain Recognized

When a corporation distributes property to the shareholders (whether as a dividend, redemption, partial or complete liquidation), it must recognize gain on the transfer. It can recognize loss on the transfer if the distribution is in complete liquidation (except in cases of built-in loss and tax avoidance purpose).

a. Value of Gain

Value is measured as if the corporation sold the entire property to an unrelated buyer in an arm's-length transaction.

2. Additional Rules

a. Liquidation of Subsidiary by Parent

Gain or loss is not recognized to the liquidated corporation in cases of section 332 liquidation (parent liquidates 80% owned subsidiary).

b. Corporate Reorganization

In a corporate reorganization where the acquired corporation receives stock of the acquiring corporation which it distributes to its shareholders, the acquired corporation does not recognize gain or loss.

c. Recognition of Loss

With a few exceptions, a corporation generally is entitled to recognize loss when it distributes assets to its shareholders in complete liquidation.

3. **Prior Law—*Court Holding* Doctrine**

Though based on a now irrelevant case, the *Court Holding* and *Cumberland Public Services* cases contain reasoning still relevant to a variety of tax issues today. Basically, the cases stand for the principle that if in substance a sale is made by one person, it cannot be attributed to another.

C. STOCK DIVIDENDS

1. General Rule—Nontaxable

Under section 305(a), a stock dividend (*i.e.*, a distribution of stock with respect to existing stock) generally is not taxable.

a. Basis

The old stock's basis is prorated over the old and new shares by the respective fair market values of each.

2. Exceptions—Taxable

A stock dividend is taxable if any shareholder can choose either stock or property and chooses stock (thus, it is taxable to the extent of corporate E & P); or if the distribution provides property for some shareholders and an increase in interests for other shareholders; or if the distribution gives preferred stock to some common shareholders and common stock to other common shareholders; or if the dividend derives from existing preferred stock.

3. Basis

If a stock dividend is *taxable*, the new stock will have a basis equal to its value at date of distribution. The basis of the old stock will stay the same.

4. Section 306 Stock

If a shareholder has section 306 stock and it is redeemed, the redemption will be treated as a dividend to the extent of current E & P. If section 306 stock is sold, part of the sales price equal to the seller's share of E & P at the time of the earlier stock dividend will be taxable as if it were a dividend. Although sales of both section 306 and non-section 306 stock give rise to capital gains tax, the *entire recovery* from a sale or redemption of section 306 stock is taxable (and cannot be offset by capital losses).

a. Definition

Section 306 stock is stock received as a *stock dividend* (other than common stock on common stock) that *was* tax-free under section 305(a).

b. Exceptions

The unfavorable tax treatment of I.R.C. section 306 does not apply if: (i) the disposition is a *complete termination* (shareholder sells his entire stock interest), (ii) stock is redeemed as part of a liquidation, (iii) the disposition is a *non-recognizing transaction*, or (iv) the IRS is satisfied that tax avoidance was *not a principal purpose*.

IV. CORPORATE TAXATION—PARENT'S PURCHASE OF SUBSIDIARY'S STOCK AND ADJUSTMENT TO BASIS OF ASSETS

A. BACKGROUND

When a purchaser ("P") buys the *assets* of a target corporation ("T"), P's basis in those assets is equal to the purchase price, and T must recognize gain on the sale. If, instead, P buys T's *stock*, the basis of T's assets will not be affected. Section 338 permits P a stepped-up basis for

T's assets without liquidating T. Few purchasers choose this election because T would have to pay tax on the appreciation of its assets.

B. ELECTION BY PARENT

1. General Requirements

If the purchasing corporation acquires at least 80% of the stock of the target corporation, it can, within nine months and 15 days, elect under section 338 to adjust the basis of the target's assets upward to approximately equal purchaser's price for the stock plus corporate liabilities.

2. Effect of Election

If the election is made, the target is treated as if it sold its assets and then bought them back.

3. Price of the Purchase

Generally, the price of the fictitious purchase is the price the buyer paid for the target's stock, plus any liabilities the target had (including any tax T paid on the "sale" of its assets) and an additional increase ("gross up") if less than 100% of the target's stock was acquired.

4. Consistency Requirement

Even if the purchaser makes no section 338 election, an election is deemed to be made if P has made certain asset purchases during the "consistency period," which begins one year before the beginning of the 12-month acquisition period and continues to one year after the acquisition date.

C. CONSOLIDATED GROUPS

If the target is part of an affiliated group, the members of the group can file a consolidated return on which transactions between members of the group will cancel each other out.

V. CORPORATE TAXATION—REORGANIZATIONS

A. DIVISIVE REORGANIZATIONS

1. General Rule—Nontaxable

The division of one corporation into two can be a tax-free reorganization, provided that the corporate division has a *business purpose*. Frequently, these are referred to as "D" reorganizations qualifying under section 355, meaning that neither the corporations nor shareholders will recognize gain or loss.

a. Corporate vs. Shareholder Business Purpose

The business purpose must be germane to the business of the corporation or a corporation to which the distributing corporation is linked. A shareholder purpose does not qualify.

b. Ruling Requests

Until recently, taxpayers could seek private rulings from the IRS on whether a proposed corporate division will qualify. However, the IRS will no longer issue such rulings; rather it will issue *revenue rulings* on common issues of concern.

2. Tax Consequences

If a divisive transaction qualifies, the tax consequences are: (i) the new corporation takes its new assets *at the same basis* the original corporation had; (ii) the original corporation *does not recognize gain or loss* on the transfer of assets to the new corporation in exchange for its stock; (iii) the **shareholders** of the original corporation **do not recognize any gain or loss** on their receipt of stock of the new corporation and they retain the same basis by splitting the basis of their original stock between it and their new stock; and (iv) if the transaction involved **boot, gain is recognized** on it.

3.   **Requirements for Tax-Free Corporate Division**

   a.   **"Device" Rule**

   The distribution of stock cannot be used as a device for the distribution of earnings and profits. The fact that shares are sold or exchanged shortly after the reorganization is evidence that it was used as such a device.

   b.   **Continuity of Interest**

   The continuity of interest requirement (*infra*, p. 146) must also be satisfied.

   c.   **Distribution of Control**

   Either **all** of the stock in the new corporation must be distributed, or **at least 80%** of it must be distributed and the rest retained for reasons other than tax avoidance.

   d.   **Five-Year Active Business**

   Most importantly, the businesses of both corporations must have been operated actively for at least five years prior to the reorganization and must carry on an active trade or business after the reorganization. However, one active business can be split into two.

4.   **Use of Divisive Reorganizations as Part of Acquisitive Transactions**

   a.   **Divisive Reorganization Plus Acquisition**

   A divisive reorganization is disqualified if the distribution is part of a plan whereby one or more persons acquire a 50% or greater interest in the stock or assets of either the distributing corporation or the controlled corporation.

   b.   **Safe Harbors**

   The Treasury Department has identified nine specific types of transactions that will not be considered part of a plan whereby one or more persons acquire a 50% or greater interest in the stock or assets of either the distributing or controlling corporation.

   c.   **Taxable Purchases of Stock Followed by "D" Reorganization**

   I.R.C. section 355 is intended to block schemes arising out of a combination of a taxable purchase of stock followed by a "D" reorganization, such as cases where there is a purchase of control followed by a division or a purchase of a stock interest followed by a division.

   d.   **Purchase of Stock Followed by Division in Which Purchaser Has at Least 50% of Controlled Corporation**

   Suppose A (an individual or corporation) purchased stock of T Corp. in a taxable transaction. Within five years, T Corp. distributes the stock of S Corp. to A in a tax-free "D" reorganization. A now has at least 50% of the stock of S Corp. The distribution is taxable to T Corp. (as if it had sold rather than distributed the stock of S Corp.). The distribution of S stock remains tax free to A.

B. LIQUIDATION AND REINCORPORATION

1. Fact Situation—Shareholder Scheme to Extract Unneeded Liquid Assets

The issue is tax treatment of shareholders of corporations with a large amount of unneeded liquid assets who want to take the unneeded assets out but do not want to pay the tax that would be due on the full amount of the dividend. They extract the unneeded assets by liquidating the corporation and paying capital gains taxes on the distribution, retaining the unneeded assets, and putting the operating assets (with a current fair market value basis) back into a newly formed corporation. The IRS has been somewhat successful in arguing that the retained assets are a dividend, and thus should be taxed as ordinary income, under the theory that the transaction was a reorganization.

a. "D" Reorganization

The IRS has had most success in arguing that the transaction amounted to a "D" reorganization with a dividend paid to the shareholders.

(1) Transfer of Assets

To be subject to "D" reorganization treatment there must have been a transfer of substantially all of the assets from the old to the new corporation. Courts have defined "substantially all" to mean the assets necessary to run the business.

(2) Control

In addition, the old corporation's shareholders must have acquired at least 50% of the new corporation's stock.

b. "E" Reorganizations

The transaction could also be attacked as an "E" reorganization (*i.e.,* recapitalization) with a dividend, but the IRS has not been very successful with such an argument.

C. COMBINING REORGANIZATIONS

1. Techniques

A statutory merger ("A" reorganization) or consolidation, a stock-for-stock exchange ("B" reorganization), or a stock-for-assets exchange ("C" reorganization) can qualify as a tax-free reorganization. In the last, both the exchange of stock and the exchange of assets are tax free, and the basis of stock and assets carries over.

2. Continuity of Interest Rule

For a reorganization to be tax free, a substantial number of the shareholders of the acquired corporation must continue as shareholders of the acquirer; otherwise, the transaction will be treated as a sale of stock or assets and not as a tax-free reorganization.

a. Case Law Development

The shareholders of the acquired corporation must receive a proprietary interest; long-term debt instruments are not sufficient. Moreover, in evaluating whether there is sufficient continuity of shareholders, the entire transaction must be scrutinized, not just the reorganization segment.

(1) Post-Reorganization Sales of Stock

Shareholders may sell the shares of acquiring corporation stock that they receive in a reorganization so long as the sales are not to the acquiring corporation or a related party.

(2) Pre-Reorganization Sales of Stock

The acquiring corporation cannot get around the continuity requirement by purchasing for cash (or arranging for a related party to purchase for cash) most of the shares of the target corporation shortly before the reorganization transaction. Nevertheless, target corporation shareholders may sell their shares for cash prior to the transaction to parties *other* than the acquiring corporation or its affiliates without violating the continuity requirement, even if such sales were made in anticipation of the transaction.

b. Statutory requirements

(1) "B" Reorganization

The acquiring corporation must use ***solely voting stock*** as the medium of exchange, and must wind up with at least 80% of the acquired corporation. No consideration other than stock may be used, even above the 80% threshold.

(2) "C" Reorganization

In a "C" reorganization, generally the acquiring corporation can use ***only voting stock*** to acquire its interest in the acquired corporation. However, there is a ***narrow exception***: The acquiring corporation can use consideration other than voting stock up to ***20% of the fair market value*** of the acquired corporation's assets. Note, however, that any liabilities of the acquired corporation taken over by the acquiring corporation count as nonstock consideration.

(3) "A" Reorganizations

There is ***no*** statutory continuity of interest rule for "A" reorganizations, although the common law rule has been adopted in the regulations.

(4) Triangular Reorganizations

In all three types of reorganizations, the acquiring corporation can use stock of its parent corporation instead of its own stock as a medium of exchange. In the ***"B" and "C"*** reorganizations, a ***parenthetical clause*** permits the use of the voting stock of a corporation in control of the acquiring corporation. In a ***forward subsidiary merger***, the target corporation transfers substantially all of its assets to a controlled subsidiary of the acquiring corporation in exchange for only voting stock of the acquiring corporation. In a ***reverse subsidiary merger***, the controlled subsidiary merges into the target corporation and an amount of target stock constituting "control" (at least 80%) converts into acquiring corporation stock. The advantage of the latter transaction is that it allows up to 20% of the consideration to be in the form of boot.

(5) Post-Reorganization Transfers to Controlled Corporations

A transaction that otherwise meets the statutory or judicial continuity requirements to qualify as an "A," "B," or "C" reorganization will not be disqualified if all or part of the assets or stock acquired are transferred to a corporation controlled (within the meaning of section 368(c)) by the corporation that acquired the assets or stock. Even successive transfers of the assets or stock will not disqualify the transaction as long as the stock or assets remain in the corporate group and the continuity of business enterprise requirement is still satisfied.

c. Contingent Stock

The acquiring corporation can use a promise to issue additional stock in the future if certain contingencies materialize, but the promise may not extend beyond five years and at least 50% of the stock ever to be issued must be issued immediately.

d. Continuity of Business Enterprise

The business of the acquired corporation must be continued.

3. "Substantially All" Requirement

In a *"C" reorganization*, substantially all of the assets must be acquired (*i.e.*, at least 90% of the fair market value of the net assets and at least 70% of the fair market value of the gross assets) or the acquisition will be taxable.

D. SINGLE CORPORATION REORGANIZATIONS

1. Recapitalizations

a. Definition

A recapitalization is a *tax-free reorganization* involving the reshuffling of stock and debt in an existing corporation.

b. Exception—Taxable

A recapitalization is taxable as a dividend if it essentially is a dividend in disguise.

2. "F" Reorganizations

"F" reorganizations are tax-free events. An "F" reorganization is a change in "identity, form, or place of organization of one corporation" (*e.g.*, a reincorporation of one corporation in another state). To qualify, there can be no significant change in existing assets or shareholders.

3. No Continuity of Interest or Continuity of Business Enterprise Requirement

Neither the continuity of shareholder interest nor the continuity of business enterprise requirements apply to an "E" or "F" reorganization.

E. BOOT IN REORGANIZATIONS

1. General Rules

Generally, no gain or loss is recognized if stock or securities in a corporation that is a party to a reorganization are exchanged solely for stock or securities of another corporation that is a party to the reorganization.

a. Treatment of Securities

If the principal amount of securities (generally long-term corporate debt, such as bonds) received in a reorganization exceeds the principal amount of securities given up, the excess is treated the same as boot.

(1) Options

Options and warrants are treated as boot.

(2) Nonqualified Preferred Stock

This is treated as boot if it resembles debt (*see supra*, p. 74).

2. Taxation

When a shareholder in a reorganization receives boot, realized *gain is recognized* up to the amount of boot. *No loss* is recognized.

a. Basis

If gain is recognized, the *basis of stock* received by shareholders of the acquired corporation is *increased by the gain* recognized but *decreased by the boot* received. The basis of the acquired *assets* remains the same as before the acquisition.

(1) Sale or Dividend

The recognized gain is capital gain with full basis recovery unless the boot "has the effect of the distribution of a dividend," in which case the amount realized is fully taxable. I.R.C. *section 302 standards* are used to decide whether the boot is like a dividend.

(2) "D" Reorganizations

If any boot is used in a spin-off, it is treated as a dividend to the extent of the distributing corporation's E & P. In all other "D" reorganizations, if boot is used, it is taxable only to the extent of recognized gain and generally constitutes a capital gain.

F. CARRY-OVER OF TAX ATTRIBUTES

1. Tax Attributes and Reorganizations

After an "A" or "C" reorganization, many tax attributes of the acquired corporation are *transferred to the acquiring corporation*. Among the most important are *loss carryforwards* of the acquired corporation. If the acquired corporation has a loss carryforward that it has not exhausted, the carryforward will pass with its assets to the acquiring corporation in an "A" or "C" reorganization. In a "B" reorganization, the loss carryforward remains in the acquired corporation.

2. Obstacles to Use of the Loss

a. Tax Avoidance Purpose

The carryforward is wiped out if the acquisition of stock or assets was effected *primarily* for tax avoidance.

b. Limitation of Use

The profits against which the loss carryforward can be used are limited. The profits that can be offset by the loss carryforward each year are equal to the value of the stock of the loss corporation immediately before acquisition times the tax-exempt bond interest rate. This rule goes into effect if there is a shift in ownership of the loss corporation of 50% or more resulting from either a stock or an asset acquisition.

G. CAPITALIZATION OF COSTS OF CORPORATE REORGANIZATION

Generally, the costs of reorganizing a corporation must be capitalized rather than deducted as an expense, because the reorganization creates a long-term benefit for the corporation. The costs of resisting a *hostile takeover*, however, are *deductible* as an expense.

VI. CORPORATE TAXATION—S CORPORATIONS

A. INTRODUCTION

Subchapter S of the Code sets forth an alternative scheme of corporate taxation. Generally, an S corporation is taxed like a partnership. It pays no tax, and its income and deductions are passed through to shareholders.

B. S CORPORATION STATUS

1. Eligibility Requirements

An S corporation must meet the following requirements:

(i) It May Not Have More than 100 shareholders;

(ii) ***It may have only individuals*** as shareholders (although decedent's estates, many trusts, charitable organizations, pension plans, and profit sharing plans can be shareholders); and

(iii) ***It may have only one class of stock*** (although differences in voting rights will ***not*** create a second class, and generally, debts cannot be reclassified as stock to create a second class).

a. Ownership of Stock

An S corporation can own stock in a C corporation (including a controlling interest in a C corporation) or in another S corporation if the second S corporation is a "qualified subchapter S subsidiary" ("QSSS").

(1) Sale of Qualified Subchapter S Subsidiary Stock

A sale of QSSS stock to a non-S corporation results in the termination of the QSSS election.

2. Election Requirement

An S corporation must correctly elect to be taxed under subchapter S and the election must not have been terminated.

a. Making the Election

A corporation must elect S treatment during the preceding year or by March 15 of the current year (unless the IRS determines that there was cause for a late election), and ***all*** shareholders must consent.

b. Termination of the Election

The election can be terminated either voluntarily or involuntarily.

(1) Voluntary Revocation

The election can be revoked by consent of ***more than half*** of the shares.

(2) Involuntary Termination

The election is involuntarily terminated if the corporation is ***no longer eligible*** (*e.g.*, has 101 shareholders). The termination creates a split year in which the corporation is an S corporation for part of the year and a C corporation for the balance.

(3) Passive Income

If a corporation has accumulated earnings and profits from a time before it made its S election ***and*** if its passive income is more than 25% of gross receipts for ***each of three years***, the election is terminated.

C. TAXATION OF S CORPORATIONS

1. General Rule

In general, an S corporation pays ***no tax***.

a. Exception—Built-In Gain

An S corporation that was formerly a C corporation must pay tax on any built-in gains (*i.e.*, the excess of the value of the S corporation's assets at the beginning of the first year it made the election over the adjusted basis of those assets) that it recognizes during the first 10 years (five years for 2011) after it elects to be an S corporation.

b.   Exception—Passive Income

Where an S corporation has earnings and profits from its years as a C corporation, and its passive income exceeds 25% of its gross receipts, it must pay tax on the excess net passive income.

2.   Pass-Thru of Items to Shareholders

All items of income, deduction, and credit pass through to shareholders. These items retain the same character in shareholders' hands (*e.g.*, capital gain or tax-free local bond income).

3.   Basis of Stock and Debts

The basis of stock is *increased* by the shareholder's pro rata share of corporate income, including tax-exempt income, and *decreased* by deductions and losses. After the basis of stock is reduced to zero by losses, the basis of corporate debts is also reduced by losses. If the basis of both stock and debt is reduced to zero, losses cannot be deducted.

4.   Distributions

Most distributions are *tax free* to shareholders.

a.   Exceptions

A distribution that *exceeds the basis* of the stock is treated as a capital gain. If a distribution *exceeds the net income* earned while the corporation has S status, it is taxable to the extent of corporate *earnings and profits accumulated* while it was a C corporation.

5.   Taxable Year of S Corporation

An S corporation must use the *calendar year* unless it persuades the IRS it has a business purpose for a different taxable year.

6.   Fringe Benefits

An S corporation is treated as a *partnership* for purposes of employee fringe benefits.

Approach to Exams

Many of the issues in a tax case involving a partnership or corporation are exactly the same as in a case involving individuals. The same problems arise:

(i)   What is income;

(ii) What is deductible;

(iii) To whom is it income;

(iv) What kind of income is it; and

(v)   When is it income?

These issues are discussed in the Taxation of Individuals Summary. This Summary covers only legal principles that are *unique* to partnerships and corporations. For exam purposes, the following points may be helpful to consider:

PARTNERSHIP TAXATION

1.   Not a Taxable Entity

The partnership pays no tax. Its income and deductions are allocated among the partners. Partners can agree to deal as outsiders with their partnerships—for example, by taking a salary; nevertheless, a partner's share of partnership income or deductions is reflected directly on the partner's tax return.

2.   Nonrecognition Provisions

Most critical events in the life of the partnership are covered by nonrecognition provisions. These include:

a.   *Formation* of the partnership and contribution of assets to it;

b.   *Most partnership distributions of cash or property*—no recognition to either the partnership or the partner; and

c.   *Most partnership complete liquidations or dissolutions*.

3.   Sales

Sales of partnership interests to outsiders and redemption of the interest by the partnership generally give rise to *capital gain* or loss, *except* to the extent that the consideration is allocable to *unrealized receivables* or *substantially appreciated inventory*.

4.   Flexibility

The accent is strongly on flexibility. The partners are given wide latitude to achieve the tax results that they want by the way they write (or amend) their partnership agreement. Thus, income can be rather freely allocated between the partners, unless the allocation does not reflect economic reality. On retirement of a partner, it is possible to have the payments to him be ordinary income and deductible by the other partners, or capital gain to him and not deductible by the other partners.

CORPORATE TAXATION

1. Separate Entity

The corporation is a tax-paying entity, separate from its shareholders, unless it makes an election under subchapter S to be taxed much like a partnership.

2. Dividends

Dividends are *not deductible* by the corporation, although they generally are taxable to the shareholders at capital gains rates. Because the money used to pay the dividend was taxed to the corporation, this creates a double tax on dividends. Consequently, there is great incentive to extract unneeded money from the corporation so that the corporation gets a deduction (salary or interest on loans). Most of the complexities of corporate taxation are traceable to the tension created by the double taxation of corporate dividends.

a. Note

Thus, there are *penalty taxes* on corporations that either unnecessarily accumulate assets or function as incorporated pocketbooks for their shareholders.

b. And Note

Many transactions that appear to be sales or exchanges of stock are treated as *dividends*. Thus, redemptions of stock are frequently treated as dividends, as are many purported complete liquidations followed by reincorporations.

3. Nonrecognition Provisions

Many of the critical events in the corporation's life are, or can be, *nonrecognition* transactions:

a. *Incorporation and transfer of assets* to the corporation;

b. *Corporate divisions;*

c. *Acquisitions of corporate stock or assets by another corporation in exchange for stock;*

d. *Most dividends paid in stock* rather than in cash; or

e. *Certain complete liquidations of subsidiary* by parent.

CORPORATE TAXATION UNDER SUBCHAPTER S

1. Not a Taxable Entity

Subchapter S of the Internal Revenue Code provides an alternative scheme of corporate taxation. Generally speaking, it treats an S corporation *like a partnership*; *i.e.,* the S corporation pays no tax, and its items of income and deduction pass through to the shareholders.

2. S Corporation Status

To be an S corporation, a corporation must meet certain *eligibility requirements* and make an *election* to be taxed under subchapter S, and the election must not be terminated.

Taxation of Business Entities

Fifteenth Edition

Chapter One

Partnership Taxation

CONTENTS	PAGE

Key Exam Issues

When answering an exam question involving the taxation of a business entity, first determine whether the entity is, for tax purposes, a partnership, corporation, or trust. Incorporated *entities* are taxed as corporations. Unincorporated *entities* (such as general or limited partnerships, limited liability companies, or limited liability partnerships) are taxed as partnerships unless they elect to be taxed as corporations. Unincorporated *businesses* with a single owner are normally taxed as sole proprietorships (*i.e.,* as a "nothing" tax-wise) unless they elect to be taxed as corporations.

Remember that generally a partnership, or other business entity taxed as a partnership, is not subject to income tax. Instead, *each partner* is liable for the income tax on his share of partnership income.

1. **Current Partnership Income**

   Current partnership income or loss is allocated among the partners according to their distributive shares as determined by the partnership agreement. When allocating income or loss on an exam question, you should:

   a. Make sure that an *item that could affect partners differently* (*e.g.,* passive income or loss) is separated from the bottom-line income or loss figure.

   b. Apply the *"substantial economic effect" test* whenever there is a *special* allocation of any item. The item must be reflected in the partner's capital account, which in turn will affect the amount that the partner receives on liquidation. Check to make sure that there is a *deficit restoration provision* or a *minimum gain chargeback provision*.

   c. Watch for situations in which the partnership has a different *taxable year* from a partner (not ordinarily permitted absent a business purpose). Make sure items of income and deduction are reflected in the correct partnership year.

2. **Contributions of Property**

   Generally, no gain or loss is recognized by the partners or the partnership when partners contribute property in exchange for a partnership interest.

   a. **Basis of Contributed Assets**

      The partnership's basis ("*inside basis*") in these assets is the same as the adjusted basis of the contributing partner. Remember, however, that on disposition of the property, the allocations of gain, loss, or deduction must take account of any unrealized gain or loss at the time of the contribution. That portion must be allocated to the contributing partner. Only *subsequent* changes in value are allocated among the partners according to the agreement.

   b. **Contribution of Services**

      If an exam question involves a promise to render services in exchange for an interest in the partnership, you should determine whether it is a *capital* interest (interest in assets) or a *profits* interest (interest in profits only). The capital interest is currently taxable, and there is a substantial risk that a profits interest might also be taxable.

   c. **Basis of Partnership Interest**

      A partner's "*outside basis*" (*i.e.,* her basis in her partnership interest) is generally equal to the adjusted basis of the contributed asset. Note that outside basis is increased by the partner's share of liabilities, but be aware that recourse and nonrecourse liabilities are allocated differently.

3. **Sales of Partnership Interests**

    When analyzing a problem involving the sale or exchange of a partnership interest, remember that the interest is treated as a capital asset; so the transferor partner will recognize capital gain or loss.

    a. Watch for *unrealized receivables or substantially appreciated inventory*. (Re-capturable depreciation is treated as an unrealized receivable.) Amounts allocated to these accounts are treated as ordinary income rather than capital gain.

    b. Be sure to point out that a partnership can make a *section 743 election*, which steps up the inside basis for a partner purchasing an interest to reflect what he paid for it. Note that the stepped-up basis applies only to the purchasing partner.

    c. Determine whether the sale *terminated the partnership* (*i.e.,* whether more than 50% of partnership interest was sold). If so, the sellers may have bunched income in the year of the sale.

4. **Partnership Distributions**

    The distribution of cash or property to the partners is generally not a taxable event, unless *money* distributed exceeds a partner's outside basis. Note, however, that outside basis is reduced by the amount of money distributed and by the basis of any property distributed. When analyzing a distribution problem, ask:

    a. Does the transaction involve a change in ownership of *unrealized receivables or substantially appreciated inventory?* If so, be aware that a distribution is often treated as a sale of these assets by either the partnership or a partner.

    b. Does a *nonliquidating cash distribution* qualify as a *guaranteed payment* (currently taxable) or a *distribution* (not taxed unless it exceeds outside basis)? If it is a guaranteed payment, determine whether it is deductible or must be capitalized (*e.g.,* expenditures with useful life in excess of one year). Keep in mind that a decrease in a partner's share of liabilities is a cash distribution.

    c. Is the *payment* by the partnership to a *retiring or deceased partner* in exchange for the partner's interest in partnership assets? If so, under *section 736(b)*, it is treated as a distribution (*i.e.,* capital gain to partner, no deduction for other partners). All other payments to a retiring or deceased partner are, under *section 736(a)*, considered to be guaranteed payments or his distributive share, and thus ordinary income. The other partners are entitled to a deduction for a section 736(a) payment (unlike a section 736(b) payment).

    d. *Will basis be lost* in a property distribution? This occurs when, for example, in a liquidation a partner cannot take any amount greater than his outside basis as a basis for distributed property. When dealing with this problem on a test, be sure to note that the lost basis can be shifted by an election under section 734, which involves adjustments to inside basis to reflect the amount of basis that would have been wasted.

A. Introduction

1. Partnership a Flow Through Entity

The provisions for the taxation of partnerships are set out in Subchapter K of the Internal Revenue Code, sections 701 through 761. Basically, under these provisions, the partnership merely files an *information return*; the partnership itself is not liable for income tax, but rather its income and deductions flow through to, and are reflected on, the tax returns of the *partners*. The Code prescribes the consequences of many different transactions involving partnerships and partners, but allows substantial flexibility so that the parties can often achieve the tax results that they desire.

2. Basis

In partnership taxation, it is often necessary to distinguish "outside basis" from "inside basis." *Outside basis* refers to a partner's *basis for the partnership interest*; this figure would be used to compute gain or loss on disposition of the interest. *Inside basis* refers to the *basis of assets held by the partnership*; this figure would be used to compute gain or loss on disposition of a particular partnership asset.

OUTSIDE VS. INSIDE BASIS—A COMPARISON	📖GILBERT
OUTSIDE BASIS	A partner's basis for his partnership interest, used to calculate gain or loss *on disposition of the interest*.
INSIDE BASIS	The basis of assets held by the partnership, used to compute gain or loss *on disposition of a particular partnership asset*.

B. Classification of Entity as Partnership or Corporation

1. Introduction

Traditionally, the courts and the Internal Revenue Service ("IRS") classified organizations as corporations (separate entities subject to corporate tax) or as partnerships (pass-through entities not subject to corporate tax) based on a four-factor test. This approach has now been abandoned, so that *unincorporated business entities* are normally taxed as partnerships unless they elect to be taxed as corporations.

2. Four-Factor Test Abandoned

Under prior law, in determining whether an organization should be taxed as a corporation, the IRS considered whether the organization had continuity of existence, centralized management, limited liability for its owners, and freely transferable ownership interests. [**Morrissey v. Commissioner,** 296 U.S. 344 (1935)] This approach was difficult to apply, particularly to limited partnerships and newer forms of unincorporated business entities, such as limited liability companies ("LLCs") and limited liability partnerships ("LLPs"). Effective January 1, 1997, the Treasury abandoned the four-factor test and substituted a "check-the-box" system under which taxpayers can elect how their unincorporated business entities should be taxed. The check-the-box system has been upheld as a valid exercise of the Treasury's authority to issue interpretative regulations under I.R.C. section 7805(a). [**Littriello v. United States,** 484 F.3d 372 (6th Cir. 2007); **McNamee v. Internal Revenue Service,** 488 F.3d 100 (2nd Cir. 2007)]

3. Check-the-Box System for Unincorporated Business Entities

The check-the-box system applies to *all unincorporated business entities*, including entities with a single owner.

a. Definition of Entity

Whether a business organization is an entity for purposes of federal tax laws is determined by federal tax law and does not depend on state law categorization. [Treas. Reg. § 301.7701–1(a)(1)] Some single-owner business organizations qualify. Joint undertakings are considered entities under federal tax laws *if* the participants carry on a trade, business, financial operation, or venture and divide the profits therefrom. [Treas. Reg. § 301.7701–1(a)(2)]

e.g. **Example:** If the co-owners of an apartment building lease space *and in addition provide services* to the occupants directly or through an agent, the joint undertaking creates a separate entity for tax purposes, but mere co-ownership of the property that is leased does not create a separate entity if no services are provided to the tenant. A joint undertaking merely to share expenses does not create a separate entity. [Treas. Reg. § 301.7701–1(a)(2)]

b. Multiple-Owner Entities

Under the "check-the-box" system, an unincorporated business entity with two or more owners, such as a partnership, limited partnership, LLC, or LLP, is referred to as an "*eligible entity*." Such an entity is taxed as a partnership unless it elects to be taxed as a corporation. [Treas. Reg. § 301.7701–3(a)]

(1) Exception—Publicly Traded Partnership

A publicly traded partnership generally is taxed as a corporation and not as a partnership. A partnership is publicly traded if interests in it are traded on an established securities market or are readily tradable on a secondary market (or the substantial equivalent of such a market). Alternatively, a publicly traded partnership that was in existence in 1987 when the publicly traded partnership rules were first adopted ("an electing 1987 partnership") can elect not to be taxed as a corporation, but if it makes such an election, it must pay a tax equal to 3.5% of its gross receipts from the active conduct of trade or business. *Note:* Partnerships whose gross income is 90% passive (*e.g.*, from interest, dividends, real property rents, etc.) or from oil operations are excluded from the publicly traded partnership rules. [I.R.C. § 7704]

c. Single-Owner Entities

As indicated above, certain single-owner unincorporated business organizations may be treated as entities under the federal tax laws. Under the "check-the-box" system, an unincorporated business entity with a single owner can elect to be taxed as a corporation or to be treated as a sole proprietorship (essentially disregarded for tax purposes). [Treas. Reg. § 301.7701–2]

d. Strategy

Normally, an unincorporated entity will prefer to be taxed as a partnership (if it has two or more members) or disregarded (if it has one member) because the partnership tax scheme is far more flexible than the corporate tax scheme. It would be unusual for an unincorporated entity to find the corporate tax structure more advantageous than the partnership structure.

(1) Advantages of Partnership Tax Scheme

For example, partnership income is taxed only once (to the partners), whereas corporate income is often taxed twice (once to the corporation, and again to shareholders when they receive dividends). Similarly, partnership losses are immediately deductible by partners, whereas corporate losses can be deducted only against corporate profits, if any. Finally, partnership liquidations are normally tax-free, whereas corporate liquidations often produce a double tax (at both the corporate and the shareholder levels).

(2) S Corporations

An entity that is incorporated may make an election under Subchapter S of the Code to be taxed in a manner similar to partnerships. (*See infra*, p. 165 *et seq.*) While Subchapter S status can mitigate many of the problems of the corporate tax, it does not solve all the problems. For example, liquidations of S corporations are taxable events. Moreover, there are numerous limitations regarding entities that qualify for S status (*e.g.*, they cannot have a foreign shareholder).

(3) Unincorporated Limited Liability Entities

By employing the newer forms of unincorporated business entities (*e.g.*, LLCs or LLPs), the owners of a business can achieve protection against business liabilities (because under state laws, the owners of such entities are not liable for debts of the entity) and still have all of the advantages of partnership taxation under the regulations unless they elect to be taxed as corporations.

4. Corporations

An entity that is incorporated under a federal or state statute (or certain foreign statutes) ***must be taxed as a corporation.*** [Treas. Reg. § 301.7701–2(b)] However, as indicated above, corporations can elect under Subchapter S to be taxed in a manner similar to partnerships. (*See infra*, p. 165 *et seq.*)

5. Trusts

Normally trusts created by a will or inter vivos declaration are subject to tax under the trust rules. However, business trusts (entities using the trust form that carry on a business) are normally taxed as corporations. Because these trusts carry on business and divide the gains between the various associates (called "beneficiaries"), they are not like the ordinary trust created by a will or inter vivos gift; rather, they are more like a corporation, with characteristics of unlimited life, centralized management, limited liability for their owners, and freely transferable ownership interests. [Treas. Reg. § 301.7701–4; **Morrissey v. Commissioner,** *supra*, p. 5]

C. Anti-Abuse Regulations

1. Introduction

The partnership tax provisions in Subchapter K are quite flexible, and taxpayers have often taken advantage of them to avoid or defer tax or shift tax burdens. A number of amendments to Subchapter K have been geared toward curbing particular forms of tax avoidance. The Treasury, however, remained concerned that the amendments left open certain unintended forms of tax avoidance using the partnership form. To curb these, the Treasury adopted a set of sweeping anti-abuse regulations. The main premise of the regulations is that Subchapter K is intended to permit taxpayers to conduct joint business activities through a flexible economic arrangement (*e.g.*, a partnership) without an entity-level tax, but only if the partnership is bona fide and only for partnership transactions entered into for a substantial business purpose. When such is not the case, the regulations empower the Commissioner to recast the transactions. [*See* Treas. Reg. § 1.701–2(a)] It is unclear what effect these regulations actually have, if any, but they are intended to exert a chilling effect on tax planners.

2. Possible Consequences

The regulations allow the Commissioner to recast a transaction involving the partnership form even though the transaction may fall within the literal words of a particular statutory provision. Among the possible consequences are:

(i)   The purported *partnership may be disregarded* and its assets and activities considered to be owned and conducted by one or more of the purported partners;

(ii) *One or more of the purported partners may not be treated as a partner*;

(iii) *Accounting methods may be adjusted to reflect clearly the partnership's or the partners' income*;

(iv) The partnership's items of *income, gain, loss, deduction, or credit may be reallocated*;

(v)   The claimed *tax treatment may be otherwise adjusted or modified*; or

(vi) The Commissioner can *treat the partnership as an aggregate of its partners rather than an entity*.

[Treas. Reg. § 1.701–2(b), –2(e)]

3. When Remedies Applicable

The anti-abuse remedies may be applied once it is determined that a partnership was formed or used for the principal purpose of reducing substantially the present value of the partners' aggregate federal tax liability in a manner inconsistent with the intent of Subchapter K. The determination must be made considering *all of the facts and circumstances* surrounding each case. The regulations provide a nonexclusive list of factors to be considered (*e.g.*, whether the present value of the partners' aggregate tax liability is substantially less than it would be had the partners acted directly; whether substantially all of the partners are related to each other; whether partners who contribute property to the partnership retain most of their ownership rights in the property, etc.) along with a series of examples. [*See* Treas. Reg. § 1.701–2(c)]

4. Anti-Abuse Case Law

In a case that arose before the anti-abuse regulations were adopted, a court found that a partnership formed exclusively for tax avoidance purposes and that functioned only to carry out an elaborate tax shelter scheme should be disregarded for tax purposes. [**ASA Investerings Partnership v. Commissioner,** 201 F.3d 505 (D.C. Cir. 2000)] In *ASA Investerings*, a United States corporation (Allied-Signal) wanted to generate a large capital loss to shelter a large gain it had already realized. Allied-Signal formed a partnership with ABN, a foreign bank. Using various partnership tax provisions and the installment sales rules, the partnership generated a large tax loss for Allied-Signal and an offsetting gain for the foreign entity (which was not taxed under its domestic law). The court held that the partnership should be disregarded and the loss disallowed because the partnership was formed and operated solely for tax avoidance purposes. Neither partner had any significant risk of gain or loss.

D. Definition of Partnership

1. What Is a Partnership?

A partnership is defined as a "syndicate, group, pool, joint venture, or other unincorporated organization, through or by means of which any business, financial operation, or venture is carried on," and which is not a trust, estate, or corporation. [I.R.C. § 761(a)]

a. Investment Partnerships

If a partnership is used for investment purposes (and not for the active conduct of a business), or for the joint production, extraction, or use of property (but not selling services or the property produced or extracted), the partnership can *elect* not to be taxed as a partnership. Instead, each partner merely accounts separately for his own share of the income and expenses from the venture. [I.R.C. § 761(a)]

b. Joint Ventures

A joint venture is a partnership created to carry out a single business venture. It is *subject to the same tax* rules as other partnerships. [**Podell v. Commissioner,** 55 T.C. 429 (1970)] A federal law standard, rather than a state law standard, is used to distinguish joint ventures from other relationships, such as employment contracts. The standard is whether the parties *intended* to go into business together, sharing profits and control. [**Wheeler v. Commissioner,** 37 T.C.M. 883 (1978)]

2. Family Partnerships

If a sole proprietor can form a partnership with her relatives, part of the income of the business will be taxed in their lower brackets, rather than her higher brackets. Thus, family partnerships have long been a popular income-splitting device. If a family partnership is not recognized for tax purposes, the tax liability remains with the sole proprietor.

a. Capital-Intensive Partnerships

If capital is a "*material income-producing factor*" in the business, the partnership will be recognized for tax purposes, even though the various interests were created by gift and the donees render no services. [I.R.C. § 704(e)]

(1) Bona Fide Transfer

However, the IRS will closely scrutinize the transaction to make sure that the interests were really transferred to the donees. The donees must have actual, bona fide ownership of their interests. The donor cannot retain control over the gifted interests, as control would be inconsistent with complete ownership by the donees. [*See* Treas. Reg. § 1.704–1(e)(2) for guidelines]

(2) Definition of Materiality

Capital is a "material income-producing factor" in a business that sells (or makes and sells) goods (*e.g.*, a restaurant or a drugstore). Capital is not material in a pure service business (*e.g.*, a real estate brokerage firm). However, some service businesses have sufficient investment in distinctive assets so that capital is considered to be material (*e.g.*, a laundry and dry cleaning business). [Treas. Reg. § 1.704–1(e)(1)(iv)]

(3) Compensation

The donor must receive reasonable compensation from the partnership for the services that the donor provides to the partnership. This rule prevents the donor from shifting income equal to the value of the services to the donees [I.R.C. § 704(e)(2)] and applies even if the family members purchase their interests rather than receive them by gift [I.R.C. § 704(e)(3)].

EXAM TIP   **GILBERT**

Be sure to carefully scrutinize family partnership fact patterns. Remember, if capital is a *material income-producing factor*, the IRS will look closely to ensure that there was a bona fide transfer of the capital to the various family member-partners. The transfer can be by gift, but if the donor *retains control* over the gifted interests, the gifts will *not be recognized*, the partnership will be treated as an improper income-splitting scheme, and all of the income will be treated as the donor's income for tax purposes. Remember, too, that the partnership must *reasonably compensate the transferor* for the value of any services that the transferor provides to the partnership; otherwise, the partnership will be treated as a scheme to shift the value of the transferor's services to the other family members.

---

b. Non-Capital-Intensive Partnerships

If capital is not a "material income-producing factor," the standards developed prior to enactment of section 704(e) govern. Under these rules, the donee must have *contributed capital or services* to be recognized as a partner. [**Commissioner v. Culbertson,** 337 U.S. 733 (1949)]

E. Current Partnership Income

1. General Rule

Partnership income and deductions are allocated among the partners according to their partnership distributive shares as determined by the partnership agreement.

a. Partners Taxed as Individuals

A partnership as such is not subject to income tax. The partners are liable for income tax on their share of partnership income in their individual or separate capacities. Thus, the partnership is considered an *"aggregate" of the partners*, not a separate entity. [I.R.C. § 701]

(1) Distinguish—Partnership Separate Entity for Some Purposes

Nevertheless, for many purposes, the partnership is viewed as a separate entity.

(a) Deferred Compensation

A partnership may be treated as an entity when it receives deferred compensation on behalf of a partner, at least when the partner's interest in the deferred compensation may be forfeited to the partnership.

Example: Deferred compensation earned by doctors in a medical partnership is paid by a hospital to a separate trust. The partnership's interest is nonforfeitable, but the interest of any particular doctor is forfeited unless he stays until retirement. *Held:* The partnership is currently taxable; as an *entity*, it earned the nonforfeitable compensation. If the doctors were viewed separately, the forfeitability of the interest of each of them would prevent current taxability. [**United States v. Basye,** 410 U.S. 441 (1972)] (For discussion of deferred compensation, *see* Taxation of Individuals Summary.)

(b) Elections

The method of depreciation for partnership property must be chosen at the partnership level, not by individual partners. Also, if partnership property is condemned, the election not to recognize gain by purchasing replacement property must be made at the partnership level. [**Demirjian v. Commissioner,** 457 F.2d 1 (3d Cir. 1972)] (For discussion of depreciation methods and the election under section 1033, *see* Taxation of Individuals Summary.)

(c) Administrative Matters

For purposes of audits and judicial review, a partnership is considered a separate entity. A "tax matters partner" represents the partnership in dealing with the IRS. However, partnerships with 10 or fewer partners (all individuals) can choose to be treated for administrative purposes as an aggregate, not an entity. [I.R.C. §§ 6221–6231]

b. Certain Items Treated Separately

Each partner takes into account separately his distributive share of certain items of the partnership, so that these items are not lumped together with all other partnership transactions. These items include, for example, passive activity losses, section 1231 gains and losses, and charitable contributions. [I.R.C. § 702(a)(1)–(4)] The foregoing must be separately stated because they will have a *different effect on each partner* depending on his particular tax position. Remaining items of partnership income or deduction are grouped together into a single item and allocated to the partners. [I.R.C. § 702(a)(9)]

Example: Alex and Becky are equal partners in the AB partnership. In 2011, AB sells a punch press at a loss of $8,000. Other than that item, it has a profit of $26,000. During 2011, Alex had a $50,000 gain from condemnation of an apartment house he owned. The $8,000 loss item from the AB partnership is reported separately from the $26,000 profit. It is a section 1231 loss, and $4,000 will be an ordinary loss to Becky. However, the other $4,000 will be a capital loss to Alex because Alex has section 1231 gains that exceed his section 1231 losses. The $26,000 profit will simply be treated as $13,000 in ordinary income to Alex and $13,000 in ordinary income to Becky. (*See* Taxation of Individuals Summary for a discussion of section 1231.)

c. Character of Items

Items of partnership income or deduction have the *same character* in the partner's hands as they would have if the partner had realized them directly rather than through the partnership. Thus, an item of capital gain realized by the partnership is treated as the same in the hands of the partners. [I.R.C. § 702(d)]

(1) Carried Interest

This rule has led to the so-called "carried interest" issue in the taxation of private funds. In such funds, the manager's carried interest in the profits of the venture, which typically arise from the sale of capital assets such as stocks, is taxed at capital gains rates rather than ordinary income rates despite the fact that the income was effectively earned from the manager's labors. One court has held in the ERISA context that such funds are operating a trade or business rather than an investment. [**Sun Capital Partners III, LP v. New England Teamsters and Trucking Industry Pension Fund**, 724 F.3d 129 (1st Cir. 2013)] Theoretically, if applied to the income tax context, this could call into question the capital gains treatment of such carried interest returns.

d. Deduction of Losses

If the partnership loses money for the year (*i.e.*, its deductions exceed its income), the losses are deductible by the partners. They take the losses into account on the last day of the partnership's taxable year.

(1) Limitation

However, the amount deductible *is limited to the partner's basis* for his partnership interest (often referred to as "outside basis"). [I.R.C. § 704(d)] (*See infra*, pp. 27–31 for a discussion of the determination of outside basis and for rules that limit the deduction of losses to amounts "at risk.") Thus, if a partner had no outside basis (because he had not paid for his interest and nothing had happened to raise basis above zero), he could not deduct his portion of partnership losses. [**Falconer v. Commissioner**, 40 T.C. 1011 (1963)] Similarly, if past losses have reduced his outside basis to zero, he can no longer deduct further losses.

EXAM TIP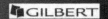

On your exam, it is very important to remember that a partner's losses from his partnership *cannot exceed his outside basis*.

---

(2) Loss Ultimately Deductible

However, if a partnership loss is not deductible because it exceeds a partner's outside basis, he is allowed to deduct the loss in a *later year* if his basis then rises above zero. [I.R.C. § 704(d)]

e. Effect on Basis

Outside basis is *increased* by a partner's distributive share of income plus his share of tax-exempt income. It is *decreased* by partnership distributions and by the partner's share of losses and nondeductible partnership expenditures. [I.R.C. § 705]

e.g. **Example:** Alex becomes a partner in the AB partnership by contributing property with a basis of $40,000 and a fair market value of $50,000. The AB partnership earns $100,000. Alex's distributive share of the income is $50,000. Alex's outside basis rises from $40,000 to $90,000 to reflect his distributive share of the AB income. This increase in outside basis ensures that Alex is taxed only once on the partnership's income—when it is earned—and not a second time when it is distributed to him.

cf. **Compare:** Suppose in the previous example that the AB partnership subsequently distributed the $50,000 in earnings to Alex. Alex's outside basis would decrease from $90,000 to $40,000 to reflect the distribution.

f. Partnership Tax Return

The partnership files a return, for information purposes, setting forth all items of income and deduction (Form 1065). However, it is not entitled to claim certain deductions to which only individuals are entitled—such as the standard deduction or the personal exemption. [I.R.C. § 703(a)]

g. Special Allocations

All items of income and deduction are divided between the partners in accordance with the provisions of the partnership agreement. [I.R.C. § 704(a), (b)(1)] However, if the partnership agreement provides for a special allocation of some items of income, deduction, or the like, and the allocation has no *substantial economic effect*, it will be disregarded and the item will be allocated in accordance with the partner's interest in the partnership. [I.R.C. § 704(b); Treas. Reg. § 1.704–1(b)(1)(i)] This rule is designed to prevent partners from allocating income and/or deductions in specific instances in order to manipulate their tax consequences.

(1) "Substantial Effect"

The economic effect of a special allocation must be "substantial" to be honored for tax purposes, both in the year of the allocation and over the life of the partnership. This means that the economic effect is weighed against the tax savings produced by the allocation. If the economic effect seems insignificant or transitory and the tax savings are large, the special allocation would be ignored. [*See* Treas. Reg. § 1.704–1(b)(2)(iii)]

(2) Economic Effect

The "substantial economic effect" test applies to any allocation of specific items of income, gain, loss, deduction, and credit, as well as to "bottom line" allocation of taxable income or loss. For an allocation to have economic effect, it must be consistent with the underlying economic arrangements of the partners. In other words, there must be an economic benefit or burden to a partner that matches the tax allocation.

Example: Alex and Becky are equal partners in a partnership that owns a building, but Alex is in a much higher tax bracket. The partnership agreement allocates all depreciation to Alex. The current depreciation deductions reduce Alex's taxable income but they also reduce his partnership capital account, which will determine the actual amount he receives when the partnership is dissolved. A partner must pay back a negative balance in his capital account at the time of dissolution. The allocation has an economic effect.

Compare: Suppose in the previous example that the agreement provided that when the building was sold, Alex would be entitled to receive half of the assets of the partnership regardless of the balance in his capital account. The allocation of depreciation has no economic effect and would be ignored for tax purposes. [*See* **Orrisch v. Commissioner,** 55 T.C. 395 (1970)]

(3) Requirements of the Regulations

The regulations under section 704(b) contain detailed provisions to assure that tax allocations match economic benefit or burden. The regulations must be complied with for special allocations in the partnership agreement to be treated as having a substantial economic effect. If an allocation does not have a substantial economic effect, the item is allocated in accordance with its actual economic benefit or burden. [Treas. Reg. § 1.704–1(b)(1)(i), (b)(3)]

(a) Capital Accounts

Capital accounts must be maintained in accordance with the regulations. Among other requirements, capital accounts must be maintained on the basis of *fair market values* of assets at the time they are contributed or distributed. [Treas. Reg. § 1.704–1(b)(2)(iv)]

(b) Liquidation

On liquidation, the assets must be distributed in accordance with positive capital account balances (after capital accounts have been appropriately adjusted for the year). [Treas. Reg. § 1.704–1(b)(2)(ii)(b)] If a partner has a negative capital account (a deficit), she must restore that amount to the creditors (or to other partners with positive capital account balances) by the end of the year in which the liquidation occurs (or, if later, 90 days after liquidation). This is called a "deficit restoration provision." [Treas. Reg. § 1.704–1(b)(2)(ii)(c)]

1) Note

Partners (especially limited partners) may not want to be obligated to restore their negative capital account on liquidation. In the alternative, the agreement can dispense with a deficit restoration provision, but in that case, no allocations can be made to a partner that would create a negative capital account. For purposes of calculating whether a partner would have a negative capital account, it is necessary to first take account of any expected distributions (because these also reduce capital accounts). If, despite this provision, capital accounts become negative because of unexpected distributions, there must be an allocation of income or gain to bring the capital account up to zero. This provision is known as a "qualified income offset." [Treas. Reg. § 1.704–1(b)(2)(ii)(d)]

(4) Nonrecourse Deductions

An additional layer of complexity arises if the partnership has nonrecourse loans outstanding. These are loans that can be satisfied only by foreclosure of the security; no partner has any personal liability for a deficiency. Losses generated by the nonrecourse liabilities are borne by the creditors, not the partners. Nevertheless, the regulations permit nonrecourse deductions (those arising out of nonrecourse loans) to be specially allocated, even though they create negative capital accounts. [Treas. Reg. § 1.704–1(b)(4)(iv)]

(a) Requirements

For an allocation of nonrecourse deductions to be respected, it must meet the above requirements: capital accounts maintained in accordance with the regulations, distributions in accordance with positive capital account balances, and either a deficit restoration provision or a qualified income offset.

(b) Minimum Gain Chargeback Provision

Also, for a partner who does not have a deficit restoration provision, there must be a "minimum gain chargeback" provision. If there is such a provision, it is permissible to allocate nonrecourse losses to a partner even though these create or increase a negative capital account.

1) "Minimum Gain"

Minimum gain is the gain that would be incurred if property subject to a nonrecourse loan were transferred to the creditor in discharge of the obligation. [*See, e.g.*, **Commissioner v. Tufts,** 461 U.S. 300 (1983)] For example, if the basis of property is $40 but it is subject to a nonrecourse loan of $57, there is a gain of $17 on foreclosure of the loan, regardless of the fair market value of the property. This gain of $17 is the "minimum gain." [Treas. Reg. § 1.704–1(b)(2)(iv)(c)]

2) "Nonrecourse Deductions"

If there is an increase in a partnership's minimum gain during the year, deductions equal to that increase are referred to as nonrecourse deductions. [Treas. Reg. § 1.704–1(b)(2)(iv)(b)]

3) "Minimum Gain Chargeback"

If there is a decrease in minimum gain (arising either from a sale of the property or a reduction of the debt), and if a partner has a negative capital account created by the allocation of nonrecourse deductions, the partnership must allocate income or gain to that partner until the negative capital account is brought up to zero. That is a "minimum gain chargeback." [*See* Treas. Reg. § 1.704–1(b)(5), example 20(i)—an illustration of minimum gain chargeback]

h. Year in Which Taxable

The various items of income and deduction from the partnership are allocated to the partners on *the last day of the partnership's taxable year*. [I.R.C. § 706(a)] For instance, if the partnership's taxable year ends on January 31, 2011, the partnership's items of income and deduction from the year that began on February 1, 2010, and ended on January 31, 2011, would appear in the tax returns of the partners for 2011, not 2010. Thus, they have *deferred* tax on 2010 income until 2011.

(1) Limitation on Choice of Taxable Year

The partner's ability to take advantage of such deferral is very limited. Partnerships are generally required to use the calendar year, with the following exceptions [I.R.C. § 706(b)(1)]:

(a) Majority Partner

A partnership must use the taxable year of one or more of its partners who have an aggregate interest in partnership profits and capital of greater than 50%. If the partners owning more than 50% do not have the same taxable year, the partnership must use the taxable year of all of the principal partners (those having a 5% interest) of the partnership—if they all have the same year. This second situation may apply if all of the principal partners have the same taxable year but they do not, in aggregate, hold a majority interest in the partnership. If neither of the preceding sentences applies, the partnership must use the calendar year. [I.R.C. § 706(b)(1)(B)]

Example: A Corp. and B Corp. are 60–40 partners of AB partnership. A Corp. has a fiscal year ending May 30. B Corp. has a fiscal year ending November 30. Because A Corp. owns more than 50% of the partnership interests in AB, AB must use a May 30 year. However, if A Corp. and B Corp. were 50–50 partners, AB would be required to use the calendar year.

(b) Business Purpose

A partnership may use a taxable year other than that prescribed by the preceding rules if it demonstrates to the IRS a business purpose for doing so. [I.R.C. § 706(b)(1)(C)] Note that convenience of the tax return preparer is *not* a business reason. [Rev. Rul. 87–57, 1987–2 C.B. 117] The IRS will, however, permit a taxpayer to use a "natural business year." A natural business year is one in which, for three consecutive years, 25% of the partnership's total receipts from sales and services fall within the last two months of the year. [Rev. Proc. 87–32, 1987–2 C.B. 396]

(c) Three-Month Deferral

A partnership may elect a taxable year that provides not more than three months of income deferral. [I.R.C. § 444] For example, a partnership generally required to use the calendar year can elect a year ending September 30, October 30, or November 30. Also, a partnership existing before 1987 can elect to retain a noncalendar year. [I.R.C. § 444(b)(3)] However, if either election is made, the partnership must pay a "toll charge" for the privilege by April 15 of the year following the end of the fiscal year. This charge is equal to an estimate of the additional tax that would have been paid if a calendar year had been used. [I.R.C. § 7519]

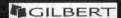

CHECKLIST OF CRITERIA JUSTIFYING NONCALENDAR TAX YEAR FOR PARTNERSHIPS

PARTNERSHIPS MUST USE THE CALENDAR YEAR FOR TAX PURPOSES UNLESS ONE OF THE FOLLOWING EXCEPTIONS APPLIES:

- ☑ The *majority partner(s)* has a tax year other than the calendar year
- ☑ *All of the principal partners* have a tax year other than the calendar year
- ☑ The partnership has a *business reason for using a different tax year* (*e.g.,* for three consecutive years, at least 25% of the partnership's total receipts from sales and services fell within the last two months of the alternative tax year)
- ☑ The partnership takes advantage of up to *three months deferral* and by April 15 of the following year pays a "toll charge" equal to an estimate of the additional tax that would have been paid if a calendar year had been used

---

(2) Closing of Partnership Year

(a) Termination of Partnership

If a partnership *terminates*, the taxable year closes as to all partners. (*See infra,* p. 37, for events that would cause a termination.)

(b) Events That Do Not Close the Year

The taxable year of a partnership does not close by reason of the death of a partner, the entry of a new partner, the liquidation of a partner's interest, or the sale or exchange of a partner's interest. [I.R.C. § 706(c)(1)] (*But see infra,* p. 37, concerning the sale or exchange of 50% or more of the interests.)

1) Sale of Individual Partner's Interest

When a partner *sells or exchanges* his entire interest in a partnership or his partnership interest is liquidated, the partnership year closes *as to him*. He will reflect in his tax return for the year *in which the sale occurs* his share of all partnership items accruing up to that time. [I.R.C. § 706(c)(2)(A)]

2) Death of Partner

The taxable year of a partner terminates if the partner's entire interest in the partnership terminates (whether by reason of death, liquidation, or otherwise). Thus if a partner of a calendar year partnership dies on April 1, the partner's year closes on that date. Profits and losses of the partnership up to April 1 are reported on the partner's final return. If the partner's estate remains as a partner, the profits and losses from April 2 to December 31 are reported on the estate's tax return. [I.R.C. § 706(c)(2)(A)] This provision changed prior law under which the profits and losses for the entire year were reported on the estate's tax return. [**Hesse v. Commissioner,** 74 T.C. 1307 (1980)]

3) Admission of New Partners

When there is a change in partnership interests during the year (as by admission of a new partner), the various items of income and deduction must be allocated between the partners for the periods before and after the change takes place. [I.R.C. § 706(c)(2)(B)] Such allocations must be done on the basis of time. Retroactive allocations to new partners are forbidden. [I.R.C. § 706(d)(1); **Richardson v. Commissioner,** 693 F.2d 1189 (5th Cir. 1982)]

a) Allocation Techniques

There are two permissible methods for allocating these items:

(i) The partnership can "*close the books*" just prior to the change in interests. Items occurring before the closure would be reflected according to the old allocation; items occurring after the closure would be reflected according to the new allocation; or

(ii) The item can simply be *allocated on a daily basis*.

e.g. **Example:** AB is a calendar year partnership in which Alex and Becky each have a 50% interest. On July 1, the firm had an ordinary loss of $36,000. On December 1, Cindy is admitted, given a one-third share, and the firm is renamed ABC. ABC is not permitted to allocate the $36,000 loss entirely to Cindy. Instead, ABC has two choices: (i) It can "close the books" on December 1. In that case, the loss would be entirely allocated to Alex and Becky, because it occurred before the "books closed." (ii) Alternatively, the loss can be allocated on a daily basis. In that case, Cindy would be entitled to deduct $1,000 of the loss. This figure is one-third of one-twelfth of the loss (one-twelfth because Cindy was a partner only for one-twelfth of the year, one-third because she is a one-third partner).

b) Cash Items

For certain "cash basis items" (of cash basis partnerships), the Code *requires* allocation on a daily basis. The "closing the books" method is not allowed. These items include interest, taxes, payments for services, payments for the use of property, or other items to be added by regulation. [I.R.C. § 706(d)(2)]

Example: Using the same assumptions as in the previous example, assume that ABC is a cash basis real estate partnership that paid interest of $36,000 on December 15 on a loan that was outstanding the entire year. If it could use the "closing the books" method, Cindy would be entitled to one-third of the interest deduction because payment occurred after Cindy became a partner. Under I.R.C. section 706(d)(2), however, this is a cash basis item. It must be allocated in accordance with the time that a person was a member of the partnership. Therefore, Cindy could deduct only about $1,000 (one-third of one-twelfth of the item).

i. Cancellation of Debt Income

A taxpayer must recognize cancellation of debt ("COD") income when a debt is canceled for less than its full amount. [I.R.C. § 61(a)(12)] However, the Code provides for numerous exceptions to COD income, including an exception that applies when a taxpayer is insolvent. [I.R.C. § 108(a)] When a partnership debt is canceled, the partnership has COD income but the various exceptions are applied at the partner level. [I.R.C. § 108(d)(6)]

Example: Alex and Becky are equal partners of AB partnership, which owed a debt of $1,000 to Cindy. The debt was canceled when Cindy accepted $600 in full payment. This produces $400 in COD income, which is taxed to Alex and Becky equally and increases their outside basis by $200 each. Note, however, that the $1,000 reduction in liabilities requires Alex and Becky each to reduce their outside basis by $500. [I.R.C. § 752(b), discussed *infra*, p. 27]

2. Transactions Between Partner and Partnership

a. Treating Partner as Stranger

If a partner engages in a transaction with the partnership *other than in his capacity as* a partner, the transaction is considered as occurring between the partnership and a *stranger*. [I.R.C. § 707(a)] For instance, if a partner loans money to the partnership, the interest on the loan will be taxed as interest income to him and an interest deduction to the partnership. The interest deduction would decrease the partnership's income and thus decrease the partner's pro rata share of that income. [**Pratt v. Commissioner,** 550 F.2d 1023 (5th Cir. 1977)]

Example—Advisory Services: Where a partner was paid for advising the partnership, a service that she also rendered to many other clients, the partner was not acting in the capacity of a partner, and payments for the advice were treated as if made to outsiders. [Rev. Rul. 81–301, 1981–2 C.B. 144]

Compare—management services: However, a partner who manages the partnership is acting in his capacity as a partner. Therefore, payments for such services are treated as distributive shares of partnership income or as guaranteed payments under I.R.C. section 707(c). [**Pratt v. Commissioner,** 64 T.C. 203 (1975), *aff'd*, 550 F.2d 1023 (5th Cir. 1977)]

b. Guaranteed Payments

A partner can agree to work for a *salary*, which is determined without reference to the partnership's income. [I.R.C. § 707(c)] Such a salary (called a "guaranteed payment") is *income* to the recipient and *deductible* to the partnership. Receipt of a guaranteed payment does not reduce the recipient partner's outside basis.

(1) Capitalization

A guaranteed payment is not automatically deductible by the partnership. Often it must be *capitalized*. [**Cagle v. Commissioner,** 63 T.C. 86 (1974), *aff'd*, 539 F.2d 409 (5th Cir. 1976)]

(a) *Section 707(c)* explicitly refers to section 263, which requires capitalization of *expenditures with useful lives in excess of one year*. In addition, payments described in section 707(a) (transactions in which a partner is treated as a stranger—*supra*, p. 18) are also nondeductible if they must be capitalized. [*See* **Zaninovich v. Commissioner,** 616 F.2d 429 (9th Cir. 1980)—prepayment extending beyond the end of the taxable year, but covering less than 12 months, need not be capitalized]

(b) *Section 709* requires capitalization of *amounts paid to organize* a partnership (these can be amortized and deducted over a period of 60 months) or to promote the sale of partnership interests (these cannot be amortized). [*See* **Surloff v. Commissioner,** 81 T.C. 210 (1983); Rev. Rul. 88–4, 1988–1 C.B. 264—cost of tax opinion in limited partnership prospectus is cost of sale of partnership interest; it must be capitalized and cannot be amortized]

(2) Definition

A "guaranteed payment" is one determined "without regard to the income of the partnership." The word "income" in this sentence means *net income*, not gross income. Consequently, a payment to a partner for managerial services, based on a percentage of the *gross* income of the partnership, is a guaranteed payment because it is determined "without regard to the income of the partnership." [Rev. Rul. 81–300, 1981–2 C.B. 143—stating that the IRS will not follow an earlier Tax Court decision, **Pratt v. Commissioner,** *supra*, p. 18, which held "income" includes both net income and gross income]

(a) Illustration—Preferred Return on Investment

A preferred return to a partner based on that partner's investment of capital also constitutes a guaranteed payment. For example, the partnership might be obligated to pay a partner 10% of the partner's initial cash contribution.

(3) Year Taxed

A guaranteed payment is taxed to the recipient as of the *close of the partnership's taxable year* regardless of when it is received by the partner. [I.R.C. § 706(a)] Moreover, a cash basis partner must include the guaranteed payment in income in the year the partnership accrued the expense, even if it was not paid in that year. [I.R.C. § 267(e); Treas. Reg. § 1.707–1(c); **Gaines v. Commissioner,** 45 T.C.M. 363 (1982)—cash basis partner taxed on guaranteed payment accrued by the partnership, even though the partnership was required to capitalize the amount accrued and the partnership never paid the partner the amount owed]

(4) Salaries vs. Other Cash Distribution

(a) Salary vs. Distribution

The treatment of payments received by partners under section 707(a) or 707(c) is quite different from other cash distributions to partners, which are *not* generally taxed to the partners and instead only reduce their outside basis (*infra*, p. 38). Whether a particular cash distribution is a nontaxable withdrawal of partnership cash or a section 707(a) or (c) payment depends on an interpretation of the partnership agreement and a careful analysis of all surrounding circumstances. [**Falconer v. Commissioner,** *supra*, p. 12]

1) Anti-Abuse Provision

Because many section 707(a) or (c) payments must be capitalized, partnerships often tried to disguise payments for services as nontaxable distributions. For example, assume a payment of $30,000 to partner Cindy in exchange for Cindy's services would be ordinary income to Cindy under section 707(a) (*see supra*, p. 19), but would have to be capitalized by ABC partnership (*see supra*, p. 19). Instead, ABC might pretend not to pay Cindy for her services and the partnership agreement might specially allocate $30,000 of income to Cindy. Then ABC would distribute $30,000 in cash to Cindy. The special allocation reduces the distributable shares of the other partners, which has the same effect as a partnership deduction. This scheme is thwarted by a Code section that treats the allocation and distribution as a disguised payment for services that must be capitalized. [I.R.C. § 707(a)(2)(A)]

(b) Stranger Payment vs. Guaranteed Payment

The treatment of guaranteed payments under section 707(c) is different from payments described in section 707(a) (when the partner is treated as a stranger; *see supra*, p. 18). Payments under section 707(a) are taxed to the recipient in accordance with his method of accounting. Thus, an interest payment under section 707(a) would be taxed to a cash basis recipient when received—not at the end of the partnership's year or when the partnership accrues a deduction. [**Pratt v. Commissioner,** *supra*, p. 19]

(5) Recipient of Salary as an "Employee"

The IRS contends that guaranteed payments are *not* treated as salary for purposes of other provisions of the Code; partners are not considered employees of the partnership for tax purposes. [Treas. Reg. § 1.707–1(c); Rev. Rul. 56–326, 1956–2 C.B. 100]

(a) But Note

Although the IRS takes the view that a partner can never be an employee of the partnership, except for the very limited purposes of I.R.C. section 707(c), there is authority to the contrary. It has been held that a partner can be treated as an employee for the purposes of receiving tax-free meals and lodging for the convenience of the employer under I.R.C. section 119. [**Armstrong v. Phinney,** 394 F.2d 661 (5th Cir. 1968)]

(6) Sale vs. Other Cash Distribution

A transfer of partnership property to a partner in satisfaction of a guaranteed payment is a sale or exchange under section 1001(a), and not a distribution under section 731. [Rev. Rul. 2007–40, 2007–1 C.B. 1426]

Example: The ABC partnership transfers property, which it had purchased for $500,000, to partner Alex in satisfaction of an $800,000 guaranteed payment due to Alex at a time when the property was worth $800,000. The transfer is treated as a sale rather than a distribution. Thus, ABC must recognize the $300,000 gain on the transfer of the property and cannot take advantage of the nonrecognition rule in section 731(b) for distributions of appreciated property.

c. Certain Losses Disallowed

Ordinarily when a partner sells property to the partnership (or the partnership sells property to a partner), the transaction will be treated like a sale between strangers—*i.e.,* gain or loss would ordinarily be recognized. [I.R.C. § 707(a)] However, a *loss* on such sale is not deductible if the partner owns, directly or indirectly, *more than 50%* of the interest in capital or profits of the partnership. [I.R.C. § 707(b)(1)(A)]

(1) Two Partnerships

Similarly, one partnership may not deduct a loss on a sale of property to another partnership if the same persons owned, directly or indirectly, more than 50% of both. [I.R.C. § 707(b)(1)(B)]

(2) Constructive Ownership

For purposes of disallowance of losses, various rules of *constructive ownership* are provided so that if close relatives of the seller or buyer are partners, the loss will still be disallowed. [I.R.C. §§ 707(b)(3), 267(c)]

d. Sales at Gain

Similarly, if assets are sold by a partner to a partnership (or a partnership to a partner) at a gain, and the partner owns, directly or indirectly, more than *50%* of the capital or profits of the partnership, the gain is *ordinary income* rather than capital gain. This rule applies only if the asset is not a capital asset in the hands of the transferee (but was a capital asset in the hands of the transferor). Similarly, a capital gain on a sale between two partnerships with 50% common ownership is treated as ordinary income if the asset is not a capital asset in the hands of the transferee. [I.R.C. § 707(b)(2)]

F. Contributions of Property to the Partnership

1. Consequences of Contributions of Property

No gain or loss is recognized to the partnership or the partners on a *contribution* of property to the partnership in exchange for a partnership interest. [I.R.C. § 721]

a. Rationale

This nonrecognition provision is based on the idea that the formation of a partnership is not an *appropriate time* to tax the partner on gain or loss on the assets contributed to the partnership.

b. Distinguish—Sale

A partner can *sell* an asset to the partnership instead of *contributing* it. In that case, the partner will recognize gain or loss on the transfer. Note that loss deductions are disallowed if the partner, directly or indirectly, owns more than 50% of the partnership (*supra,* p. 21). The Code provides that a sale disguised as a contribution (followed by an allocation or distribution to the partner which in substance is payment for the property) must be treated as a sale and not as a contribution. [I.R.C. § 707(a)(2)(B)] This Code section throws doubt on cases that had upheld such transactions as contributions. [*See* **Otey v. Commissioner,** 70 T.C. 312, *aff'd,* 634 F.2d 1046 (6th Cir. 1980)—held contribution, not sale]

(1) Rebuttable presumption

Contributions and distributions made within two years of each other are presumed to constitute sales unless the facts and circumstances suggest otherwise. [Treas. Reg. §1.707–3(c)]

(2) Facts and circumstances

Treasury Regulations identify a variety of facts and circumstances to consider in determining whether to characterize a transfer as a contribution or a sale, including whether the transferor has the right to enforce the subsequent transfer or whether a third party has relied upon the transfer in committing funds. [Treas. Reg. § 1.707–3(b)(2); see **Virginia Historic Tax Credit Fund 2001 LP v. Commissioner**, 639 F.3d 129 (4th Cir. 2011)—citing § 707(a)(2)(B) and Treas. Reg. § 1.707–3 to recharacterize a transfer of cash in exchange for historic tax credits as a purchase rather than a contribution]

2. Basis of Contributed Assets

The basis of property contributed to a partnership by a partner is the same as the adjusted basis of the property to the contributing partner. [I.R.C. § 723] The *partnership's basis* for its assets is often referred to as *"inside basis."*

a. Subsequent Partnership Dispositions

Thus, when the partnership sells the property, any previously unrecognized gain or loss will be recognized and divided among the partners (according to the allocation explained in the next paragraph).

b. Allocations with Respect to Contributed Property

The allocations of gain, loss, and deduction with respect to contributed property must take account of any unrealized gain or loss at the time the property was first contributed. This must be allocated to the partner who contributed the property. Only *subsequent* appreciation or depreciation is allocated among the partners according to their agreement. Similar principles govern the assumption of liabilities by the partnership from cash basis partners (who have incurred but not yet deducted the item). When the partnership pays the debt, the entire deduction will be allocated to the contributing partner. [I.R.C. § 704(c)]

Example: Alex contributes Blackacre to the ABC partnership at a time when its basis is $400 but its value is $1,200. While ABC holds Blackacre, its value further appreciates to $1,500 and it is sold to Xavier for $1,500. ABC's inside basis for Blackacre is $400. However, its gain of $1,100 is not divided equally among Alex, Becky, and Cindy. The $800 unrecognized gain at the time of contribution must be allocated to Alex; the balance of the gain ($300) is divided among Alex, Becky, and Cindy in accordance with the profit sharing ratio of their partnership agreement.

(1) Contribution and Distribution

Suppose in the previous example that within five years after Alex contributes Blackacre to ABC, the partnership distributes Blackacre to Becky. Ordinarily, partnership distributions are not taxable events to the partnership or to the distributee partner. (*See infra,* pp. 38–40.) However, in this situation, the built-in gain of $800 on Blackacre is taxed to Alex at the time of the distribution to Becky. [I.R.C. § 704(c)(1)(B), discussed *infra,* p. 43]

(2) Departure of Contributing Partner

If the contributing partner is no longer a partner at the time of the disposition of the asset, pre-contribution gain is allocated to the transferee partner. [Treas. Reg. § 1.704–3(a)(7)] Pre-contribution loss, however, may be allocated only to the contributing partner to prevent partners from shifting losses among themselves. The asset will be considered to be held at fair market value for purposes of allocating gain or loss to the non-contributing partners. [I.R.C. § 704(c)(1)(C)]

c. Distinguish—Sale to Partnership

Another option would be for the partner to *sell* the property to the partnership, rather than contribute it, in which case the partner will be treated under I.R.C. section 707(a) as an unrelated party. The partnership's inside basis will then be equal to the purchase price.

d. Character of Subsequent Gain

If contributed property was an unrealized receivable or was an inventory item to the contributing partners, any gain or loss on disposition of the asset by the partnership is ordinary rather than capital. (For definitions of unrealized receivables and inventory items, *see infra,* p. 34.) The taint on inventory items lasts only five years after they are contributed to the partnership, but the taint on unrealized receivables lasts indefinitely. [I.R.C. § 724]

Example: Alex held Blackacre for sale to customers in the ordinary course of business. [*See* I.R.C. §§ 1221(1), 1231(b)(1)(B)] However, to Alex's ABC partnership, it was a capital asset or an I.R.C. section 1231 asset. Three years later, ABC sells Blackacre at a gain. The gain is ordinary income. Note also that any portion of the gain that relates back to the time before Blackacre was contributed to ABC must be allocated to Alex (*see supra,* p. 22).

e. Character of Subsequent Loss

If contributed property is a capital asset in the hands of the contributing partner, any loss recognized on the disposition of the property for the next *five years* will be a capital loss to the extent of the "built-in loss" on the asset at the time it was contributed. [I.R.C. § 724(c)]

Example: In year 1, Alex contributes to ABC land that is a capital asset in Alex's hands. Its basis to Alex was $100,000, but it is worth only $40,000. The asset is not a capital asset in the hands of ABC (for example, because it is property held for sale in the ordinary course of business under I.R.C. section 1221(1)). The "built-in loss" was $60,000. ABC sells the land for $26,000 in year 3. ABC has a $76,000 loss, of which $60,000 is capital loss and only $16,000 is ordinary loss. Moreover, the $60,000 capital loss must be allocated to Alex. [I.R.C. § 704(c), discussed *supra,* p. 22]

3. Contribution of Services

If a partner promises to render services, and in exchange receives an interest in the *capital* of the partnership, she is immediately taxable on the value of that interest because the interest is considered property paid to the partner in exchange for rendering services. [I.R.C. § 83; Treas. Reg. § 1.721–1(b)] The law is unclear on whether a partner who receives an interest in future *profits* in exchange for a promise of services is currently taxable on the value of the interest or whether she is not taxable until the profits are received.

a. Capital Interest vs. Profits Interest

A *"capital interest"* in a partnership entitles its owner to a pro rata share of the partnership's *assets* if the partnership is dissolved. A *"profits interest"* entitles the partner *only* to a share of the profits, not to any part of the assets that other partners have contributed or earned.

e.g. **Example:** Keisha, an associate of law partnership ABC, is made a 10% partner on December 31. This entitles her to 10% of the future profits or losses of ABC. But if ABC were dissolved later on December 31, she would receive nothing because she is not entitled to any part of the assets owned by the partnership on that date. In other words, Keisha has only a profits interest, not a capital interest. Although her profits interest is valuable, she may not be taxed on receiving it (*but see infra*, pp. 25–27).

b. Capital Interest—the *Frazell* Case

Wheless and Woolf formed a partnership to prospect for oil. They hired Frazell, a geologist, to check certain properties for them. If the partnership proved successful, Frazell was to receive a capital interest in the partnership after Wheless and Woolf recovered all their expenses. Frazell found oil, but the proposed partnership was never formed; instead, a new corporation was formed in which Frazell took one-sixth of the stock, worth $91,000. *Held:* Frazell has ordinary income. [**United States v. Frazell,** 335 F.2d 487 (5th Cir. 1964)]

(1) Note

The court held that there were two ways to interpret the facts. One was to say that the partnership was actually formed, following which, it was incorporated. Frazell's receipt of an interest in this short-lived partnership would result in realization of income under Treasury Regulation section 1.721–1(b). Another view of the facts was that the partnership was never formed, and so Frazell merely received stock for services. However, such a transaction is also taxable. [I.R.C. § 351(a), discussed *infra,* p. 68]

(2) And Note

Frazell also contributed a valuable oil map. The receipt of either stock or a partnership interest for the map would be a nonrecognizing transaction under I.R.C. section 721 or 351. Therefore, the map and the services had to be valued so as to determine how much of the $91,000 was currently taxable.

c. Profits Interest—the *Diamond* and *Campbell* Cases

It is unclear whether a person who receives an interest solely in future profits in exchange for services is currently taxable on the fair market value of the profits interest. The regulations contain a strong hint that a profits interest, as opposed to a capital interest, is not currently taxable. [Treas. Reg. § 1.721–1(b)] Note the element of double taxation if a profits interest is currently taxed: The partner is taxed when he receives the profits interest, then again when he receives partnership profits. Finally, an interest in future profits is extremely difficult to value. How, for example, would a young associate of a law firm value a 1% interest in the future profits of the firm at the time the associate is promoted to partner? Despite these arguments against current taxation, some case law indicates that a profits interest received for services is currently taxable to the service provider if it is susceptible to valuation.

(1) *Diamond* Case

Diamond performed services and received an interest in a partnership entitling him to 60% of future partnership profits and losses, but no interest in existing partnership capital. Diamond promptly sold the interest for $40,000. It was held that the fair market value of this interest was taxable when received. The case might be distinguishable because the interest was earned solely for past (not future) services, and it was easy to value because it was immediately sold for cash. [**Diamond v. Commissioner,** 56 T.C. 530 (1971), *aff'd,* 492 F.2d 286 (7th Cir. 1974)]

TREATMENT OF CONTRIBUTIONS TO PARTNERSHIP— A SUMMARY		⬛GILBERT
TYPE OF CONTRIBUTION	**DESCRIPTION**	**TAX EFFECT**
GUARANTEED PAYMENT	Cash payments made to partners without regard to *net* income (*e.g.,* an annual salary of $75,000 or 10% of *gross* profits)	*Ordinary income* to the recipient; *deductible* by partnership, but must be *capitalized* if it confers a long-term benefit
OTHER CASH DISTRIBUTIONS	Cash payments made to partners that are *not* guaranteed payments	Generally *not taxable to partner,* but reduces partner's outside basis; generally *not deductible by partnership*
CONTRIBUTIONS OF PROPERTY	Partner transfers property to the partnership under circumstances *not* constituting a sale of the property to the partnership	No gain or loss is recognized at the *time of contribution,* but on subsequent disposition by partnership, gain or loss accrued before the contribution must be *allocated to the contributing partner,* and gain or loss accrued after contribution is *allocated among the partners*

SALE OF ASSETS TO PARTNERSHIP	Partner transfers property to partnership under *circumstances constituting a sale*	Generally *partner must recognize gain or loss* at the time of the sale; but if partner owns more than 50% of the capital or profits of the partnership, a loss is *not* deductible and a gain is treated as *ordinary income*
CONTRIBUTION OF SERVICES IN EXCHANGE FOR CAPITAL INTEREST IN PARTNERSHIP	Partner promises to render services in exchange for a *right to a pro rata share of the partnership's assets upon dissolution*	Partner is *currently taxable* on the value of the interest
CONTRIBUTION OF SERVICES IN EXCHANGE FOR PROFITS INTEREST IN PARTNERSHIP	Partner promises to render services in exchange for a promise of a share of *future profits*	Law is unclear whether partner is currently taxable or only when profits are received; *IRS* taxes interest only if it: (i) relates to a substantially certain stream of commerce; (ii) the partner disposes of the interest within two years of receiving it; *or* (iii) the interest is a limited partnership interest in a publicly traded partnership

(2) *Campbell* Case

Campbell performed services for partnerships (selling interests in the partnerships). As compensation, Campbell received profits interests in those partnerships. Campbell was not taxed on the receipt of these interests because the valuation was too speculative. Dictum in the decision suggests that the court believed that a profit interest received by a person who intends to continue as a partner should not be currently taxable even if it is subject to valuation. [**Campbell v. Commissioner,** 943 F.2d 815 (8th Cir. 1991)]

(3) **IRS View**

In most cases, the IRS will not assert that a partner who has or will perform services for the partnership has income from receipt of a profits interest. It will assert that the profits interest *is* taxable only if: (i) the profits interest relates to a *substantially certain stream of income* from the partnership, (ii) the partner *disposes of the interest within two years* of its receipt, *or* (iii) the interest is a *limited partnership interest in a publicly traded partnership*. [Rev. Proc. 93–27, 1993–2 C.B. 343] *Note:* For purposes of determining whether the partner has disposed of the interest within two years of its receipt, the IRS has clarified that a service provider receives a profits interest on the date of the grant, even if the interest is nonvested. [Rev. Proc. 2001–43] In the absence of such a rule, a post-vesting sale would have made the original issuance of the profits interest taxable.

d. **Proposed Regulations**

Under proposed regulations issued in 2005, the receipt of a partnership interest in connection with the performance of services would be considered "property" under section 83 and therefore would be taxed as a guaranteed payment, if substantially vested, regardless of whether it was considered a profits interest or a capital interest. The partners and the partnership could elect to value it at its liquidation value, however, which would effectively result in the non-taxation of profits interests and the taxation of capital interests. The regulations would also prevent the other partners from taking a deduction for the payment, which would preserve the goal of symmetry of treatment. [Prop. Treas. Reg. §§ 1.721–1(b)(4)(i), 1.83–3(l); IRS Notice 2005–43, 2005–1 C.B. 1221] This issue remains unresolved as Congress attempts to address the proper treatment of the carried interest for managers in private equity funds.

e. Assignment of Income

Suppose Paul Partner has a client, Yolanda, for whom Paul worked before Paul became a partner of ABC. When Paul joined ABC as a partner, he transferred to ABC the right to all future fees earned from Yolanda. When fees from Yolanda are later collected by ABC as a result of Paul's services, are the fees taxed to ABC or to Paul? The IRS contended that under traditional assignment of income principles, the fee should be taxed to Paul. [*See, e.g.,* **Lucas v. Earl,** 281 U.S. 111 (1930)—husband taxed on personal service earnings he had transferred to his wife] But the Tax Court held that under partnership principles, especially the principle that a partnership is a separate entity, fees earned by Paul after he became a partner should be taxed to ABC rather than to Paul. [**Schneer v. Commissioner,** 97 T.C. 643 (1991)]

4. Basis of Partnership Interest

It is frequently necessary to determine the basis for a partner's interest in the partnership (referred to as his "outside basis"). In general, when a partner contributes property to a partnership, his outside basis is equal to the adjusted basis of the contributed asset. [I.R.C. § 722]

a. Effect of Liabilities

Changes in partnership liabilities affect a partner's outside basis as if cash were contributed or distributed by the partnership. Thus an increase in partnership liabilities increases a partner's outside basis—as if he had contributed cash to the partnership. [I.R.C. § 752(a)] A decrease in partnership liabilities decreases outside basis—as if the partnership had distributed cash to the partner. [I.R.C. § 752(b); *see infra,* p. 38 *et seq.* for discussion of distributions] Similarly, if a partnership takes over a partner's liability, this decreases the partner's outside basis. [I.R.C. § 752(b)]

DETERMINING PARTNER'S BASIS IN PARTNERSHIP (OUTSIDE BASIS)	GILBERT
TO DETERMINE A PARTNER'S OUTSIDE BASIS:	
Start with:	Adjusted basis of property partner contributes
Add:	Any increase in partner's liability for partnership debts
Subtract:	Any decrease in partner's liability for partnership debts
Equals:	Outside basis

Example: Alex contributes Blackacre to AB, a 50–50 general partnership. The basis of Blackacre in Alex's hands is $12,000; its value is $20,000. Blackacre is subject to a $3,000 liability. Alex's outside basis is increased $10,500: $12,000 (basis of Blackacre), decreased by $3,000 (partnership took over his liability), increased by $1,500 (Alex's share of the increase in AB's liabilities). The other partner's outside basis is also increased $1,500 (her share of the increase in AB's liabilities). If AB pays off the liability, the partners would each decrease their outside basis by $1,500.

(1) Caution

A decrease in a partner's share of liabilities, or an assumption by a partnership of a partner's personal liability, is treated as a distribution of money. If the "distribution" exceeds a partner's outside basis, gain is recognized. [I.R.C. § 731(a)(1); *see infra,* p. 38 *et seq.*] Thus, in the above example, if Alex's basis for Blackacre had been only $100, Alex would have a $1,400 gain on the contribution ($3,000 less the sum of $100 and $1,500). [Rev. Rul. 84–15, 1984–1 C.B. 158]

(a) Note

The deemed distribution from a reduction of partnership liabilities is considered to occur **at the end of the partnership's taxable year**, not at the date the liabilities are reduced. [Rev. Rul. 94–4, 1994–1 C.B. 196] This ruling could, in some cases, permit a partner to avoid recognizing gain on the deemed distribution because outside basis at the end of the year would first be increased by the partner's distributive share of income before being decreased by the reduction in liabilities.

(2) Cash Basis

Accrued but unpaid liabilities of cash basis partnerships are **not** treated as liabilities for purposes of section 752. [Rev. Rul. 88–77, 1988–2 C.B. 128]

e.g. **Example:** Suppose Attorney Aldo (who uses the cash method of accounting) contributes his solo law practice to the ABC partnership. The basis for the contributed assets is $300. Aldo owes $700 in debts for rent, salary, etc., which he has not paid. His outside basis is $300, and he does not have gain on the contribution. When ABC pays the $700, the deduction is allocated entirely to Aldo. [I.R.C. § 704(c)(3)]

(3) Accrual Basis

A partnership on the accrual basis cannot deduct a liability until all the events have occurred that determine that it is obligated to pay. (*See* Taxation of Individuals Summary for discussion of the "all events" test.) For that reason, contingent liabilities of a partnership do not increase the outside basis of the partners. [Treas. Reg. § 1.752–2(b)(4); **La Rue v. Commissioner,** 90 T.C. 465 (1988)—stock brokerage firm owed money to customers because of back-office technical foul-ups, but the amounts owed to particular customers had not yet been fixed; therefore, the partners' outside bases were not increased]

b. Allocation of Liabilities

Detailed regulations control the allocation of partnership liabilities among the partners. [Treas. Reg. §§ 1.752–1 through –4] These regulations are coordinated with the regulations concerning special allocations and the substantial economic effect test (*supra,* p. 13 *et seq.*).

(1) Recourse Liabilities

Recourse liabilities are debts that one or more partners are personally liable to repay (meaning that the creditor can sue the partners for any deficiency after foreclosing on the security for the loan). Recourse liabilities are allocated among partners in accordance with the economic risk that each bears with respect to the liability.

(a) Worst-Case Scenario

Under the regulations, this allocation is done according to a worst-case scenario. Assume that all partnership assets (including cash) are gone or worthless; assets are sold for zero dollars and all liabilities are immediately payable. The fictitious loss on sale of assets is allocated in accordance with the partners' loss-sharing ratio (assuming this ratio is valid under the substantial economic effect test discussed *supra,* p. 13 *et seq.*). Now determine how much each partner must contribute to the creditors or to the partnership, taking into account any contractual provisions that would shift the loss to other partners (such as reimbursement agreements). This figure measures a partner's ultimate risk with regard to the liability. The recourse liabilities are allocated in accordance with this determination. [Treas. Reg. § 1.752–2]

e.g. **Example:** Alex and Becky each contribute $100 to AB, a general partnership. AB borrows $800 from Cindy. AB purchases a building for $1,000. The building secures the loan; however, the loan is a recourse loan, meaning that Cindy can sue Alex and Becky for a deficiency if the value of the building is insufficient to pay back the loan. The partnership agreement provides that losses are allocated 60% to Alex, 40% to Becky. Assume that this special allocation meets the substantial economic effect test. (*See supra,* p. 13 *et seq.*) In a worst-case scenario, the building would be sold for $0, producing a $1,000 loss that would be allocated 60% to Alex ($600), 40% to Becky ($400). This will produce a $500 negative capital account to Alex and a $300 negative capital account to Becky. A negative capital account means that Alex would owe $500 to the partnership for the benefit of Cindy; Becky would owe $300 to the partnership for the benefit of Cindy. As a result, the $800 liability owed to Cindy is allocated $500 to Alex, $300 to Becky. Alex increases outside basis by $500, Becky increases outside basis by $300. [Treas. Reg. § 1.752–2(f), example 1]

1) Reimbursements

In the previous example, suppose Alex and Becky agreed that if the debt to Cindy is not paid, Alex will relieve Becky of any liability to Cindy. In that case, the entire economic risk of loss is borne by Alex and the entire liability would be allocated to Alex. [Treas. Reg. § 1.752–2(b)(3), (b)(5)]

(2) Limited Partnerships

In a limited partnership, only a general partner is responsible for paying recourse liabilities in the event the worst-case scenario occurs. Consequently, all recourse liabilities are allocated to the general partner or partners. ***In unusual situations***, the partnership agreement might require a limited partner to repay any deficit in the partner's capital account or to reimburse the general partner(s) for any loss. In such situations, recourse liabilities are allocated to the limited partners. [Treas. Reg. § 1.752–2(f), example 3]

(3) Nonrecourse Liabilities

Nonrecourse liabilities are debts that the debtor has no personal obligation to repay even if the security for the debt is insufficient to repay the creditor. In general, nonrecourse liabilities are shared between the partners based on their share of partnership *profits*. As a result, *both limited and general partners* increase outside basis by reason of nonrecourse liabilities. [Treas. Reg. § 1.752–3]

e.g. **Example:** Alex and Becky each contribute $100 to AB, a general partnership. AB borrows $800 on a nonrecourse loan. AB purchases a building for $1,000. The agreement provides that losses are allocated 60% to Alex and 40% to Becky, but profits are split 50–50. Alex and Becky each increase outside basis by $400.

(a) Nonrecourse Liabilities and Minimum Gain

"Minimum gain" is the gain that would occur on foreclosure of a nonrecourse loan. This gain is the excess of the principal balance of a nonrecourse loan over the adjusted basis of the property that secures the loan. [**Commissioner v. Tufts,** 461 U.S. 300 (1983)] Recall that the regulations permit special allocations of loss arising out of nonrecourse debt if a partner (including a limited partner) is bound by a minimum gain chargeback provision. (*See supra,* pp. 14–15.) If minimum gain is present (*i.e.,* the adjusted basis of the asset has fallen below the principal balance of the loan), the nonrecourse liabilities are first allocated to each partner based on that partner's share of minimum gain (*i.e.,* based on the nonrecourse deductions allocated to the partner that create minimum gain). The balance of the nonrecourse loan is allocated in accordance with profit sharing ratios. [*See* Treas. Reg. § 1.752–3]

5. Limits on Deduction of Partnership Losses

a. At-Risk Rules

A partner can deduct partnership losses only to the extent of her outside basis. [I.R.C. § 704(d); *and see supra,* p. 12] However, a partner is not permitted to deduct partnership losses beyond the amount she has placed "at risk" in the partnership. Thus, a partner may not deduct losses of the partnership by reason of increases in her basis occurring because of partnership liabilities *for which she is not personally liable.* [I.R.C. § 465]

e.g. **Example:** AB is a 50–50 partnership (general *or* limited) that makes stock market investments. AB borrows $50,000 to buy stocks but has *no* liability to repay it (the stocks being pledged to secure the loan). Neither partner can use her share of the $50,000 debt for purposes of deducting partnership losses. However, each can add the debt to their outside basis for any purpose other than deducting losses, *e.g.,* to avoid tax on a cash distribution (*see infra,* p. 38).

EXAM TIP   **⬛GILBERT**

The at-risk rules come into play often on law school exams. Be sure to remember the basics: A partner generally is *not allowed to deduct partnership losses* beyond the amount that the partner has placed at risk in the partnership (*i.e.,* beyond the value of cash or property that the partner has contributed and debts for which the partner is personally liable).

---

(1) Exception for Real Estate Loans

The at-risk rules apply to real estate investments in the same way that they apply to all other investments. However, there are several exceptions: A taxpayer is treated as being at risk with respect to nonrecourse loans *provided by government entities*. In addition, a taxpayer is at risk for loans provided by *qualified persons*. Qualified persons are actively and regularly engaged in lending money (*e.g.*, banks or savings and loans). However, financing provided by the seller of the property to the taxpayer does not qualify under this exception, even if the lender is a qualified person. [I.R.C. § 465(b)(6)]

It is important to remember that while the at-risk rules may apply to real estate, they often do not because of the exceptions for nonrecourse loans from government entities and banks and the like. On your exam, you must pay particular attention to *who has financed a purchase of real property* for a partnership. If it was the seller and the loan was nonrecourse, the at-risk rules come into play. But if the partnership obtained a nonrecourse loan from a government entity or a financial institution, the at-risk rules do not apply.

(2) Definition of Amounts at Risk

A partner cannot deduct partnership losses except to the extent of amounts she has placed at risk in the partnership. This means investments of cash or other assets, or partnership liabilities for which the partner is liable, but not partnership liabilities (other than qualified real estate loans) for which she has no personal liability.

(a) *Even if the partner has no personal liability for a partnership debt,* she will be at risk if she has pledged her own property (but not the partnership's property) to secure the debt. [I.R.C. § 465(b)(2)(B)]

(b) *Even if a partner is apparently liable for a partnership debt*, it cannot be used for the purpose of deducting loss if the amount is owed to another partner (or a close relative of another partner). Nor can the partner use the liability if she is indirectly protected against loss, *e.g.*, by someone else's guarantee of the loan. [I.R.C. § 465(b)(3), (4); Rev. Rul. 77–401, 1977–2 C.B. 197]

(3) Later Deduction Possible

If a partner is denied a loss deduction because she lacks sufficient amounts at risk, the deduction may be taken in future years if she has amounts at risk in those years. [I.R.C. § 465(a)(2)]

(4) Overvalued Property

Whether or not the at-risk rules apply, partners cannot increase outside basis by reason of a liability if the liability is speculative or contingent or the property securing it is overvalued. [**Brountas v. Commissioner,** 692 F.2d 152 (1st Cir. 1982), *cert. denied,* 459 U.S. 1106 (1983); **Estate of Franklin v. Commissioner,** 544 F.2d 1045 (9th Cir. 1976)]

b. Passive Losses

Generally, a partner may deduct losses from "passive activities" only against income from "passive activities"; a partner *cannot* deduct losses from "passive activities" against other income (such as income from a profession or income from investments). [I.R.C. § 469] This provision essentially destroys almost all "tax shelters." A "passive activity" is a trade or business in which the partner does not "*materially participate*." To materially participate, the taxpayer must be involved on a "regular, continuous, and substantial" basis. A limited partner never materially participates. A general partner may or may not materially participate. The regulations state a series of tests and safe harbors to help taxpayers meet the "material participation" requirement. [Treas. Reg. § 1.469–5T] For example, a taxpayer who participates in the business for more than 500 hours per year satisfies the material participation standard. [Treas. Reg. § 1.469–5T(a)(1); *compare* **Mordkin v. Commissioner,** T.C. Memo 1996–187—75–130 hours per year managing a partnership ski lodge is not material participation]

EXAM TIP

Like the at-risk rules, the passive loss rule has a good chance of arising in a law school exam question. Be sure to remember that a partner cannot deduct losses from passive activities *against other income*.

---

(1) Rentals

All rental activity is deemed passive.

(a) Exception—Moderate Income Taxpayer

A taxpayer (as an individual or as a general partner) is allowed to deduct up to $25,000 in passive loss from real estate activity if the taxpayer "*actively participates*" (*e.g.,* by finding tenants, arranging for repairs, etc.). But this applies only to taxpayers with adjusted gross incomes under $100,000. If AGI exceeds $100,000, the $25,000 figure is phased out at the rate of 50¢ for each dollar by which AGI exceeds $100,000. Note, however, that this exception for real property rental is *not* available to a *limited partner*.

(b) Exception—Real Estate Professionals

A real estate professional can deduct passive losses from rental real estate without limit. A real estate professional is a taxpayer who performs more than 750 hours of service in real property trades or businesses in which the taxpayer materially participates. [I.R.C. § 469(c)(7)]

(2) Disallowed Loss May Be Carried Forward

If a taxpayer's losses from passive activities exceed the taxpayer's income from passive activities, the excess loss is disallowed in the current tax year. However, disallowed passive loss is carried forward and can be used against passive income in future years. A previously disallowed loss can also be deducted upon a taxable disposition of the property.

(3) Application to Corporations

The passive loss rule [I.R.C. § 469] applies to personal service corporations and S corporations as well as to individuals and partnerships. It also applies in more limited form to closely held C corporations. In a closely held C corporation, more than 50% of the stock is owned by five or fewer persons. A closely held C corporation can subtract passive losses from its net active income but not from its investment income.

G. Sales of Partnership Interests

DETERMINING CAPITAL GAIN OR LOSS ON SALE OF PARTNERSHIP INTEREST—AN APPROACH

Start with:	Sale price
Add:	Partner's share of partnership debt
Subtract:	Amount of sale price allocable to hot assets
Subtract:	Partner's outside basis before the sale not allocable to hot assets
Equals:	Capital gain or loss*

* If the result is positive and the partner held the interest for more than a year, it is a long-term capital gain. If the result is negative, the loss can be deducted only to the extent of capital gains plus $3,000, although an individual partner can carry forward greater losses for deduction in future years.

1. General Rule

A partnership interest is treated as a capital asset. When it is sold or exchanged, gain or loss is recognized to the transferor partner. It is *capital gain or loss*, except as provided in I.R.C. section 751 (*infra,* p. 33). [I.R.C. § 741] An *exchange* of partnership interests does not qualify for nonrecognition as a "like-kind" exchange under section 1031. [I.R.C. § 1031(a)(2)(D)] (*See* Taxation of Individuals Summary for discussion of section 1031.)

a. Importance of Capital Treatment

(1) Long-Term Capital Gain

For *individuals*, long-term capital gain is taxed at a lower rate than ordinary income. Although ordinary income can be taxed at rates up to 39.6%, capital gain is taxed at a maximum rate of 20% for assets held more than one year. [I.R.C. § 1(h)] *Corporate* capital gain, however, is taxed at a rate of 35%. [I.R.C. § 1201(a)]

(2) Capital Loss

Corporations can deduct capital loss only to the extent of capital gain. In the case of individuals, capital loss in excess of capital gain can be deducted to the extent of $3,000 per year [I.R.C. § 1211(a), (b)], and the amount exceeding that limit can be carried forward to future years and deducted against capital gains plus $3,000 in future years [I.R.C. § 1212(b)]. In the case of corporate capital loss, the excess of capital loss over capital gain can be carried back three years and forward only five years. [I.R.C. § 1211(a)]

2. Exception—Hot Assets

When a partnership interest is sold, the consideration allocable to the partnership's *unrealized receivables and inventory* items becomes *ordinary income* to the selling partner. [I.R.C. § 751(a)] Thus, for this purpose, the partnership is treated like an *aggregate* rather than an *entity*; the consequences to the selling partner are the same as if he had sold the underlying assets instead of the partnership interest. Unrealized receivables and inventory items are often referred to as "hot assets."

a. Unrealized Receivables

"Unrealized receivables" are rights to payment, not previously includible in income, for past or future sales of goods or services. [I.R.C. § 751(c)] This provision is designed to insure that ordinary income will not be avoided in situations where the partnership has not yet recognized it because it uses the cash basis.

 Example: Restitutionary rights to payment for unbilled legal services are unrealized receivables. [**Logan v. Commissioner,** 51 T.C. 482 (1968)]

(1) Depreciation Recapture

Suppose the partnership owns assets on which depreciation would be recaptured as ordinary income if the partnership had sold the assets. [I.R.C. §§ 1245, 1250—discussed in the Taxation of Individuals Summary] This recapturable depreciation is considered to be an "unrealized receivable." [I.R.C. § 751(c)] Thus, on a sale of a partnership interest, the amount received allocable to the recapturable depreciation becomes ordinary income.

(2) Judicial Construction of Unrealized Receivables

The term "unrealized receivables" has been broadly construed. For example, a contract to manage a dog racing track was treated as an unrealized receivable because it was considered a right to payment for *services to be rendered in the future*. [**Ledoux v. Commissioner,** 77 T.C. 293 (1981), *aff'd*, 695 F.2d 1320 (11th Cir. 1983)]

b. "Inventory Items"

The term "inventory items" refers to any assets which, if sold by the partnership, would not be capital assets or property described in I.R.C. section 1231. Thus, parcels of real property subdivided primarily for sale to customers in the ordinary course of business are inventory items. [I.R.C. §§ 1221(1), 1231(b)(1)(B); **Estate of Freeland v. Commissioner,** 393 F.2d 573 (9th Cir. 1968)]

c. Basis of Section 751 Property

In making the necessary computations under I.R.C. section 751, the basis of unrealized receivables and inventory items is the same as their inside basis. Of course, the inside basis for an unrealized receivable for rendering services would generally be zero. [Treas. Reg. § 1.751–1(a)(2); I.R.C. § 732] The amount allocated to section 751 items in a contract of sale of the partnership will generally be regarded by the IRS as correct. [Treas. Reg. § 1.751–1(a)(2)]

 Example: The AB partnership is on the cash basis and has unrealized accounts receivable of $15,000. Thus, Alexa's interest in the receivables is $7,500. Alexa's outside basis in her partnership interest is $20,000, and she sells it for $23,000. However, she first must allocate $7,500 of the sale price to the unrealized receivables, the basis of which is zero. Thus, she has $7,500 of ordinary income. The remaining $15,500 of the sale price is allocated to the balance of the partnership interest. She has a $4,500 capital loss on the balance of her partnership interest ($20,000 less $15,500). [*See* Treas. Reg. § 1.751–1(g)—additional examples]

3. Liabilities of Partnership

If a partner sells a partnership interest, her amount realized includes her share of partnership liabilities. [I.R.C. § 752(b), (d)] (*See supra*, p. 28 *et seq.* for discussion of allocation of liabilities between partners.)

 Example: Alexa sells her partnership interest for $20,000 cash. Her share of partnership liabilities was $8,000. Her amount realized is $28,000.

a. Nonrecourse Liabilities

This rule does not change even if the loan is nonrecourse and is secured by property worth less than the loan. The selling partner is still considered to realize the full amount of the loan. [I.R.C. § 7701(g); **Commissioner v. Tufts,** 461 U.S. 300 (1983)]

4. Basis of Partnership Assets After Transfer of Partnership Interest

a. General Rule

Ordinarily the inside basis of a partnership asset is not changed merely because a partnership interest has been sold. [I.R.C. § 743(a)]

b. Special Basis Adjustment

However, the Code provides that inside basis can be adjusted on a transfer of a partnership interest. If the partnership *makes an election* pursuant to I.R.C. section 754, inside basis will be adjusted *as to the partner who acquired the interest* so that it is the same as what that partner paid for the interest. [I.R.C. § 743(b)]

 Example: The inside basis of the assets in the hands of the AB partnership is $6,000. However, the fair market value of the assets is $15,000. Cindy purchases Beckett's 50% partnership interest for $7,500. If the partnership makes the election provided in sections 743(b) and 754, the inside basis is adjusted *as to Cindy only*. It remains the same as to partner Alexa ($3,000) but is increased to $7,500 as to Cindy. Thus, if the partnership then sold the assets for their fair market value of $15,000, there would be a $4,500 gain to Alexa but no gain or loss to Cindy. This reflects the fact that when she bought the interest, Cindy paid the fair market value of the asset.

(1) Death of Partner

Sections 743(b) and 754 also apply when a partner dies. The person inheriting the partnership interest takes as his basis the fair market value of the partnership interest at the date of death. [I.R.C. § 1014] As to the legatee, the basis of partnership assets is adjusted if the election under section 754 is made.

(a) Exception

No step-up in basis is allowed for unrealized receivables. An increase in basis of those assets would run counter to the policy of I.R.C. section 691, relating to income in respect of a decedent. (*See* Taxation of Individuals Summary.) [**Quick Trust v. Commissioner,** 54 T.C. 1336, *aff'd*, 444 F.2d 90 (8th Cir. 1971)]

(2) Permanency of Election

The election operates permanently so that it might later involve a disadvantageous *downward* adjustment of the basis of partnership property on later transfers of partnership interests.

(3) Allocation of Basis

Section 755 provides that when a section 754 election is made, the inside basis is to be adjusted, insofar as possible, so as to conform the bases of the assets with their *market values*. The basis is then allocated between the capital and noncapital assets to eliminate the gain on a subsequent sale. An amount equal to the gain or loss on a hypothetical sale of the noncapital assets is allocated to the noncapital assets, and the remaining basis adjustment is allocated to the capital assets. The maximum amount of the basis adjustment is the excess of the purchase price over the buyer's share of the total inside basis of the assets. [*See* Treas. Reg. § 1.755–1(c)]

Example: In the previous example (*supra,* p. 35), assume that the value of the AB partnership's assets exceeded the inside basis because of the following: (i) $4,000 of unrealized appreciation with respect to a partnership building that had an inside basis of $3,000 and a current fair market value of $7,000, and (ii) $5,000 of unrealized gain with respect to section 751 property that had an inside basis of $3,000 and a fair market value of $8,000. When Beckett sold his 50% partnership interest to Cindy for $7,500, $2,000 ($3,500–$1,500) is allocable to section 751 property and the remaining $2,500 of the gain ($4,000–$1,500) is capital gains. If the partnership elects after the sale of Beckett's interest to Cindy to step up the inside basis of the assets with respect to Cindy under sections 743(b) and 754, the inside basis of the building would increase from $1,500 to $2,500 and the inside basis of the section 751 property would increase from $1,500 to $2,000. This increase in the inside basis of the assets with respect to Cindy would prevent the double taxation of gain to her in the event of a sale of the assets.

(4) Case Law

In a district court case, a partnership was given the benefit of an election under sections 743 and 754 even though the partnership had failed to make the election. The court did so in order to prevent double taxation of the gain from unrealized receivables. That is, the seller of the partnership interest was taxed and the IRS sought to tax the buyer on the same gain when the receivables were collected. [**Barnes v. United States,** 253 F. Supp. 116 (S.D. Ill. 1966)]

c. Required Basis Adjustment

If there is a substantial built-in loss (in excess of $250,000) immediately following a transfer of a partnership interest, then the partnership *must* adjust the inside basis of partnership property downward with respect to the transferee partner's interest. [I.R.C. § 743(a), (d)] This is designed to prevent loss-shifting among partners.

(1) Exception

The required downward adjustment to inside basis is optional for certain investment partnerships, such as venture capital and other similar funds holding almost exclusively investment assets. [I.R.C. § 743(e)(1)] Instead, the partnership may choose to apply a partnership loss limitation rule. Under this alternative, the transferee is not permitted to share in the losses from the transfer of partnership property unless she can show that the losses exceed the loss recognized on the original transfer of the partnership interest. [I.R.C. § 743(e)(2)]

5. Termination of Partnerships

a. Consequence

(1) Timing

If a partnership "terminates," all income or loss to the date of termination must be reflected on the returns of the partners for the *year in which the termination occurs*.

e.g. **Example:** The taxable year of AB partnership ends on January 31 of year 1. The partnership is *terminated* on December 1 of year 1. The partners must reflect on their year 1 returns both the results for the 12 months ending January 31, and also the results for the 10 months between February 1 and December 1 of year 1. The result is to telescope 22 months of profits into a single taxable year, because both the tax year of the partnership and the year of its termination are within the individual partner's tax year.

(2) Distribution

On "termination," the assets of the partnership are deemed distributed to the partners. Note, however, on a termination that occurs by reason of the sale or exchange of 50% or more of the partnership interests of a continuing partnership (*see infra*, p. 37), the old partnership is deemed to have contributed its assets to a new partnership. The old partnership then distributes the interests in the new partnership to the new partners. [Treas. Reg. § 1.708–1(b)(4)] This approach avoids the problems that could arise if the old partnership's assets were deemed distributed to partners in a partnership liquidation, particularly under the mixing bowl provisions discussed *infra*, at p. 42 *et seq.*

b. Events That Terminate Partnership

(1) Discontinuance of Business

If no part of the business or the financial operation of the partnership continues to be carried on by any of its partners, the partnership is terminated. [I.R.C. § 708(b)(1)(A)]

(a) Death

However, if one partner of a two-partner firm dies or retires, the partnership remains in existence until all payments due to that partner or the estate have been made. [Treas. Reg. §§ 1.736–1(a)(6), 1.708–1(b)(1)(i)]

(b) Winding up

If the partnership sells its assets but is still in the process of winding up, it is not terminated, although it may be considered dissolved for state law purposes.

(2) Sale of Interest

If, during a 12-month period, there is a *sale or exchange* of *50%* or more of the partnership interest in capital and profits, the partnership terminates as to *all partners*. [I.R.C. § 708(b)(1)(B); **McCauslen v. Commissioner,** 45 T.C. 588 (1966)—sale by one 50% partner of his interest to other partner]

(a) But Note

A *gift* of the partnership interest does not trigger this result, neither does the death of a partner and a bequest of the interest to survivors. [Treas. Reg. § 1.708–1(b)(1)(ii); **Maxcy v. Commissioner,** 59 T.C. 716 (1973)]

(b) Partnership Conversions

Conversion of a general partnership to a limited partnership is not considered a sale or exchange under section 708. Therefore, the partnership does not terminate. [Rev. Rul. 84–52, 1984–1 C.B 157] The same is true of conversion of a partnership to an LLC or LLP. [Rev. Rul. 95–37, 1995–1 C.B. 137; Rev. Rul. 95–55, 1995–2 C.B. 313] (*Note:* For discussion of LLCs and LLPs, *see supra,* pp. 5–6.)

(c) Distribution of Subpartnership

Suppose Partnership AB owns a 60% interest in partnership S. AB distributes its interest in S to its partners Alexa and Beckett. This is treated as a sale or exchange of the 60% interest in partnership S for the purpose of terminating partnership S. [I.R.C. § 761(e)(1)] For other purposes, however, the distribution of an interest in a subpartnership is treated under the distribution rules (*see infra,* p. 38 *et seq.*) rather than the sale rules (*supra,* p. 33 *et seq.*).

(d) Partnership Mergers and Divisions

In the case of a merger or consolidation of two or more partnerships, or a division of a partnership into two or more partnerships, the surviving or resulting partnership(s) is considered a continuation of the merging, consolidating, or prior partnership whose members own an interest of more than 50% of the capital and profits of the surviving or resulting partnership(s). [I.R.C. § 708(b)(2)]

H. Partnership Distributions and Basis Adjustments

1. General Rule

The *distribution* of cash or property by a partnership to a partner generally is *not* a taxable event, either to the partnership or to the partner. Instead the partner's outside basis is *reduced* (but not below zero) by the amount of *any money* distributed to the partner and by the *basis* to such partner of *distributed property* other than money. [I.R.C. § 733]

a. Exception—Distribution of Cash or Marketable Securities

If a partnership distributes cash or marketable securities to a partner, the partner recognizes gain *if* the cash plus the fair market value of the marketable securities *exceeds the partner's outside basis*. [I.R.C. § 731(a)(1), (c)]

(1) Definition of "Marketable Securities"

The term "marketable securities" means financial instruments (such as stocks, bonds, options, etc.) and foreign currencies. The instruments or currencies must be *actively traded* as of the date of distribution. The term "marketable securities" also covers a variety of other instruments which are the economic equivalent of actively traded instruments. [I.R.C. § 731(c)(2)]

(2) Exceptions

A distribution of marketable securities will not be treated as a cash distribution in a few narrowly defined situations, including certain investment partnerships or situations in which the recipient partner contributed the security in question to the partnership. [I.R.C. § 731(c)(3)(A)]

e.g. **Example:** Antoine's outside basis in ABC is $100 but Antoine's partnership interest is worth $250. ABC distributes IBM stock to Antoine worth $250 in liquidation of Antoine's partnership interest. Under the general rule, Antoine would recognize no gain and the IBM stock would have a basis of $100. [I.R.C. § 731(a)(1)] As a result, Antoine could defer recognition of gain until he sold the IBM stock. Because IBM stock is a marketable security, section 731(c) requires that the distribution be treated as if Antoine received $250 in cash. Antoine has an immediate $150 capital gain. The IBM stock has a basis of $250 in Antoine's hands.

b. Exception—Guaranteed Payments

Receipt of a guaranteed payment is taxable to the partner as ordinary income. (*See supra,* p. 19.)

c. Exception—Hot Assets

A distribution of cash or other assets in exchange for a partner's interest in hot assets (*i.e.*, unrealized receivables or substantially appreciated inventory) may be taxed to that partner. (*See infra,* p. 41.) Similarly, a distribution of hot assets by a partnership to a partner may be taxable to the partnership. (*See infra,* p. 40.)

d. Exception—Disguised Sales

A distribution of property that follows closely after a contribution of money or other property to the partnership by a partner may be characterized as a disguised sale. (*See supra*, p. 21)

e. Caution—Partnership Liabilities

Recall that a reduction in a partner's share of partnership liabilities is treated as a distribution of money and can, if it exceeds outside basis, trigger gain recognition. [I.R.C. § 752(b); *see supra*, p. 28]

e.g. **Example:** Partnership AB distributes Blackacre to Abby and Greenacre to Ben. Blackacre was subject to a partnership liability of $1,600 and Greenacre was subject to a partnership liability of $2,800. Abby's and Ben's shares of partnership liabilities each decrease by $2,200 (because neither is subject to his one-half share of the AB liabilities totaling $4,400). This is considered as if it were a $2,200 cash distribution to Abby and Ben, which reduces their outside basis. [I.R.C. § 752(b)] But Abby's individual debt increases by $1,600 and Ben's individual debt increases by $2,800. These individual debt increases are treated like contributions of money to the partnership. [I.R.C. § 752(a)] The increases and decreases are netted out, so that Abby has a $600 decrease in outside basis and Ben has a $600 increase in outside basis. In addition, Abby and Ben must reduce outside basis by an amount equal to AB's basis in Blackacre and Greenacre, respectively. (*See supra*, p. 38; and *see infra*, p. 40.) [Rev. Rul. 79–205, 1979–2 C.B. 255]

f. Draws

A "draw" is an advance payment of a partner's expected year-end distribution. A draw is treated as a loan to the partner which is not taxable until the end of the partnership's taxable year. [Treas. Reg. § 1.731–1(a)(1)(ii)]

g. Loss recognition

Loss can be recognized only in connection with a liquidation of the partner's interest. (*See infra,* p. 44 *et seq.*)

2. Distributions of Property

If a partnership distributes property other than money, the partnership's inside basis becomes the distributee partner's basis for the property. [I.R.C. § 732(a)] As already noted, that partner's outside basis is reduced by that same amount.

a. Exception

However, the basis to the distributee partner cannot exceed the outside basis of her partnership interest, reduced by any money distributed in the same transaction. [I.R.C. § 732(a)(2)] The result may be that some of the inside basis of the distributed property could disappear. (A provision that may solve this problem is considered *infra,* p. 49.) There is a different rule for distributions in liquidation (*see infra,* p. 47).

e.g. **Example:** Abby's outside basis in AB partnership is $20,000. The partnership makes a nonliquidating distribution to Abby of $12,000 cash and also land having an inside basis of $10,000 and a fair market value of $50,000. Abby first reduces her outside basis to $8,000 by reason of the cash distribution; she has no gain on the cash distribution. Then she takes into account the distribution of land by reducing her outside basis to zero. The land ordinarily would have a basis to her of $10,000 (the partnership's inside basis), but in this case the basis of the land to her is only $8,000 (which was her remaining outside basis). Basis of $2,000 has disappeared (*but see infra,* p. 49). [*See* Rev. Rul. 79–205, *supra,* p. 39—distribution of property subject to liabilities: increase and decrease in outside basis owing to liability adjustments are netted; then remaining outside basis is applied to establish basis of property received]

3. Disproportionate Distributions of Receivables or Inventory

If the partnership distributes hot assets (unrealized receivables or substantially appreciated inventory items) to a partner *in exchange for her interest in other partnership assets,* the partnership realizes ordinary income on the distribution as if it had sold those assets to an outsider. [I.R.C. § 751(b)(1)(A)]

DISTRIBUTION TYPE	EFFECT
DISTRIBUTIONS OF *CASH OR MARKETABLE SECURITIES* OTHER THAN GUARANTEED PAYMENTS	*Reduces partner's outside basis* (but not below zero); amounts exceeding outside basis are treated as gain
DISTRIBUTIONS OF *PROPERTY*	Partnership's *inside basis becomes distributee's* basis up to an amount equal to the distributee's outside basis reduced by any cash distributed to the partner in the same transaction
DISTRIBUTIONS OF *HOT ASSETS* TO PARTNER IN EXCHANGE FOR PARTNER'S INTEREST IN OTHER PARTNERSHIP ASSETS	Partnership realizes *ordinary income*
DISTRIBUTIONS OF *CASH OR OTHER PROPERTY* TO A PARTNER IN EXCHANGE FOR PARTNER'S INTEREST IN HOT ASSETS	The partner has *ordinary income* to the extent of the interest transferred

a. Substantially Appreciated Inventory Items

Recall that on a sale of a partnership interest, amounts allocated to inventory items (whether or not the inventory items have appreciated in value) can produce ordinary income rather than capital gain to the selling partner. (*See supra*, p. 33 *et seq.*) For purposes of the disproportionate distribution rules, however, the inventory items must be "substantially appreciated" to be treated as hot assets. For this purpose, "substantial appreciation" means that the fair market value of the inventory items exceeds 120% of the partnership's inside basis for the items. [I.R.C. § 751(b)(3)(A)]

b. Note—Where Roles Reversed

Similarly, if a partnership distributes cash or other assets to a partner *in exchange for her interest* in hot assets, the distribution is taxable to the partner as ordinary income to the extent of her transfer of an interest in those assets.[I.R.C. § 751(b)(1)(B)]

(1) Exceptions

The rules of I.R.C. section 751(b)(1) do not apply to a distribution of property that the partner *originally contributed* to the partnership. They also do not apply to payments to a retiring partner described in I.R.C. section 736(a), but they do apply to payments described in I.R.C. section 736(b) (*see infra*, pp. 45–49). [I.R.C. § 751(b)(2); Treas. Reg. § 1.751(b)(4)]

c. Effect

The effect of section 751(b) is to take certain distributions out of the general rules of section 731, which provide that most distributions are not taxable to the partnership or the partner. Instead, the distribution is made taxable to the partnership or the partner, depending on which of them sold an interest in the receivables or inventory. There is no problem if the partners receive a *pro rata distribution* of cash, or of receivables or inventory, because then none of them has increased or decreased his interest in the receivables or inventory. [Treas. Reg. § 1.751–1(b)(1)(ii)]

e.g. **Example:** Section 751(b) can be extremely complex in operation. Mechanically, the regulations treat distributions covered by section 751(b) as a "double distribution." Suppose Bella has an outside basis of $10,000 for her interest in ABC and receives a $6,000 distribution in exchange for her interest in unrealized receivables, which had an inside basis of zero. This is treated as if ABC first distributed the receivables to Bella and then *bought them back*. The fictitious distribution of the receivables to Bella produces no gain to Bella or ABC, and the receivables have a zero basis in Bella's hands. Her outside basis remains $10,000. When Bella "sells" the receivables back to ABC, she has $6,000 of ordinary income on the "sale." ABC now has an inside basis of $6,000 for these receivables.

4. Further Effects of Distribution

a. Holding Period

When a partner *sells* property previously distributed to her by the partnership, she is entitled to include in her holding period the partnership's holding period for the same property. [I.R.C. § 735(b)]

b. Unrealized Receivables

If the partnership distributes unrealized receivables to the partner, her gain or loss on the subsequent sale or collection of the items is ordinary income. [I.R.C. § 735(a)(1)]

c. Inventory Items

If the partnership distributed inventory items (whether or not substantially appreciated) to the partner, and she sells them within five years of the date of the distribution, her gain or loss will be ordinary rather than capital. [I.R.C. § 735(a)(2)]

5. Mixing Bowl Transactions

While most partnership distributions are tax-free to both the partnership and the partner, Congress became concerned with strategies to avoid tax on precontribution gains, or to shift or defer tax on those gains, through the device of contributions to and distributions of appreciated property from a partnership. These are often referred to as "mixing bowl transactions." The Code sections relating to mixing bowl transactions apply only if the related contribution and distribution occur *within seven years* of each other.

a. Illustration of Mixing Bowl Transactions

Alex, Becky, and Cindy form partnership ABC as equal partners. Alex contributes Blackacre, which has a basis of $100 and a value of $1,000. Becky contributes Greenacre, which has a basis and a value of $1,000. Cindy contributes $1,000 cash. Recall that if ABC sold Blackacre for $1,300, $900 of its gain would be allocated to Alex; the remaining $300 would be allocated equally among Alex, Becky, and Cindy. [I.R.C. § 704(c)(1); *see supra,* p. 22] Now imagine two possibilities:

(1) ABC distributes Blackacre to Becky at a time when it is worth $1,300 in liquidation of Becky's interest. Under the normal rules, Becky has no gain on this transfer and her basis for Blackacre is $1,000 (assuming $1,000 is Becky's outside basis for her interest in ABC). [I.R.C. §§ 731(a)(1), 732(b)] Becky now sells Blackacre and has

a gain of only $300. *Effect:* The $900 precontribution gain on Blackacre has not been recognized even though Blackacre has been sold.

(2) ABC distributes Greenacre to Alex when Greenacre is worth $1,300. Because Alex's outside basis was only $100, Alex's basis for Greenacre is $100, meaning that the basis for Greenacre was reduced by $900. [I.R.C. § 732(a)(2)] Assume that Alex is not planning to sell Greenacre anytime soon. By making the election under sections 734 and 754, ABC can increase the basis of Blackacre by $900. (*See infra,* p. 49.) Now ABC can sell Blackacre without recognizing the precontribution gain of $900.

b. Code Sections to Restrict Mixing Bowl Transactions

(1) Contribution of Appreciated Property by One Partner, Distribution to Another

In the first mixing bowl illustration above (contribution of Blackacre by Alex, distribution of Blackacre to Becky), the normal rules allowed a step-up in basis of Blackacre and allowed Blackacre to be sold by Becky without recognition of the precontribution gain. However, the Code now requires that the $900 precontribution gain be taxed to Alex, as if ABC had sold the property rather than distributing it. [I.R.C. § 704(c)(1)(B)] This section applies only if the distribution occurs within seven years of the contribution of Blackacre to ABC. Alex's outside basis is increased by $900, and the basis of Blackacre is increased by $900 before it is distributed to Becky.

(2) Contribution of Appreciated Property by One Partner, Distribution of Different Property to That Partner

In the second mixing bowl example above (contribution of Blackacre by Alex, distribution of Greenacre to Alex), the normal rules would allow ABC to sell Blackacre after the distribution without recognition of the precontribution gain. Instead, the Code requires taxation of the precontribution gain on Blackacre ($900) to Alex. [I.R.C. § 737] This gain is in addition to any gain recognized under section 731.

(a) Amount of Gain Recognized

The amount of gain that the partner must recognize under section 737 is limited to the least of:

(i) The partner's net precontribution gain (above, $900), or

(ii) The excess of the value of the property (above, $1,300) over the partner's outside basis in the partnership immediately before the distribution (reduced by any money received in the distribution) (above, $100). [I.R.C. § 737(a)] Thus, in the example above, Alex recognizes $900 in gain (the lesser of $900 and $1,200).

(b) Basis Rules

The partner's outside basis is increased by gain recognized under section 737 ($900) and that amount becomes the basis of the distributed property. Also the inside basis of Blackacre is increased by $900. [I.R.C. § 737(c)]

6. Consequence to Partnership Inside Basis

Generally, the distribution of cash or property does not affect the inside basis of the property retained by the partnership. This, however, may create circumstances where the remaining partners would be temporarily overtaxed or undertaxed if the average basis of the distributed property is higher or lower than the average basis of the retained property. Thus, Congress allows the parties to make an optional adjustment to basis through a section 754 election (*see supra,* p. 35). [I.R.C. § 734(b)] Even if the partnership does not make a section 754 election, a downward adjustment is mandatory if there is a "substantial basis reduction" with respect to a distribution, which occurs when the sum of the following exceeds $250,000: (i) the loss recognized to the distributee partner under section 731(a)(2), and (ii) the excess of the basis in the partnership interest over the basis of the property in the hands of the partnership before the distribution. [I.R.C. § 734(d)(1)]

I. Partnership Liquidations

1. Flexible Treatment

The Code provides for flexible treatment when the interest of one partner is bought *by the partnership. Caution:* Entirely different rules apply if the interest is sold to another partner. (*See supra,* p. 33 *et seq.*)

a. Section 736(a) Payments

Payments made to a retiring or deceased partner are, except as provided below, considered as a *distributive share* or as a *guaranteed payment*.

(1) Characterization

Payments are treated as a *distributive share* if their amount is determined by a percentage of the partnership's income. They are treated as a *guaranteed payment* if their amount is determined without regard to the income of the partnership.

(2) Effect on Recipient

The amount received is *ordinary income to the recipient* if it is a guaranteed payment, and it is either ordinary income or capital gain, depending on the underlying character of the partnership income, if it is a distributive share. If it is a distributive share, it also increases the recipient's outside basis by the amount of the distributive share; outside basis is then reduced by the amount of cash actually distributed. If it is treated as a guaranteed payment, it does not affect outside basis at all. [I.R.C. § 736(a)] (*See* discussion of distributive shares, guaranteed payments, and effect on basis, *supra,* pp. 11, 12, 19.) Moreover, a payment described in section 736(a) to a deceased partner's estate is treated as "income in respect of a decedent" and thus is fully taxable to the deceased partner's estate or other successor. [I.R.C. § 753; Rev. Rul. 66–325, 1966–2 C.B. 249]

(3) Effect on Other Partners

Payments described in section 736(a) are *deductible by the remaining partner* or partners. If the payment is considered a distributive share, it simply reduces the distributive shares allocable to the remaining partners—which has the same effect as a deduction. If the payment is a guaranteed payment, it is deductible by the partnership.

b. Section 736(b) Payments

If a payment to a retiring or deceased partner is described as made *in exchange for the interest* of the partner in partnership property, it is treated as a *distribution* by the partnership and not as a distributive share or a guaranteed payment.

(1) Effect—General Rule

If the distribution of cash or marketable securities exceeds the recipient's outside basis, it gives rise to *capital gain*, and if it is less than outside basis, it gives rise to *capital loss*. There is *no deduction* to other partners. [I.R.C. § 736(b)]

(2) Distinguish—Unrealized Receivables

However, payments in exchange for the partner's interest in unrealized receivables must be treated under section 736(a) rather than section 736(b). [I.R.C. § 736(b)(2)(A)] *But note:* This provision applies only in cases where capital was not a material income-producing factor for the partnership (*see supra*, p. 9, for a discussion of this phrase) *and* the retiring or deceased partner was a general partner. [I.R.C. § 736(b)(3)]

(3) Substantially Appreciated Inventory Items

A payment in exchange for the partner's interest in substantially appreciated inventory items (*i.e.*, "hot assets") is dealt with under section 736(b). However, it produces ordinary income rather than capital gain. [I.R.C. § 751(b); *see* discussion of I.R.C. § 751, *supra*, p. 33 *et seq.*]

(4) Payments for Goodwill

Amounts received in exchange for the partner's interest in the goodwill of the partnership are taxed under section 736(a) as ordinary income, rather than under section 736(b) as made in exchange for the interest, *unless the partnership agreement specifically provides for a payment with respect to goodwill*. [I.R.C. § 736(b)(2)(B)] This reference must be *specific*. [**Smith v. Commissioner,** 313 F.2d 16 (10th Cir. 1962)]

(a) Caution

However, this provision relating to payments for goodwill applies only in cases where capital was not a material income-producing factor for the partnership (*see supra,* p. 9, for discussion of this phrase) *and* the retiring or deceased partner was a general partner. [I.R.C. § 736(b)(3)] Thus, in cases where capital *is* a material income-producing factor, *or* the retiring or deceased partner was a *limited* partner, payments in exchange for goodwill are treated under I.R.C. section 736(b) *regardless* of what the partnership agreement provides.

(b) Modifications

Even if the partnership agreement failed to provide for a payment for goodwill, it can be modified, and the modification will be given effect for tax purposes. The partnership agreement can be effectively modified at any time prior to the date on which the partnership return for the taxable year is due. Thus, even *after* the payment is made, the agreement can be retroactively amended up to the due date of the return. [I.R.C. § 761(c)] A modification to provide for a goodwill payment has been upheld. [**Commissioner v. Jackson Investment Co.,** 346 F.2d 187 (9th Cir. 1965)]

If an exam question involves a partner selling his interest **back to the partnership**, a good place to begin your tax analysis is I.R.C. section 736(a). Most payments received upon liquidation are governed by section 736(a) and are treated as **ordinary income** to the recipient. However, if the payment is described as being made in exchange for the partner's interest, it generally is governed by I.R.C. section 736(b) and gives rise to a **capital gain or loss**, with three exceptions:

- Payments made for a partner's interest in **unrealized receivables** are treated under section 736(a) **if** capital was **not** a material income-producing factor for the partnership and the partner was a **general partner;**
- Payments for **goodwill** are taxed under section 736(a) unless the **partnership agreement specifically provides** for payment with respect to goodwill (note that the agreement can be modified **retroactively** to so provide); and
- Payments made in exchange for the partner's interest in **substantially appreciated inventory** are treated under section 736(b), but nevertheless are taxed as ordinary income.

(5) Sale of Interest or Liquidation

There are real differences between the *sale of a partnership interest* to the other partners (which is governed by I.R.C. sections 741 and 751) and the sale of the same interest back to the partnership (which is dealt with under the complicated provisions of I.R.C. section 736). Sometimes it is difficult to know whether a partnership interest was sold to the other partners or back to the partnership, especially in a two-person partnership. [*See* **Foxman v. Commissioner,** 352 F.2d 466 (3d Cir. 1965)— partnership interest was sold to the other partners, not to the partnership, even though the payment was made by the partnership]

(6) Illustrations

Assume that Becky's outside basis in AB partnership is $20,000. On Becky's retirement, AB partnership (as opposed to Alex as an individual) purchases Becky's interest.

(a) The partnership (which has no unrealized receivables or substantially appreciated inventory) pays Becky $32,000 in cash *in exchange for her interest in partnership assets*. Becky has a $12,000 capital gain; AB has no deduction. [I.R.C. § 736(b)]

(b) AB pays Becky $18,000 cash in exchange for her interest in the assets *and* an additional $7,000, which is *not in exchange for her interest in assets*. Becky has a $2,000 capital loss and $7,000 ordinary income (because the $7,000 payment is a guaranteed payment under I.R.C. section 736(a)). AB has a $7,000 deduction.

(c) AB pays Becky $32,000 in exchange for her interest in AB's assets, of which $7,000 is in exchange for her *interest in goodwill*. AB is a general partnership and capital is not a material income-producing factor. The partnership agreement does *not* provide for any payment for goodwill. Becky has $7,000 of ordinary income and $5,000 of capital gain (because the payment for goodwill must be reflected under section 736(a)). AB has a $7,000 deduction.

(d) Suppose in illustration (c) that the agreement *did* provide for a payment for *goodwill*. Becky has a $12,000 capital gain and AB has no deduction.

(e) AB pays Becky $32,000 for her interest in partnership assets. However, $7,000 of those assets are *unrealized receivables* having a zero basis in AB's hands. AB is a general partnership and capital is not a material income-producing factor. Becky has $7,000 of ordinary income and $5,000 of capital gain. AB has a $7,000 deduction. Payments for unrealized receivables must be reflected under section 736(a).

(f) AB pays Becky $32,000 for her interest in partnership assets. However, $7,000 of this payment is in exchange for Becky's interest in *substantially appreciated inventory* having a basis of $4,000 in AB's hands. Becky has $3,000 of ordinary income and $9,000 of capital gain, because she is treated as if she had directly sold her interest in the inventory. [*See* I.R.C. § 751(b), described *supra*, pp. 40–41] AB has no deduction.

    1) Mechanically, this result can be reached by using the fictitious "double distribution" technique described *supra,* pp. 40–41. Using this approach, AB is treated as if it had first distributed the inventory to Becky. This fictitious distribution reduces Becky's outside basis from $20,000 to $16,000 and gives her a basis of $4,000 for the inventory. She is then treated as "selling" the inventory back to AB, which produces $3,000 in ordinary income to Becky and gives AB a $7,000 basis for the "purchased" inventory. Finally, the remaining $25,000 cash distribution produces a $9,000 capital gain ($25,000 less $16,000 in remaining basis).

2. Distributions of Property in Liquidation

a. Distributions of Money

If the partnership distributes *only money* in liquidation of a partnership interest, the partner recognizes gain if the money distributed exceeds his outside basis. [I.R.C. § 731(a)(1)] He recognizes loss if the money distributed is less than his basis. [I.R.C. § 731(a)(2)] These rules apply *both* to complete liquidations and to purchases of the interest of one partner under section 736(b). *Note:* For purposes of measuring *gain but not loss*, the word "money" includes marketable securities. [I.R.C. § 731(c)]

b. Distributions of Property

If the partnership distributes *property* (other than marketable securities) in liquidation, there is *usually no gain or loss recognized* to the partner. The property received takes a *basis equal to the partner's outside basis* (less any money also distributed). [I.R.C. §§ 732(b), 731(a)(2)] However, *see* the discussion of mixing bowl transactions, *supra,* p. 42 *et seq*.

e.g. **Example:** AB partnership is completely liquidated. Alex, whose outside basis was $20,000, receives cash of $6,000 and Blackacre, whose inside basis was $29,000. Blackacre's basis in Alex's hands is $14,000 ($20,000 less $6,000). Note that $15,000 in basis has been "wasted" in this example. (*See infra,* p. 49 for a provision for conserving this basis.)

(1) Distributions of Unrealized Receivables or Inventory

If the partnership distributes hot assets (*i.e.,* unrealized receivables or inventory items) to the partner in liquidation of his interest, their basis to him remains the *same as it was in the hands of the partnership*. [I.R.C. § 732(c)]

(a) Loss Possible

In this situation, the partner could realize a *loss* on the liquidation. Suppose Alex's outside basis was $20,000 and in complete liquidation of his interest, he received $6,000 cash and unrealized receivables worth $18,000. The receivables had an inside zero basis, and therefore Alex's basis for them is also zero. Consequently, he has a $14,000 capital loss on the liquidation. [I.R.C. § 731(a)(2)(B)]

1) Distinguish

But, in the previous example, if the property distributed was a patent with an inside basis of zero (not an unrealized receivable or inventory item), Alex would *not* realize a loss. His basis for the patent would be $14,000 (*i.e.,* his basis of $20,000 less the cash distributed).

(b) Allocation of Basis

If a partnership distributes several assets in liquidation of a partner's interest, the partner's outside basis must be allocated between those assets after it is reduced by the amount of cash or marketable securities received in the distribution. [*See* I.R.C. § 732(c)]

1) Hot Assets

Hot assets (unrealized receivables and inventory items) are allocated a basis equal to the partnership's basis in those items.

2) Other Assets—Tentative Basis

All other assets receive a tentative basis equal to the partnership's basis in those assets.

3) Increase in Tentative Basis

If it is necessary to increase the tentative basis of the assets to make the aggregate bases of the assets equal to the liquidated partner's outside basis, the tentative basis is adjusted in the following manner: first to assets with unrealized appreciation, in proportion to the amount of appreciation in each asset, but not in excess of an asset's unrealized appreciation. If an additional increase is needed, the necessary amount is added in proportion to the respective fair market values of the assets.

4) Decrease in Tentative Basis

If it is necessary to decrease the tentative basis of the assets, the tentative basis is first adjusted downward by an amount in proportion to the unrealized depreciation of the assets (but only to the extent of an asset's unrealized depreciation). If an additional decrease is needed, the necessary amount is subtracted in proportion to the respective tentative bases after they have been decreased.

(c) Scope of Application—Caution

I.R.C. section 751(b) may apply to any distributions of unrealized receivables or substantially appreciated inventory items (whether or not in liquidation). This occurs, for example, when the distribution is not pro rata among all partners. [Rev. Rul. 77–412, 1977–2 C.B. 223—liquidation of two-person partnership] In the example *supra*, p. 48, if section 751(b) were applicable, the partnership would be treated as if it had "sold" the receivable to Alex for $18,000 rather than distributed it. (This example assumes that $18,000 is the excess over Alex's pro rata share of the receivables.)

Example: Mechanically, under the section 751 regulations, ABC first fictitiously distributes $18,000 in cash to Alex, reducing Alex's outside basis to $2,000. Alex takes the cash and "buys" the receivables. This produces an $18,000 gain to ABC (which is taxed to Becky and Cindy, not to Alex). It also gives Alex an $18,000 basis for the receivables. Finally, Alex is taxed in the usual manner on the $6,000 in cash he actually receives. It produces a $4,000 capital gain ($6,000 less $2,000 in remaining basis).

3. Loss on Liquidation

A partner recognizes loss on a liquidation if the partner receives no consideration except cash, marketable securities, or hot assets (unrealized receivables or inventory). [I.R.C. § 731(a)(2)] Normally the loss is a *capital loss*. [I.R.C. §§ 731(a)(2) (last sentence), 741]

a. Exception—Abandonment Loss

However, if a partner receives nothing at all in exchange for a partnership interest that has become worthless, the partner has an ordinary loss rather than a capital loss because this transaction does not satisfy the "sale or exchange" requirement for capital gain or loss. An abandonment occurs when: (i) a partner notifies the partnership in writing that he has abandoned his interest, (ii) the partnership agreement is amended to exclude him as a partner, and (iii) the interest is in fact worthless. [Rev. Rul. 93–80, 1993–2 C.B. 239]

b. Caution—Decrease in Liabilities

Assume that partnership liabilities are allocated to a partner (*see supra*, p. 47 *et seq.* for discussion of the allocation of partnership liabilities). When that partner abandons his partnership interest, he is treated as having received money on the abandonment owing to a decrease in the liabilities to which he is subject [I.R.C. § 752(b)]. As a result, that partner's loss is capital rather than ordinary. [Rev. Rul. 93–80, *supra*—general partner was allocated portion of partnership nonrecourse loan: loss is capital] Whereas if no partnership liabilities are allocated to the partner, he receives no money on the abandonment and has ordinary loss. [Rev. Rul. 93–80, *supra*—limited partner allocated no part of partnership nonrecourse loan: loss is ordinary]

4. Basis Adjustment After Distributions

Occasionally, the basis of property might be wasted in connection with a distribution.

Example: In a distribution in liquidation, the partner cannot take as the basis for the distributed property any greater basis than his former outside basis. [I.R.C. § 732(b); *and see supra*, p. 47] Similarly, in a nonliquidating distribution, the basis of the assets ordinarily remains the same in the partner's hands as its former inside basis. However, basis could be lost if the inside basis exceeds a partner's outside basis. [I.R.C. § 732(a)(2), discussed *supra*, p. 40]

a. Election

If an election is made under I.R.C. section 754 (*see supra*, p. 35 *et seq*.), the partnership *increases the inside basis of remaining partnership property* by the amount of basis that would be wasted in connection with the distribution. [I.R.C. § 734]

b. Additional Adjustments Required by Section 734

Section 734 also requires a downward adjustment in the inside basis of remaining partnership assets if a distributee partner got a stepped-up basis for distributed assets. (*See* the example concerning the patent, *supra,* p. 48.) In addition, section 734 permits an upward adjustment of remaining assets if a distributee partner recognized gain on a distribution. But it requires a downward adjustment if the partner recognized loss on the distribution that would result in a substantial basis reduction in an amount in excess of $250,000. [I.R.C. § 734(d)(1)]

Chapter Two

Corporate Taxation— Problems of Entity, Penalty Taxes, and Formation

CONTENTS

PAGE

Key Exam Issues

1. Corporation as a Taxable Entity

The two entity issues that exam questions commonly focus on are: (i) whether an entity should be taxed as a corporation (as opposed to a partnership or trust), and (ii) whether the corporate entity should be ignored.

a. ***Incorporated entities are taxed as corporations***. Unincorporated entities are normally taxed as partnerships unless they elect to be taxed as corporations.

b. Courts are far less likely to **ignore the corporate entity** under tax law than under corporate law. For tax purposes, a corporation will be recognized as a separate entity if it carries on *any* business (*i.e.,* does anything more than hold title). Watch for a fact situation, however, where a corporation is an agent of the shareholder. In that case, its income will be taxed to the shareholder.

c. When analyzing a fact situation involving *multiple corporations*, keep in mind that, under *section 482*, the IRS may *reallocate items of income and deduction* among businesses controlled by the same interests.

2. Penalty Taxes

Sometimes a corporation will be required to pay a special tax instead of, or in addition to, the regular corporate income tax. In answering an exam question, be particularly watchful for the applicability of the following taxes:

a. The Code imposes an ***alternative minimum tax*** on corporations similar to that imposed on individuals.

b. If a corporation seems to have accumulated assets in excess of its reasonable business needs, the ***accumulated earnings tax*** may apply.

c. If a corporation is receiving mostly passive, investment forms of income, determine whether it is a personal holding company. If it is, it may be subject to the ***personal holding company tax*** on undistributed income.

3. Creating the Corporation

Formation problems are a favorite exam topic. When confronted with such a problem, start from the assumption that the nonrecognition rule of section 351 controls. (Section 351 provides that no gain or loss is recognized when property is conveyed to a corporation for stock or securities.) Then, examine the consequences of the transaction to all of the shareholders and the corporation. Address the following issues:

a. Do the transferring shareholders have ***control of the corporation*** (80% of voting stock and 80% of all other classes of stock) immediately after the exchange? This is a requirement of section 351. Note that, for this purpose, several transferors and transactions may be linked together into a control group.

b. Was any ***stock received for services***? If so, it is ordinary income. Be careful not to include a person receiving solely stock for services when calculating whether property transfers by other transferors qualify for nonrecognition under section 351.

c. Is there "***boot***"? If the corporation distributes property other than stock ("boot") to the transferor, ***gain*** (but not loss) is recognized up to the value of that property. In addition to calculating realized and recognized gain, you must ***increase the basis*** of the stock by the amount of gain recognized.

d. Did the corporation *assume, or take property subject to, liabilities*? Assumed liabilities decrease basis and occasionally trigger gain under section 357(b) or (c).

e. Is the *transfer of assets called a sale*? If so, the seller recognizes gain or loss and the basis will be stepped up. Most importantly, consider whether the sale characterization will be followed. Often these sales are *reclassified* as section 351 exchanges with boot.

A. Corporation as a Taxable Entity

1. Introduction

A corporation is taxed as a *separate entity*. Dividends paid by the corporation are taxed to the shareholders but are not deductible to the corporation. This is *double taxation* of dividends and leads to many methods of tax avoidance. These in turn have caused the considerable complexity of the corporate tax provisions. Also, many corporate transactions are covered by *nonrecognition* provisions.

2. Tax Rates

a. Rate Structure

The corporate income tax has four brackets: 15% on the first $50,000 of income, 25% on income between $50,000 and $75,000, 34% on income between $75,000 and $10 million, and 35% on income in excess of $10 million. [I.R.C. § 11(b)(1)]

(1) Phase-Out

A corporation with taxable income in excess of $100,000 pays an additional tax equal to the lesser of 5% of the excess over $100,000 or $11,750. This provision denies larger corporations the benefit of the lower tax brackets on income below $75,000. In addition, corporations with income over $15 million must pay an additional tax equal to the lesser of 3% of the excess over $15 million or $100,000. This provision denies very large corporations the benefit of the lower tax brackets on income below $10 million.

(2) Personal Service Corporations

Personal service corporations are denied the benefit of the graduated rates. Such corporations pay tax on all income at the flat rate of 35%. [I.R.C. § 11(b)]

b. Multiple corporations

(1) Problem

The rate structure encourages multiple corporations because each new corporation would have another $75,000 of income to be taxed in the two lower brackets.

(2) Statutory Solution

However, there is usually no advantage in splitting up a business into separate corporate entities. The Code requires corporations in a single "controlled group" to share the lower brackets. Thus, even if there are six controlled corporations, they can use the lower brackets only once. [I.R.C. §§ 1561, 1563]

(3) Controlled Group

Corporations are in a "controlled group" and thus subject to the limitations of sections 1561 and 1563 in the following cases.

(a) Parent-Subsidiary

Corporations are in a "controlled group" if they are in a ***parent-subsidiary chain*** and the parent owns at least 80% of the voting power or 80% of the total value of all classes of stock. [I.R.C. § 1563(a)(1)]

(b) Brother-Sister

Corporations are in a "controlled group" if: (i) they are in a ***brother-sister relationship;*** and (ii) ***five or fewer persons*** own more than 50% of the voting power or more than 50% of the total value of all stock classes of each corporation, considering a particular person's stock only to the extent that it is owned identically with regard to each corporation (*e.g.,* if a stockholder owns 40% of Corp. A and 30% of Corp. B, his interest is identical only to the extent of 30%). [I.R.C. § 1563(a)(2)]

> **e.g.** **Example:** Aldo and Bianca each own 30% of X Corp., and Carlo owns the remaining 40%. Aldo owns 60% of the stock of Y Corp.; Bianca and Carlo each own 20%. Aldo, Bianca, and Carlo meet the 50% test because five or fewer individuals own at least 50% of both corporations. Taking into account only the amount owned identically in each corporation, Aldo owns 30% in each corporation and Bianca and Carlo each own 20%, for a combined total ownership of 70%. Corps. X and Y are brother-sister corporations, and together they can use the low tax brackets on income below $75,000 only once.

(c) Comment

These rules are even more complicated than they sound because elaborate "attribution rules" are provided by which stock owned by related entities or close relatives is constructively owned by the stockholders, in order to bring their holdings up to 50%. [I.R.C. § 1563(e)]

c. Capital Transactions

Unlike individuals, corporations receive no benefit from long-term capital gain; it is taxed at a maximum rate of 35%, which is at or above a corporation's top marginal tax rate. [I.R.C. § 1201(a)] Corporate capital loss is deductible only to the extent of corporate capital gain (in contrast to individuals who can deduct an additional $3,000 of capital loss in excess of capital gain). [I.R.C. § 1211(a)] If corporate capital loss exceeds capital gain, the excess can be carried back three years and forward five years (in contrast to individuals who carry forward such excess for an unlimited period). [I.R.C. § 1212(a)]

d. Charitable Contributions

A corporation can deduct charitable contributions up to 10% of taxable income. An individual can deduct contributions up to 50% of adjusted gross income (30% or 20% in certain cases). [I.R.C. § 170(b)(2)]

3. Consolidated Returns

If one corporation owns ***at least 80%*** of the voting stock (and 80% of the total value of stock excluding nonvoting preferred stock) of another, the two corporations can ***elect*** to file "consolidated returns." [I.R.C. §§ 1501, 1504] Under this election, the corporations are treated for many purposes like a single corporation. For example, intercorporate sales of goods or services are not taxed, and losses of one member can be offset against the profits of another. Elaborate regulations provide the ground rules for consolidated returns. [Treas. Reg. §§ 1.1502.1 *et seq.*]

4. Allocation Between Corporations—Section 482

a. Problem

Frequently, related corporations deal with one another. Sometimes, there are advantages in having the corporations not deal at arm's length. For example, if A Corp. has a loss for the year but B Corp. is profitable, and both are owned by the same shareholders, it is advantageous for A Corp. to sell goods at an artificially high price to B Corp., which would then resell the goods to outsiders. Because the resale would produce an artificially low profit, the effect is to shift the group's profit to A Corp., which would pay no tax because it is operating at a loss. Similar schemes are often employed with foreign entities. If A Corp. is domestic but B Corp. is in a low-tax foreign jurisdiction, A might sell goods or services to B at an artificially low price to shift income to the lower tax rate country.

b. Solution—Reallocation

I.R.C. section 482 gives the IRS discretionary power to *reallocate* items of income or deduction between businesses controlled directly or indirectly by the same interests in order to reflect income. Although it is possible to prove that the IRS abused its discretion in making a section 482 reallocation, it is difficult to do so. In general, the standard is that a transaction between related entities must be at "arm's length." If it is not, the transaction will be restructured so that it is at arm's length. [*See* I.R.C. § 482 *and* the Regulations thereunder; **Eli Lilly & Co. v. United States,** 372 F.2d 990 (Ct. Cl. 1967)]

c. Application

Under the regulations, there are five categories of transactions between commonly controlled entities that are most likely to trigger reallocation. These include:

(1) *Loans and advances* [*see, e.g.*, **B. Forman Co. v. Commissioner,** 453 F.2d 1144 (2d Cir. 1972), *cert. denied,* 407 U.S. 934 (1973)—interest-free loan requires charging lender with interest income, crediting borrower with a deduction];

(2) *Performance of services*;

(3) *Use of tangible property*, such as a lease of business premises;

(4) *Sales of tangible property;* and

(5) *Sale or use of intangible property.*

THE FOLLOWING FIVE CATEGORIES OF TRANSACTIONS ARE LIKELY TO TRIGGER AN IRS
REALLOCATION OF INCOME OR DEDUCTIONS BETWEEN CORPORATIONS BELONGING TO A
SINGLE CONTROLLED GROUP:

- ☑ *Loans and advances*
- ☑ Performance of *services*
- ☑ Use of *tangible property*
- ☑ Sales of *tangible property*
- ☑ Sale or use of *intangible property*

d. Super-Royalty Provision

It is difficult for the IRS to decide what is an arm's length charge for the use of intangible assets such as copyrights, patents, or trademarks. Therefore, a different approach is used in the case of such assets (the so-called super-royalty provision). If there has been a transfer or license of intangible property, for purposes of section 482, the transferor's income must be commensurate with the total income generated by the transferee from the use of the intangible. [I.R.C. § 482, second sentence] Thus if the transferee actually earned income from a trademark of $2 million, it must compensate the transferor an appropriate percentage of the $2 million.

e. Advance Pricing Agreements

The IRS will enter into a negotiated agreement with taxpayers concerning the application of section 482 to any transactions between commonly controlled entities. [*See* Rev. Proc. 91–22, 1991–1 C.B. 526] Such advance pricing agreements avoid highly burdensome disputes when the IRS seeks to apply section 482 to past transactions.

f. Relationship to Constructive Dividends

A bargain transfer between two controlled corporations may result not only in an increased price under section 482, but also in a constructive dividend to the controlling shareholder. [Rev. Rul. 69–630, 1969–2 C.B. 112] Thus if sole shareholder A causes X Corp. to sell Blackacre to Y Corp. for $100,000, when Blackacre was really worth $300,000, the consequences are: X Corp. realizes $200,000 additional income, Y Corp. has $200,000 additional basis, A has a $200,000 dividend, and A increases her basis in Y Corp. stock by $200,000. [Rev. Rul. 69–630, *supra*]

g. Other Law

The Supreme Court has held that a section 482 reallocation of income is impermissible if other law would have prevented the corporation from receiving that kind of income. [**Commissioner v. First Security Bank of Utah,** 405 U.S. 394 (1972)—IRS could not reallocate part of insurance policy income—equal to customary commissions in the insurance industry—from an insurance company to a bank that initiated the sale of the policy, even though both were subsidiaries of the same holding company, where law prohibited the bank from acting as an insurance agent]

h. Corporation and Shareholder

Section 482 has also been used to reallocate income between a corporation and shareholder if the shareholder is not receiving sufficient compensation. Frequently, corporations "loan out" their shareholders to tender services to outsiders. This often occurs in corporations owned by entertainers. The corporation must compensate the employee-shareholder adequately. Otherwise, part of the corporation's income will be allocated to the shareholder-employee. [**Rubin v. Commissioner,** 429 F.2d 650 (2d Cir. 1970)] There is a split in authority, however, as to whether section 482 applies when a shareholder-employee works exclusively for the controlled corporation. [*See* **Foglesong v. Commissioner,** 691 F.2d 848 (7th Cir. 1982)—section 482 inapplicable; **Haag v. Commissioner,** 88 T.C. 604 (1987), *aff'd,* 855 F.2d 855 (8th Cir. 1988)—section 482 applicable]

i. Personal Service Corporations

A provision similar to section 482 empowers the IRS to reallocate income or deductions of certain personal service corporations. [I.R.C. § 269A]

(1) Note

This provision applies only if a personal service corporation renders substantially all of its services on behalf of one other corporation or partnership. Thus, section 269A is primarily applicable to professional corporations that serve as partners in service partnerships (such as law firms or medical practices).

(2) Allocation

If the principal purpose of forming the corporation was tax avoidance, the IRS can reallocate its income, deductions, or credits to the corporation's employee-owners. "Employee-owners" are persons who own at least 10% of the outstanding stock of the corporation. Tax avoidance, for this purpose, means tax benefits not available without incorporation, such as various fringe benefits.

(3) Comment

This provision was intended to overrule a Tax Court decision upholding the use of a professional corporation as a partner in a pathology partnership. The doctor formed the corporation to take advantage of both a medical reimbursement plan and a pension plan. [**Keller v. Commissioner,** 77 T.C. 1014 (1981), *aff'd,* 723 F.2d 58 (10th Cir. 1983)]

5. When Will the Corporate Entity Be Ignored?

a. Corporate Law vs. Tax Standards

Under corporate law, a corporate entity can be ignored and the shareholders held liable for corporate debts in many circumstances. (*See* Corporations Summary.) However, for tax purposes, the courts are much *less* likely to ignore the entity of corporations.

b. Tax Criteria

If the corporation carries on *any* business—such as securing a loan or doing something more than merely holding title—it will be recognized as a separate entity. [**Moline Properties, Inc. v. Commissioner,** 319 U.S. 436 (1943)] However, if the corporation does virtually nothing except hold title, and serves no business purpose other than to obtain limited liability for the shareholders, the corporate entity will be ignored. [**Paymer v. Commissioner,** 150 F.2d 334 (2d Cir. 1945)]

(1) Illustration—Corporation as Nominee

Real estate investors frequently use corporations to borrow money and hold title to land (*e.g.*, to avoid state usury limitations). They assert that the corporate entity should be ignored and its income and deductions be reflected directly on the investors' returns. This argument fails. Avoiding usury laws is a business purpose. Borrowing money and mortgaging property is business activity. [**Strong v. Commissioner,** 66 T.C. 12 (1976), *aff'd,* 553 F.2d 94 (2d Cir. 1977)]

(2) Exception—Corporation as Agent

When an agent acts on behalf of a principal, the resulting income is taxed to the principal. For example, when a store employee makes a sale, the income is taxed to the owner of the store, not to the employee. This rule might apply in the corporation-shareholder context: If a corporation is an agent of the shareholder, the shareholder is the proper taxpayer. The arrangement between the corporation and the shareholder must unequivocally show an agency relationship, but there is no need for payment of a fee by the principal to the agent. [**Commissioner v. Bollinger,** 485 U.S. 340 (1988)—all documents and representations to third parties indicated that corporation was mere agent]

(3) Exception—Sham Corporations

If a taxpayer employs multiple corporations for a single project (like a real estate development in which numerous corporations merely hold title to property and sell it) without a business purpose for doing so, the separate corporations can be treated as a single corporation on the theory that they are "shams." [**Greenberg v. Commissioner,** 62 T.C. 331 (1974), *aff'd,* 526 F.2d 588 (4th Cir. 1975), *cert. denied,* 423 U.S. 1052 (1976)]

EXAM TIP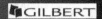

If the facts of an exam question lead you to the issue of whether a corporate entity should be ignored for tax purposes, do not let your knowledge of corporate law cloud your answer. While courts will seldom ignore a corporate entity under corporate law, it is ***even rarer to ignore a corporate entity for tax purposes***. Be sure to state the test: The corporate entity will be ignored for tax purposes only if the corporation neither performs *any* business nor serves *any* business purpose. Because the business criteria here are interpreted broadly (*e.g.*, holding a loan in a corporate name is a sufficient business purpose), your answer probably should conclude that the corporate entity should *not* be ignored, unless the corporation was merely acting as an agent for its shareholder, or the corporation is one of several corporations formed to undertake a single venture.

---

6. Transactions Between Shareholder and Corporation

Generally, sales of property between a corporation and shareholder, or between related corporations, are treated as if the parties were independent entities. However, there are a number of *exceptions*.

a. Sales of Depreciable Property at a Gain

If an individual owns *more than 50% in value* of the corporate stock, any gain recognized on sales of depreciable property (including patent applications) between the shareholder and corporation produces *ordinary income*, rather than capital gain. [I.R.C. § 1239(a)] Furthermore, there is attribution—in computing the 50% figure, the shareholder must also count stock owned by his spouse, children, and grandchildren.

(1) Application

The section 1239 test applies if a shareholder owns "more than 50% *in value*." This means that if he owns 50% of the stock and has an option to buy the remaining stock at a favorable price, he actually owns more than 50% "in value" of the stock. [**United States v. Parker,** 376 F.2d 402 (5th Cir. 1967); *but see* **Trotz v. Commissioner,** 26 T.C.M. (CCH) 632 (1967)—refusing to give an option any additional value]

(a) Note

Section 1239 also applies to sales between two or more corporations if the same individual owns 50% or more in value of each of them. [I.R.C. § 1239(b)(3)]

(b) Distinguish—Recapture

Even if section 1239 does not apply, I.R.C. sections 1245 and 1250 convert capital gain into ordinary income to the extent of depreciation recapture. (*See* Taxation of Individuals Summary.)

b. Sales at a Loss

If a shareholder owns *more than 50% in value* of the stock, any losses arising on sales between the shareholder and corporation are disallowed. [I.R.C. § 267(a)(1), (b)(2)]

(1) Note

Elaborate attribution rules are provided in section 267(c) so that stock owned by family members or related entities is counted in figuring whether an individual meets the 50% control standard.

(2) Distinguish—Related Corporations

Sales between related corporations are covered if more than 50% of the stock of each is owned, directly or indirectly, by the same individual, *and* either of the corporations was a *personal holding company* in the preceding year (*see infra*, p. 65 *et seq.*). [I.R.C. § 267(b)(3)]

EXAM TIP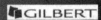

Be on the lookout for exam fact patterns in which a majority owner of a corporation sells *appreciated property* to, or buys such property from, the corporation. The general rule treating the parties as separate entities does not apply. *Gain* from such a sale is treated as *ordinary income* rather than capital gain, and *loss* from such a sale is *not recognized*.

---

7. Alternative Minimum Tax

The Code imposes a minimum tax on corporations that is similar to that imposed on individuals. (For a summary of the alternative minimum tax, *see* Taxation of Individuals Summary.) However, there are some important differences.

a. Tax Rates

The corporate minimum tax is 20% of alternative minimum taxable income ("AMTI") in excess of $40,000—but only to the extent that the minimum tax exceeds the regular tax. [I.R.C. § 55(a), (b)(1)(B), (d)(2)] Thus, the minimum tax operates in cases where Congress thinks that a corporation has reduced its regular tax by using too many tax preferences (*i.e.,* loopholes).

b. Small Corporate Exemption

Certain small corporations are exempt from the AMT. To qualify for the exemption initially, the corporation's average annual gross receipts from the previous three taxable years cannot exceed $5 million. To retain the exemption in subsequent years, the corporation's annual average gross receipts cannot exceed $7.5 million for the previous three years. [I.R.C. § 55(e)]

c. Computation of AMTI

AMTI is computed by starting with corporate taxable income. Tax preferences are added. Then taxable income must also be "adjusted."

(1) Tax Preferences

Under I.R.C. section 57(a), the following tax preferences are added to taxable income:

(a) *Percentage depletion* in excess of adjusted basis;

(b) *Intangible drilling costs* in excess of the amount that would be recovered using straight-line depreciation; and

(c) *Tax-exempt interest* on certain private-purpose state and local bonds.

(2) Adjustments

The following adjustments to taxable income are then made to arrive at AMTI:

(a) Depreciation

It is necessary to use 150% (instead of 200%) declining balance depreciation for assets depreciated using the accelerated cost recovery system ("ACRS"; *see* Taxation of Individuals Summary) rather than using the straight-line method. [I.R.C. § 56(a)]

(b) Adjusted Current Earnings

AMTI must be increased by 75% of the excess of adjusted current earnings ("ACE") of the corporation over AMTI. If ACE is less than AMTI, AMTI is decreased by 75% of the difference.

1) Definition of ACE

The term "adjusted current earnings" means those items that increase current earnings and profits (*see infra,* p. 92) but that are not included in gross income (or that decrease earnings and profits but that are not deductible from gross income). As explained *infra,* on p. 92, earnings and profits (but not gross income) are increased by such items as interest on tax-free state and local bonds and deferred income on installment sales, and are decreased by such items as unreasonable compensation. Conversely, although earnings and profits are decreased by federal income taxes, this item does not decrease ACE. Note that ACE is computed by using straight-line depreciation over longer useful life periods than generally allowed under the ACRS.

e.g. **Example:** Taxable income of T Corp. is $5 million. Thus its income tax under the regular rate (34%) is $1.7 million. However, assume that T Corp. deducted depreciation in the amount of $2 million. If depreciation were computed at 150% rather than 200% declining balance, depreciation would have been only $1.5 million. Thus T Corp.'s AMTI is $5.5 million. Moreover, assume that ACE was $7 million because T had income from city of Chicago bonds and because for ACE purposes only straight-line depreciation (over longer than usual useful lives) can be used. The ACE adjustment is $1,125,000 (*i.e.,* 75% of $1.5 million—the excess of ACE over AMTI). Therefore, total AMTI is $6,625,000. The minimum tax (at the rate of 20%) is $1,325,000. Because T's minimum tax ($1,325,000) does not exceed its regular tax ($1.7 million), it pays no minimum tax.

B. Penalty Taxes on Corporations That Do Not Pay Dividends

1. Accumulated Earnings Tax

a. Purpose of Tax

The accumulated earnings tax is intended to force dividend distributions of unneeded corporate assets. In the past, the problem was that closely held corporations (and sometimes publicly held corporations as well) tended to hold on to assets because dividends were subject to tax at the high individual rates. Now that dividends are subject to tax only at capital gains rates (*see infra*, p. 94), the incentive to retain earnings is reduced, although not completely. [I.R.C. § 532(c)]

b. Basic Standard

The tax is imposed on corporations "formed or availed of for the *purpose* of avoiding the income tax with respect to its shareholders . . . by permitting earnings and profits to *accumulate* instead of being divided or distributed." [I.R.C. § 532(a)] Therefore, this tax is imposed only if the forbidden *purpose* is found.

(1) Broad Application

However, the Supreme Court has held that if tax avoidance is merely *one* of the purposes for accumulation, the tax can be imposed. [**United States v. Donruss Co.,**

393 U.S. 297 (1969)] Consequently, taxpayers can seldom disprove the IRS's assertion of the proscribed purpose.

(a) Veto Power

The tax has been imposed even where most of the shareholders *wanted* to pay dividends but because of a shareholder voting agreement, a 25% shareholder was able to *veto* all corporate dividends. [**Atlantic Properties, Inc. v. Commissioner,** 519 F.2d 1233 (1st Cir. 1975)]

c. Reasonable Needs Test

The fact that the earnings and profits are permitted to accumulate beyond the *reasonable needs of the business* establishes that the corporation has been availed of for the purpose of tax avoidance, unless the corporation proves the contrary. [I.R.C. § 533(a)]

(1) Critical Issue

Thus, the critical issue in most accumulated earnings tax cases is whether the earnings and profits have accumulated beyond the reasonable needs of the business. If there has been such an accumulation, it will be almost impossible to prove that the corporation was not formed or availed of for the proscribed purpose.

(a) Note

As a practical matter, the reasonable needs issue turns on whether the *assets* have accumulated beyond reasonable needs of the business. For this purpose, marketable assets must be valued at current fair market value, less disposition costs, *not book value*. [**Ivan Allen Co. v. United States,** 422 U.S. 617 (1975)] The reasonable needs issue requires a careful economic analysis of why the directors failed to pay dividends and what kinds of assets the corporation needed to operate.

(2) Possible Needs

If the directors can show that they accumulated for the purpose of constructing a new building, acquiring a competitor, replacing expensive fixed assets or the like, they can establish that the accumulation was for the reasonable needs of the business.

(3) Working Capital

In many cases, the accumulation of assets will be to provide adequate working capital for the business in order to permit it to pay its bills during the manufacturing and accounts receivable collection period. Many cases have made what is called an "operating cycle analysis" in order to determine how long this period of time is in a given business and how much money is needed to pay bills during that period. [**Bardahl Manufacturing Co. v. Commissioner,** 24 T.C.M. (CCH) 1030 (1965)]

(4) Unfavorable Factors

The fact that the directors have invested surplus assets in stocks and bonds would tend to show that they had more assets than were needed. Similarly, a pattern of loans to the shareholders is unfavorable because it tends to show that the same money could have been distributed as a dividend. On the other hand, a pattern of paying reasonable dividends is very helpful to the corporation.

(5) Additional Reasonable Needs

The law provides for certain additional purposes that are deemed reasonable. These include accumulation to make an I.R.C. section 303 redemption (defined *infra*, p. 110) in the year in which a shareholder dies or in later years. Also, reasonably *anticipated* needs (*e.g.*, saving to build a bigger factory) are as permissible as present needs. [I.R.C. § 537]

EXAM TIP   **GILBERT**

On your exam, be on the lookout for corporations that have earnings but that do not pay dividends. Remember, if the IRS finds that one purpose of such nonpayment is tax avoidance, it will impose the accumulated earnings tax. Corporations cannot keep earnings and profits— generally measured by the net market value of marketable assets—beyond those necessary to meet the *reasonable needs of the business*.

---

d. Burden of Proof

A unique provision of the Code allows the taxpayer to shift the burden of proof to the Commissioner on the question of whether earnings were accumulated beyond the reasonable needs of the business. A taxpayer does this by filing a *specific statement* of the grounds relied upon to establish that the earnings did not accumulate beyond the reasonable needs of the business. This provision, however, applies only to litigation in the Tax Court, not in the district court or the Court of Claims. [I.R.C. § 534]

e. Calculation of the Tax

The accumulated earnings tax is imposed on an *annual basis* on "accumulated taxable income" ("ATI"). The rate is 15% of ATI.

(1) Calculation of ATI

ATI is equal to taxable income minus a number of special deductions. These include *taxes* (including federal income taxes) and dividends *paid*. Also, with some modifications, a taxpayer can deduct the entire amount of capital gain and loss. The idea, in other words, is to arrive at the amount that would be available to pay dividends. [I.R.C. § 535(a), (b)(1), (b)(6)–(8)]

(2) Minimum Deduction

If accumulated earnings and profits (defined *infra*, p. 93) are less than $250,000 at the *beginning of the year*, a deduction is given in the amount of the difference between $250,000 and accumulated earnings and profits at the beginning of the year. [I.R.C. § 535(c)(2)]

(a) Distinguish—Professional Corporations

The minimum deduction is only $150,000, not $250,000, for professional corporations (such as law or medical corporations) or those engaged in the performing arts. [I.R.C. § 535(c)(2)(B)]

(3) Reasonable Needs

In addition, if the taxpayer has shown that *some assets* were retained to meet the reasonable needs of the business (even though some were not), the amount that was retained to meet reasonable needs is allowable as a deduction. [I.R.C. § 535(c)(1)] However, this deduction is an alternative to the "minimum deduction" described *supra,* p. 64. The taxpayer is entitled to whichever is greater—but *not* to both the "minimum deduction'' and the "reasonable needs" deduction.

e.g. **Example:** The taxable income of T Corp. was $200,000. It had no capital gains. It had capital losses of $20,000, paid income taxes of $45,000, and paid dividends of $20,000. It proved that it had retained $50,000 for the reasonably anticipated needs of the business. Its accumulated earnings and profits ("E&P") at the beginning of the year were $240,000. What is its ATI?

Taxable Income			$200,000
Deductions:			
Capital losses		$20,000	
Income taxes		45,000	
Dividends paid		20,000	
Minimum deduction:			
Amount by which E&P at beginning of the year were less than $250,000	$10,000		
Assets retained for reasonable needs of the business	50,000		
Greater of these two amounts	50,000	50,000	
Total deductions			135,000
Accumulated Taxable Income			$65,000

Thus, the tax due would be 15% of $65,000, or $9,750.

2. Personal Holding Company Tax

a. Purpose

I.R.C. sections 541 through 547 impose a tax on undistributed income of a personal holding company ("PHC"). Generally speaking, a PHC is a corporation that *receives passive forms of income*; it is an incorporated "pocketbook" for its shareholders. When dividends were taxed at ordinary income rates, the motivation for the PHC was to force distribution of the PHC's income so that it would be taxed in the shareholders' brackets. Now that dividends are subject to tax only at capital gains rates, the incentive to retain earnings is reduced, although not completely.

b. Requirements Concerning Ownership

The PHC tax cannot be imposed unless 50% in value of the corporation's outstanding stock is owned directly or indirectly by *not more than five people*. For this purpose, elaborate *attribution* rules are provided so that stock owned by members of a shareholder's family is attributed to him, as are shares owned by corporations or partnerships in which the shareholder is involved. [I.R.C. § 544(a)]

c. Definition of Personal Holding Company

A corporation is a PHC if at least 60% of its adjusted ordinary gross income is PHC income. [I.R.C. § 542(a)]

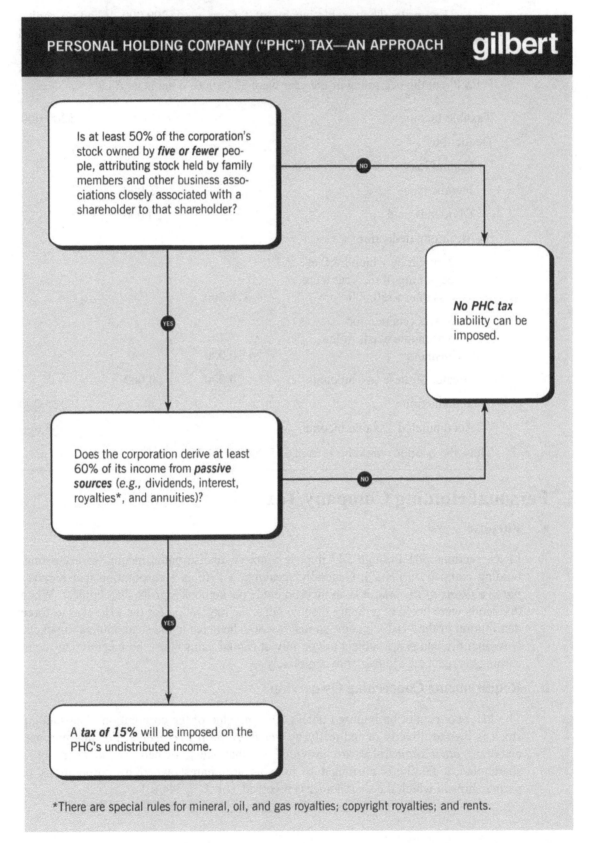

PERSONAL HOLDING COMPANY ("PHC") TAX—AN APPROACH **gilbert**

Is at least 50% of the corporation's stock owned by *five or fewer* people, attributing stock held by family members and other business associations closely associated with a shareholder to that shareholder?

NO → **No PHC tax** liability can be imposed.

YES ↓

Does the corporation derive at least 60% of its income from *passive sources* (e.g., dividends, interest, royalties*, and annuities)?

NO →

YES ↓

A *tax of 15%* will be imposed on the PHC's undistributed income.

*There are special rules for mineral, oil, and gas royalties; copyright royalties; and rents.

d. PHC Income

The PHC tax is imposed on PHC income. PHC income is defined in I.R.C. section 543(a) and includes:

(1) Dividends, Interest, Royalties, and Annuities

Dividends, interest, royalties, and annuities are PHC income. However, *mineral, oil, and gas royalties* are not counted if they constitute 50% or more of adjusted ordinary gross income. Similarly, *copyright royalties* are not included if they constitute 50% or more of adjusted ordinary income. In addition, to exclude copyright royalties, other PHC income cannot exceed 10% of ordinary income, and section 162 deductions allocable to the royalties must exceed 25% of gross income. However, royalties from licensing of computer software developed by a corporation actively engaged in developing and producing such software are not PHC income.

(2) Rents

Rents are PHC income. However, rents will *not* be treated as PHC income if the taxpayer can meet two tests [I.R.C. § 543(a)(2)]:

(a) *Rents* are 50% or more of adjusted ordinary gross income ("adjusted ordinary gross income" means ordinary income less deductions attributable to rentals); *and*

(b) *Dividends* paid during the year exceed the amount by which PHC income (*other than rents*) exceeds 10% of ordinary income.

(3) Produced Film Rents

Payments obtained through the rental of films produced by the taxpayer (or acquired before substantial completion of the production of the film) are treated like rents rather than copyright royalties. That means that they are not PHC income if they meet the above tests for rents; they need not meet the strict limits placed on copyright royalties.

(4) Shareholder Rentals

Payments received through rental of a corporation's property to *a shareholder* who owns 25% or more of the corporation's stock are PHC income.

(5) Personal Service Income

Personal service income is classified as PHC income if the corporation's contract with an outsider names the individual who will perform the services or the outsider can *choose* the individual. Such individual would have to own at least 25% of the stock.

(a) Primary Application

This provision applies mainly to corporations that make available the services of particular *entertainers*. It might also apply to professional service corporations of doctors or lawyers where the patient or client has the right to name which doctor or lawyer she will see.

1) Note

However, the IRS has ruled that a doctor in solo practice does not ordinarily have PHC income, because the doctor generally has the power to substitute another doctor. The ruling assumed that the doctor's services were not in some way unique. It also assumed that there was no contract that would prevent the substitution of another doctor in the taxpayer's place. [Rev. Rul. 75–67, 1975–1 C.B. 169]

(b) Distinguish—Nonshareholder Employees

If the contract requires the performance of services by persons other than the 25% shareholder, and these are important and essential services, the amounts received can be allocated to the other persons, and this would reduce the personal holding company income. However, this exception is strictly construed. [**Kurt Frings Agency, Inc. v. Commissioner,** 351 F.2d 951 (9th Cir. 1965)]

e. Computation of the Tax

If the corporation is a PHC, it is necessary to compute "undistributed PHC income." The tax is imposed at the rate of 15% of undistributed PHC income. [I.R.C. § 541] This figure is obtained by starting with taxable income and subtracting such items as income taxes, disallowed charitable contributions, long-term capital gains, and dividends paid.

C. Creating the Corporation

1. Nonrecognition

Ordinarily, the formation of the corporation and conveyance of property to it in return for stock is a transaction in which gain or loss is not recognized. [I.R.C. § 351] The policy is that, normally, the formation of a corporation is not an appropriate time to recognize gain or loss on appreciation or depreciation of assets employed in the incorporated business. The theory is that incorporation represents a mere change in the form in which assets are held, rather than a substantial change that would warrant collection of a tax (or deduction of a loss).

2. Summary of Requirements for Application of Nonrecognition Rule

For the nonrecognition rule of I.R.C. section 351 to apply, the "transferors" of "property" to the "corporation" must, as a group, have "control" of the corporation "immediately after the exchange." No gain or loss is recognized if the transferors receive solely stock. Gain, but not loss, is recognized if the transferors receive "other property" in addition to stock.

3. Definition of Control

Control means at least 80% of the voting stock *and* at least 80% of the total number of shares of all other classes of stock. [I.R.C. §§ 351(a), 368(c)(1)]

a. Multi-Class Structures

According to the IRS, to have control, the transferors of property must have at least 80% of the voting power and at least 80% of *each class* of nonvoting stock. [Rev. Rul. 59–259, 1959–2 C.B. 115]

Example: The stock of X Corp. is entirely owned by Antoine. Antoine transfers Blackacre to X Corp. without receiving any additional stock. This is called a "contribution to capital." Because Antoine has control of X immediately after the transfer, Antoine does not recognize gain or loss.

cf. **Compare:** In the previous example, assume that Blackacre is transferred by Bert in exchange for 50% of the voting stock of X. Bert must recognize gain or loss on this exchange because he did not have control of X.

e.g. **Example:** Assume again that Antoine had 100% of the stock of X Corp. (100 shares). Antoine transfers Blackacre to X Corp. and Bert transfers Whiteacre to X Corp. Each receives an additional 50 shares. Because Antoine and Bert *as a group* have control over X Corp. immediately after the transfers, neither recognizes gain or loss on the transfer.

4. Immediately After the Exchange

For section 351 to apply, the transferors of property must have control "immediately after the exchange."

a. All Transactions Considered

All related transactions are considered together to see whether this requirement has been met.

e.g. **Example:** Existing X Corp. has 50 shares outstanding, all owned by Zedora. On January 5, Antoine contributes Blackacre for an additional 50 shares. On January 10, as part of the same plan, Bert contributes Whiteacre for an additional 300 shares. The transfers by Antoine and Bert are viewed together, and Antoine and Bert have control of X Corp. (350 out of 400 shares). It was necessary to view Antoine's and Bert's transfers together; viewed separately, neither of them had control of X Corp. immediately after their own exchanges.

(1) Regulations

This principle is expressed in the regulations: The phrase "immediately after the exchange" does not necessarily require simultaneous exchanges by two or more persons, but comprehends a situation where the rights of the parties have been previously defined and the execution of the agreement proceeds with an expedition consistent with orderly procedure. [Treas. Reg. § 1.351–1(a)(1)]

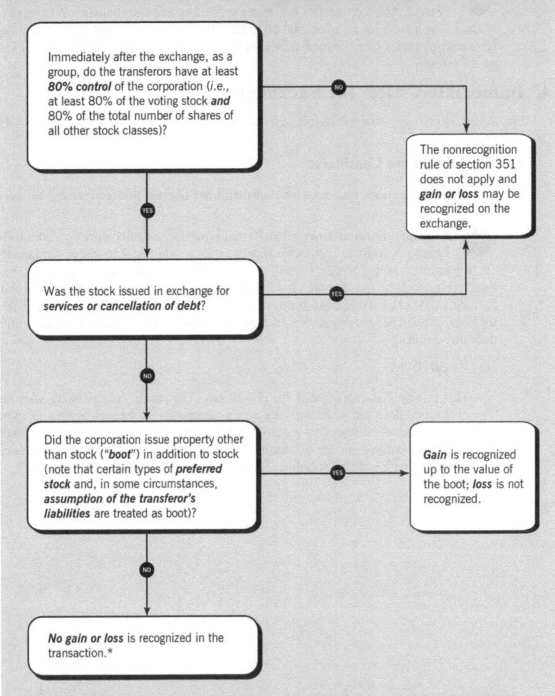

Immediately after the exchange, as a group, do the transferors have at least **80% control** of the corporation (*i.e.,* at least 80% of the voting stock **and** 80% of the total number of shares of all other stock classes)?

NO →

The nonrecognition rule of section 351 does not apply and **gain or loss** may be recognized on the exchange.

YES ↓

Was the stock issued in exchange for **services or cancellation of debt**?

YES →

NO ↓

Did the corporation issue property other than stock ("**boot**") in addition to stock (note that certain types of **preferred stock** and, in some circumstances, **assumption of the transferor's liabilities** are treated as boot)?

YES →

Gain is recognized up to the value of the boot; **loss** is not recognized.

NO ↓

No gain or loss is recognized in the transaction.*

*Remember that even when assets are "sold" to a corporation, the transfer may be reclassified as a section 351 exchange if it seems to be part of the overall transaction in which the corporation is formed and capitalized.

b. Gifts

If a transferor had control of the corporation but gave away part of the stock received, so she fell below 80%, the section 351 nonrecognition rule nevertheless applies to her transfer. [**Stanton v. United States,** 512 F.2d 13 (3d Cir. 1975); **Wilgard Realty Co. v. Commissioner,** 127 F.2d 514 (2d Cir. 1942)]

Example: Antoine transfers Blackacre to newly formed X Corp. in exchange for 75 shares. X Corp. issues 25 more shares to a trust for Antoine's children. The transfer to the children was a gift from Antoine. Section 351 applies to the transfer even though Antoine (the only transferor of property) never formally had control of X Corp., because he is treated as if he received 100 shares and gave 25 shares to his children. [*See* **D'Angelo Associates, Inc. v. Commissioner,** 70 T.C. 121 (1978)]

c. Contractual Transfers

If the transferor loses control of the corporation because she is ***contractually obligated*** to transfer part of the stock to another, the nonrecognition rule does not apply. [**Fahs v. Florida Machine & Foundry Co.,** 168 F.2d 957 (5th Cir. 1948); **Intermountain Lumber Co. v. Commissioner,** 65 T.C. 1025 (1976); Rev. Rul. 79–70, 1979–1 C.B. 144]

Example: In the previous example, assume Antoine had agreed to transfer 25% of the stock he would receive when he formed X Corp. to Claude, a creditor of the business, in discharge of the debt Antoine owed to Claude. Antoine does not have control immediately after the transfer and section 351 does not apply.

(1) Exception

Nonrecognition treatment may still apply despite a contractual obligation to transfer the stock received in a section 351 exchange if the transfer is part of a nonrecognition transaction that the transferor could have done in a different way while still qualifying for nonrecognition treatment.

Example: W corporation conducted business A, among other activities. It sought to combine business A with a similar business conducted by Y corporation, a wholly owned subsidiary of X corporation, and both parties wanted the combined business to ultimately reside in the subsidiary of a holding company. Thus, W created Newco and transferred the assets of business A to Newco. Pursuant to a preexisting contractual commitment, W transferred the stock of Newco to Y in exchange for Y stock. At the same time, Y transferred its business to Newco. W's transfer of the Newco stock did not violate the "control" requirement because W could have transferred its business A assets directly to Y in exchange for Y stock. [Rev. Rul. 2003–51; 2003–21 IRB 938]

5. Exceptions to Nonrecognition Rule

a. Stock for Services

Stock issued for services (past, present, or future) is not issued in exchange for property. [I.R.C. § 351(a)]

(1) Consequences to Recipient

The person who receives stock for services has ***ordinary income*** on the exchange. [I.R.C. § 83—*see* Taxation of Individuals Summary; **James v. Commissioner,** 53 T.C. 63 (1972)]

(2) Consequences to Other Transferors

If some recipients of stock transfer only services and others transfer only property, the transferors of property might not (as a group) receive control. Consequently, they would recognize gain or loss on the exchange.

Example: Antoine receives 50% of the stock of newly formed X Corp. for his promise to render managerial services in the future. Bert receives the other 50% for a patent to be used in the business. The basis of the patent is zero and the value is $50,000. Assume that Antoine's promise is also worth $50,000, so that the stock of X Corp. is worth $100,000. Antoine has $50,000 of ordinary income. Bert has $50,000 of gain on transfer of the patent (it is ordinary income; *see* I.R.C. section 1235(d)). Bert's gain is recognized because he is the only transferor of property and he has only 50% of the stock, which is not "control." X Corp. receives no deduction for Antoine's services because they will be rendered in the future. It is treated as having paid $50,000 to Antoine, but the "expenditure" must be capitalized and amortized over the term that Antoine will render the services. Bert's basis for his stock is $50,000. Antoine's basis for his stock is also $50,000. X Corp.'s basis for the patent is $50,000.

(3) Distinguish—Stock for Both Property and Services

If a transferor receives stock for *both* property *and* services, he is counted *in full* as a transferor of property for purposes of the 80% *control requirement*. However, the value of the stock received for services still counts as *ordinary income*. [Treas. Reg. § 1.351–1(a)(1)]

Example: Bert transfers Blackacre for 50% of the stock in newly formed X Corp. Antoine transfers Whiteacre in exchange for 15% of the stock and his promise to render services for the remaining 35% of the stock. Because both Antoine and Bert are transferors of property, no gain or loss is recognized on either Blackacre or Whiteacre. However, the value of the 35% of the stock received for services is still taxed as ordinary income to Antoine. [Treas. Reg. § 1.351–1(a)(2), example (3)]

b. De Minimis Property

To qualify a transfer of property to an existing corporation as tax-free under section 351, existing shareholders might also receive a few shares of stock. Under the regulations, this scheme will not work. [Treas. Reg. § 1.351–1(a)(1)(ii); **Estate of Kamborian v. Commissioner,** 469 F.2d 219 (1st Cir. 1972)]

Example: Antoine wants to transfer appreciated property to C Corp. in exchange for its stock. After receiving the stock, Antoine will own 10% of C Corp. stock. Thus Antoine's transfer will not qualify under section 351 (because Antoine will not be in control). To make Antoine's transfer tax-free, Bert will purchase one share at the same time for $1. Bert owns 75% of the stock of C Corp. Antoine and Bert argue that together they have control of C Corp. (85%) so that Antoine's transfer qualifies under section 351. The plan will not work because the stock issued to Bert is "of relatively small value" in comparison to the value of stock that Bert already owns.

(1) Guideline

According to the IRS, "relatively small" means *less than 10%* of the stock or securities already owned by the transferor. [Rev. Proc. 77–37, 1977–2 C.B. § 3.07]

c. Stock for debt

When a corporation issues stock in discharge of its own outstanding debt, both the corporation and the shareholder may have income on the exchange.

(1) Income to Corporation

The corporation has debt cancellation income if the *value of the new stock* is less than the amount of the debt. [I.R.C. § 108(e)(8)(A); *see* Taxation of Individuals Summary for discussion of debt cancellation income] Suppose C Corp. owes Antoine $1,000. Antoine's basis for the debt is $900. C Corp. cancels the debt in exchange for C stock worth $600. C Corp. has $400 of income. However, C Corp. would not have income in this situation if it is insolvent, if the exchange occurred pursuant to a bankruptcy reorganization, or if the exchange occurred in a "qualified workout" of its debts. [I.R.C. § 108(e)(10)(B), (C)]

(a) Contribution to Capital

A slightly different rule applies if the shareholder contributed the debt to capital (*i.e.,* forgave it and received no stock in exchange). The corporation's income is measured by the difference between the amount of the debt and the *shareholder's basis for the debt* (*i.e.,* $100 in the above example). [I.R.C. § 108(e)(6)]

(2) Bad Debt to Shareholder

If no nonrecognition section (such as section 351) is applicable, a shareholder recognizes gain or loss on the exchange of a corporate debt for corporate stock. Thus, in the above example, if section 351 were inapplicable, Antoine would have a bad debt of $300 when he exchanged a debt having a $900 basis in his hands for $600 of stock. However, if section 351 were applicable, Antoine would recognize no gain or loss on the exchange. Also, the loss may be nondeductible if the exchange occurs as part of a tax-free recapitalization (*see infra,* p. 155).

(a) Exceptions

Section 351 can apply in this situation *only* if the debt is evidenced by a *security* (a relatively long-term corporate debt, such as a long-term corporate bond). [I.R.C. § 351(d)(2)] Moreover, stock issued in exchange for unpaid *interest* of the debtor corporation (which accrued on or after the beginning of the transferor's holding period for the debt) is not issued in exchange for "property" and thus is not tax-free under section 351. [I.R.C. § 351(d)(3)] Thus, receipt of stock for accrued interest would be ordinary income to the creditor. (Although special treatment for "securities" has been repealed for most section 351 purposes, this reference to securities remains in the amended Code.)

6. Recognition of Gain

a. Distribution of Other Property

If the corporation distributes other property (*i.e.,* other than stock) to the transferor, *gain* is recognized up to the value of the other property. [I.R.C. § 351(b)] Loss is *not* recognized. Such other property is generally referred to as "boot."

b. Preferred Stock as Boot

Normally, the corporation can distribute any kind of stock—common or preferred—as part of an incorporation transaction. However, "nonqualified preferred stock" (*see infra*) is not treated as stock for this purpose; instead it is treated as boot. [I.R.C. § 351(g)] *Rationale:* Preferred stock structured to more closely resemble debt than stock should be treated like debt.

(1) Preferred Stock

For this purpose, preferred stock means stock which is limited and preferred as to dividends and does not participate in corporate growth to any significant extent.

(2) Nonqualified Preferred

Preferred stock is nonqualified if:

(i) The *holder has the right* to require the issuer or a related person to *redeem or purchase* the stock;

(ii) The *issuer* or a related person is *required to redeem or purchase* the stock;

(iii) The *issuer* or a related person has the *right to redeem or purchase* the stock and, as of the issue date, it is more likely than not that such right will be exercised; or

(iv) The *dividend rate on the stock varies with reference to interest rates, commodity prices, or similar indices*.

Note that (i)–(iii) apply only if the right or obligation may be exercised within the 20-year period starting on the issue date and there is no contingency that, as of the issue date, makes the chances of redemption or sale less likely.

c. Ceiling on Recognized Gain

The transferor never *recognizes* more gain than is *realized* on the transfer. (However, note the exception to this rule under section 357(c), *infra,* p. 76.)

 Example: Ariel transfers Blackacre to X Corp. in exchange for 50 shares of stock and $10,000 in cash. Belle transfers Whiteacre to X Corp. in exchange for only 50 shares. They are the only shareholders. The basis of Blackacre in Ariel's hands is $42,000 and the value is $50,000. Ariel recognizes only $8,000 in gain (her entire realized gain), even though she received boot of $10,000.

 Example: In the previous example, assume Ariel's basis for Blackacre was $36,000. Now her realized gain is $14,000. She recognizes $10,000 of gain (the amount of the boot).

 Example: Assume, in the previous example, that Ariel's basis for Blackacre was $61,000. Although she realized an $11,000 loss, she recognizes none of it.

d. Liabilities as Boot

Frequently, a corporation will assume or take subject to liabilities of the transferor when she transfers assets to the corporation. The general rule is that such assumption of liabilities is *not* treated as boot to the transferor and no gain is recognized. [I.R.C. § 357(a)]

 Example: Ariel transfers the assets of her sole proprietorship business to newly formed X Corp. in exchange for 100% of the stock. The assets have a basis of

$40,000 and a value of $100,000. The corporation also assumes the liabilities of the business ($30,000). Under section 357(a), the $30,000 is not treated as boot and no gain is recognized.

(1) Subject to Debts

For all purposes under section 357, it does not matter whether the corporation assumes the debts or merely takes subject to the debts. Either way, the liabilities are not treated as boot under section 357(a).

(2) Exception for Tax Avoidance

If the nature of the liability, and the circumstances of its acquisition by the corporation, indicate that there was a tax avoidance purpose (or an absence of a bona fide business purpose) on the exchange, *all* liabilities assumed (or that the corporation takes subject to) are treated as boot. [I.R.C. § 357(b)]

(a) Note

It is likely that section 357(b) will apply when the liabilities are personal, rather than business, or when they were incurred just before incorporation. [*See* **Drybrough v. Commissioner,** 376 F.2d 350 (6th Cir. 1967)]

Example: In the previous example (*supra,* p. 74), suppose that $20,000 of the $30,000 liability was actually Ariel's delinquent alimony payments. Or assume that $20,000 of the $30,000 in liabilities was created a week before incorporation by mortgaging property in the business. It would probably be found that Ariel's purpose was tax avoidance, and section 357(b) would apply. The entire $30,000 in liabilities would be treated as boot (not just the $20,000 as to which a tax avoidance purpose applied). Ariel must recognize $30,000 of her $60,000 realized gain.

(3) Liabilities in Excess of Basis

If the liabilities transferred exceed the basis of the assets transferred, gain is recognized in the amount of the excess. [I.R.C. § 357(c)] For instance, in a section 351 exchange, Ariel transfers a ranch to X Corp. having a basis of $120,000. The ranch is subject to a mortgage of $160,000. The ranch is the only asset transferred. Ariel must recognize gain of $40,000 on the transfer.

(a) Cash Basis Transferors

A serious problem can be created when a cash basis service business (like a law firm) is incorporated. Because it has a zero basis for its accounts receivable (*see* Taxation of Individuals Summary for explanation of the cash basis), its liabilities frequently exceed the basis of its assets. However, section 357(c) has been amended to avoid recognition of gain in most such cases.

1) Rule

In the case of a cash basis transferor, *accounts payable are disregarded* for purposes of the section 357(c) calculation. An account payable is a liability the payment of which will give rise to a deduction. [I.R.C. § 357(c)(3)(A)—codifying the reasoning in **Focht v. Commissioner,** 68 T.C. 223 (1977)]

2) But Note

If the liability gave rise to an increase in the basis of any asset, it is not excluded for purposes of section 357(c). [I.R.C. § 357(c)(3)(B)]

Example: Ariel incorporates her law firm. There are $20,000 of accounts receivable, which have a zero basis. The basis and value of the other assets is $6,000. There are liabilities of $10,000. These consist of rent and salaries payable of $7,000 and a liability of $3,000 for the purchase of law books. The rent and salaries payable are disregarded under section 357(c) because they are accounts payable; when the corporation pays them, it will receive a deduction. But the $3,000 liability is not disregarded; it was a purchase money liability for the books, and so the liability was included in the basis of the books (*see* Taxation of Individuals Summary for discussion of including purchase money liabilities in basis). Because the total basis of assets is $6,000 and only $3,000 in liabilities are taken into account under section 357(c), Ariel recognizes no gain on the incorporation.

(b) Accrual Method Transferors

Accrual method transferors may have certain liabilities that have not yet become deductible. Under the rule of section 357(c)(3), these liabilities also may be ignored for purposes of section 357. [*See* Rev. Rul. 95–74, 1995–2 C.B. 36—accrual basis parent can ignore environmental cleanup liabilities for purposes of measuring gain under section 357; subsidiary will either deduct the cleanup costs or capitalize them]

(c) Lack of Realized Gain Immaterial

Gain is recognized under section 357(c) even if there is no realized gain. In other words, even if the value of the assets is not greater than their adjusted basis, gain must still be recognized if the liabilities exceed the adjusted basis. Furthermore, the section 357(c) gain is still recognized even if the shareholder remains liable on the liabilities and the creditors look only to him, not to the corporation. [**Rosen v. Commissioner,** 62 T.C. 11 (1974)]

Example: Ariel transfers Blackacre to X Corp. in a section 351 exchange. The basis of Blackacre is $100,000 but it is worth only $70,000. It is subject to a liability of $105,000. Despite the fact that Ariel has a realized loss on Blackacre, she must recognize $5,000 in gain (which will be capital gain if Blackacre is a capital asset).

(d) Shareholder Debt to Corporation

A taxpayer might be able to avoid gain under section 357(c) by promising to pay the corporation the excess of liabilities over the basis of the assets. In a questionable decision, one court has held that the corporation could count as an asset the debt owed to it by the shareholder; the basis of that asset is the face value of the debt. Therefore, the total basis of the corporation's assets would be equal to its liabilities. [**Lessinger v. Commissioner,** 872 F.2d 519 (2d Cir. 1989)] A second court reached the same conclusion. It found that the shareholder's promissory note had a basis equal to its face value (on the theory that the shareholder could have borrowed the amount of the note from a third-party lender and contributed cash). The court also held (overruling the Tax

Court's decision on this point) that the note was bona fide, not a sham, even though the taxpayer never started making payments on the note until after the IRS began auditing the transaction. [**Peracchi v. Commissioner,** 143 F.3d 487 (9th Cir. 1998)]

1) Distinguish—Personal Guarantee

While a promissory note might be sufficient to avoid gain, a taxpayer's personal guarantee has been held to be insufficient. [*See, e.g.,* **Owen v. Commissioner,** 881 F.2d 832 (9th Cir. 1989); **Seggerman Farms v. Commissioner,** 308 F.3d 803 (7th Cir. 2002)]

e. Allocation of Gain [§ 305]

If the transferor transfers several assets and receives boot, he must allocate the boot among the various assets transferred. After the boot is allocated, he can then compute the correct amount of the recognized gain. This allocation is done by prorating the boot among the assets in proportion to their *fair market values*—not their bases. [Rev. Rul. 68–55, 1968–1 C.B. 140]

Example: Art transfers three assets to newly formed X Corp. in exchange for 80% of its stock and $10,000; Blackacre (basis $60,000, value $100,000); Whiteacre (basis $48,000, value $50,000); and Tanacre (basis $70,000, value $50,000). The boot is allocated in proportion to the values of the assets: $5,000 to Blackacre, $2,500 to Whiteacre, and $2,500 to Tanacre. Thus, Art recognizes gain of $5,000 on Blackacre and $2,000 on Whiteacre. No gain is recognized on Tanacre because there was no realized gain.

f. Recapture of Depreciation

If no gain is recognized on a section 351 exchange, depreciation is not recaptured on the transferred assets under section 1245 or 1250. [*See* I.R.C. §§ 1245(b)(3), 1250(d)(3)] But if gain is recognized because boot is received, depreciation on the assets is recaptured as ordinary income to the extent of the recognized gain. (*See* Taxation of Individuals Summary for explanation of depreciation recapture.)

g. Installment Obligations

Similarly, if an obligation accounted for under the installment method of section 453 is transferred to the corporation, in a section 351 exchange, the transfer is not treated as a disposition of the obligation that would trigger recognition of the previously unrecognized gain. (*See* Taxation of Individuals Summary for explanation of the installment method.)

h. Sale of Assets to Corporation

A taxpayer who seeks to avoid section 351 (in order to recognize loss or to get a step-up in basis at the corporate level) may *sell* the asset to the corporation rather than contribute it in exchange for stock or securities. However, such sales are frequently reclassified as section 351 exchanges.

(1) Consequence of Sale

If the transaction is treated as a sale, the *seller recognizes gain or loss in its entirety*. The corporation's basis for the purchased asset is its purchase price.

(a) Restriction on Losses

If the shareholder (and her relatives) owns more than 50% of the stock, loss is disallowed. [I.R.C. § 267(a)(1), (b)(2)]

(b) Ordinary Income

If an individual sells property to the corporation that is depreciable in the hands of the corporation, and she owns directly or indirectly 80% or more in value of the stock, the gain is ordinary income. [I.R.C. § 1239(a), (b)(2)] Note also that depreciation is recaptured on such a sale, which also produces ordinary income. [I.R.C. §§ 1245, 1250]

(2) Reclassification of the Sale as a Section 351 Exchange

If the "sale" seems to be part of an overall transaction in which the corporation is formed and capitalized, the IRS will contend that the true substance of the "sale" is that it is part of the issuance of stock. The result is that the sale will be treated as part of the section 351 exchange.

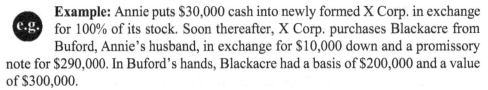 **Example:** Annie puts $30,000 cash into newly formed X Corp. in exchange for 100% of its stock. Soon thereafter, X Corp. purchases Blackacre from Buford, Annie's husband, in exchange for $10,000 down and a promissory note for $290,000. In Buford's hands, Blackacre had a basis of $200,000 and a value of $300,000.

1) If the transaction is upheld, Buford would have a $100,000 capital gain and X Corp.'s basis would be $300,000 for Blackacre.

2) However, the IRS would contend that the cash and property transactions should be treated as a single section 351 exchange in which the Annie-Buford family placed $20,000 in cash (*i.e.,* $30,000 less $10,000) and Blackacre into X Corp. in exchange for stock plus a debt. In addition, the IRS would undoubtedly contend that the debt should be reclassified as equity. (*See infra,* pp. 85–86.) Buford would recognize no gain, and X Corp.'s basis would be only $200,000. [*See, e.g.,* **Aqualane Shores, Inc. v. Commissioner,** 269 F.2d 116 (5th Cir. 1959); **D'Angelo Associates, Inc. v. Commissioner,** *supra,* p. 71; *but see* **Sun Properties, Inc. v. United States,** 220 F.2d 171 (5th Cir. 1955)—decision much more favorable to the taxpayers]

i. Contribution to Capital

A shareholder may contribute shares of a corporation's stock back to the corporation to increase the percentage of stock held by other shareholders. The contributing shareholder is not permitted to recognize loss on the contribution. Instead, the basis of the contributed shares is simply added to the basis of her remaining shares. [**Commissioner v. Fink,** 483 U.S. 89 (1987)]

7. Basis Adjustments and Related Problems Under Section 351

a. Corporation's Basis

If section 351 applies, the transferee corporation retains the same basis for the property as it had in the transferor's hands. If the transferor recognized gain on the exchange, however, the corporation increases its basis by the amount of the gain. [I.R.C. § 362(a)]

(1) Note

If several assets are transferred, gain may be recognized on some of them, but not others. [*See* Rev. Rul. 68–55. 1968–1 C.B. 140, discussed *supra,* p. 77] In such a case, the corporation would increase the basis of only those assets on which gain had been recognized.

(2) Built-In Loss Property

An exception to the general carryover basis rule in section 362(a) applies if the transferred properties have a net built-in loss (*i.e.*, the aggregate adjusted bases of the transferred properties exceed the aggregate fair market value). Under this circumstance, in the absence of an election to reduce the transferor shareholder's basis in the stock received in the transfer, the transferee corporation's aggregated adjusted basis in the transferred properties must be reduced to the fair market value of the properties at the time of the transfer. [I.R.C. § 362(e)(2)(A), (C)] The aggregate adjusted bases are allocated among the transferred properties in proportion to their respective built-in losses immediately prior to the transfer. [I.R.C. § 362(e)(2)(B)]

b. Shareholder's Basis

The shareholder has the same basis for his stock received in a section 351 exchange as he had in the property transferred to the corporation [I.R.C. § 358(a)(1)]:

(i) ***The basis of stock received must be reduced by the amount of any liability*** the corporation assumed or took subject to, even if the corporation's acquisition of the liability was not treated as boot. [I.R.C. § 358(d)] One exception to this rule is for any liability assumed that is excluded under section 357(c)(3), discussed *supra*, p. 75 [I.R.C. § 358(d)(2)], unless the trade or business with which the liability is associated is not transferred. [I.R.C. § 358(h)(2)(A); *see also* Treas. Reg. 1.358–5—making § 358(h)(2)(B), which added "substantially all of the assets" to the "trade or business" exception, inapplicable for transactions occurring after May 9, 2008]

(ii) ***The basis of the stock received must be decreased by the amount of boot*** received by the shareholder—either money or the value of any property received as boot. [I.R.C. § 358(a)(1)(A)(i), (ii)]

(iii) ***The basis of the stock received must be increased by the amount of gain*** recognized on the exchange. [I.R.C. § 358(a)(1)(B)(ii)]

(iv) ***The basis of any boot received is equal to its value.*** [I.R.C. § 358(a)(2)]

(v) ***In the event that basis must be allocated between several different assets*** (such as several classes of stock or stock and securities), it is done by a formula that allocates the basis in proportion to the respective values of the different assets. [Treas. Reg. § 1.358–2]

(vi) ***The basis of stock received in exchange for built-in loss property may be reduced to the fair market value*** of the property transferred, at the election of the transferor and transferee corporation. [I.R.C. § 362(e)(2)(C)]

> **Example:** Assume that Anson transfers Blackacre to X Corp. in exchange for 100% of its stock and a corporate debt of $10,000. Blackacre had a basis of $21,000 and a value of $24,000 in Anson's hands. It was subject to a $4,000 debt and X Corp. takes subject to that debt. Assume also that the X Corp. $10,000 debt is treated as ***boot***. Anson's realized gain was $3,000, all of which is recognized. The basis of the $10,000 debt is $10,000 in Anson's hands. The basis of Anson's stock is the basis of

Blackacre ($21,000), reduced by the debt to which X Corp. took subject ($4,000), decreased by the value of the boot ($10,000), and increased by the recognized gain ($3,000). Thus, the basis of the stock in Anson's hands is $10,000. The basis of Blackacre in X Corp.'s hands is $24,000 (the former basis of $21,000 plus gain recognized to Anson of $3,000).

c. Holding Period

For purposes of determining whether capital gain is long-term or short-term, it is necessary to know a taxpayer's holding period for the asset sold. The holding period for stock obtained as a result of a section 351 exchange includes that of the property exchanged for the stock. *Exception:* If the property exchanged for the stock was not a capital asset or an asset described in section 1231, the shareholder's holding period for the stock begins at the date of the exchange. [I.R.C. § 1223(1)] The *corporation's holding period* for acquired assets includes the shareholder's holding period for those assets. [I.R.C. § 1223(2)]

d. Corporation's Gain

The corporation has no gain or loss from issuing its own stock in exchange for property. This is so even if it issued treasury stock (*i.e.,* stock it had bought previously from a shareholder). [I.R.C. § 1032]

e.g. **Example:** The corporation's basis in its own treasury stock is zero. Thus, suppose A Corp. puts its own treasury stock into B Corp., in exchange for 80% of B Corp. stock. The exchange is under section 351. A Corp.'s basis for its B Corp. stock is zero— because A Corp.'s basis for the property that it transferred to B Corp. was zero. [Rev. Rul. 74–503, 1974–2 C.B. 117]

e. Assignments of Income

Suppose that partners on the cash basis render services for which they have not yet been paid. The zero-basis receivables are transferred to the corporation in a section 351 exchange. It has been held that the corporation, not the shareholders, is taxed when the corporation collects the receivables. Also, the corporation can deduct the accounts payable. [**Hempt Bros., Inc. v. United States,** 490 F.2d 1172 (3d Cir. 1974); Rev. Rul. 80–198, 1980–2 C.B. 113]

8. Corporate Tax Shelters and Economic Substance Doctrine

A new corporation is sometimes established under section 351 to facilitate corporate tax shelter transactions. Such transactions must not violate the economic substance doctrine. This judicial doctrine, which is related to the sham transaction doctrine and the business purpose requirement (*infra*, pp. 132–134), inquires whether a transaction has any economic consequences apart from the tax benefits. It applies outside the context of incorporations to cover other transactions as well.

a. Contingent Liability Tax Shelters

An example of such a transaction is the contingent liability tax shelter, which was later the subject of litigation in **Black & Decker Corp. v. United States,** 436 F.3d 431 (4th Cir. 2006), and **Coltec Industries, Inc. v. United States,** 454 F.3d 1340 (Fed. Cir. 2006). In each of these cases, a contingent liability (for asbestos product liability claims in *Coltec,* and for employee and retiree healthcare benefit claims in *Black & Decker*) was transferred to a newly created subsidiary, along with cash with a value slightly above the value of the contingent liability, in exchange for the subsidiary's assumption of the contingent liability plus the transfer of a small amount of stock (equal in value to the difference between the value of the cash and the value of the liabilities assumed) in a transaction that was designed to qualify as a section 351 nonrecognition exchange. Under section 358(d)(2), the parent corporation held the subsidiary stock at a basis equal to the cash transferred, undiminished by the liability assumed. Subsequently, the parent sold the stock for its small economic value and claimed a large loss because of its high basis in the subsidiary stock under section 358(d)(2). Since the facts in each case arose prior to the enactment of section 358(h) (*supra*, p. 79), the courts remanded (in *Black & Decker*) and reversed (in *Coltec*) on considerations of whether the transactions violated the economic substance doctrine.

b. Codification of Economic Substance Doctrine

In 2010, Congress codified the economic substance doctrine [I.R.C. § 7701(o)] by identifying the components of economic substance. Under section 7701(o), a transaction is treated as having economic substance if (i) the transaction changes the taxpayer's pre-tax economic position in a meaningful way, **and** (ii) the taxpayer has a substantial non-tax business purpose for entering into the transaction. This resolved some split in the circuit courts about whether both prongs of the economic substance doctrine were required. The provision was not intended to supplant the court's view on whether the economic substance doctrine is relevant to a particular transaction, but rather to clarify the appropriate elements of the doctrine when it was applied.

D. Corporation's Capital Structure—Debt or Equity?

1. Why the Dispute

A frequently litigated problem in corporate taxation is whether corporate debt should be reclassified as equity (*i.e.,* as stock). This presents a difficult issue of whether the "true substance" of the instrument is different from its form.

a. Advantages of Using Debt

There are a number of incentives to use corporate debt rather than equity:

(1) Interest

The interest on debt is deductible while dividends on stock are not. [I.R.C. § 163]

(a) Original Issue Discount

If a corporation issues debt that fails to call for a market rate of interest, interest will be *imputed* on the debt.

e.g. **Example:** Z Corp. issues a "zero coupon bond" to Ted. Ted pays $10,000 cash. The bond pays no interest but will pay Ted $17,500 at the end of five years. This $7,500 difference reflects a return of 12%, which is a substitute for interest. That $7,500 difference between the "issue price" ($10,000) and the redemption price at maturity ($17,500) is called "original issue discount" ("OID"). The amount of OID is deductible to the borrower (Z Corp.) and ordinary income to the lender (Ted) over the period of the loan. [I.R.C. §§ 1272, 1273, 163(e)]

(b) Repayment

When a corporation repays a debt that it owes to its shareholder, the shareholder is allowed to recover his basis. In many cases, therefore, the repayment will produce no tax. If there is a gain on repayment, the gain will be capital. [I.R.C. § 1271(a)]

e.g. **Example:** In year 1, Z Corp. borrowed $10,000 from Amy. The debt pays 15% interest and is due in year 8. In year 4, Bob purchased that debt from Amy for $7,000. In year 8, Z Corp. paid Bob $10,000. Bob's $3,000 gain is long-term capital gain.

1) Caution

In many cases, corporate debt is reclassified as equity (*i.e.,* as corporate stock). In that case, "repayment" of the "debt" is likely to be taxed as a dividend without any recovery of basis (*see infra,* p. 102).

(2) Reasonable Needs

The accumulation of assets for the purpose of repaying outstanding corporate debt is a reasonable need of the business for accumulated earnings tax purposes, while the accumulation of assets for the purpose of redeeming stock ordinarily is not. (*See supra,* p. 62 *et seq.*)

(3) Sharing with Creditors

If the corporation becomes insolvent, the debt holder can hope to share in competition with outside creditors. A shareholder, however, cannot be paid until all creditors are paid.

b. Disadvantages of Using Debt

(1) Corporate Shareholder

If a corporation is the shareholder of another corporation, it might prefer to have stock rather than debt. *Rationale:* Interest on debts is fully taxable as ordinary income but the corporate shareholder can deduct 70% (sometimes 100%) of dividends received from income. [*See* I.R.C. § 243, discussed *infra,* p. 95]

(2) Higher Rate

Dividends received from most domestic corporations are taxed to the recipient at the long-term capital gains rate, currently 15%. [I.R.C. § 1(h)(11)] By contrast, interest received is subject to taxation at the individual's taxable rate, as much as 35%. [I.R.C. § 1(i)(2)] Notwithstanding the higher rate, the effective rate on income paid out as interest may still be less than the effective rate on income paid out as dividends because of the deductibility of interest payments at the corporate level.

e.g. **Example:** In 2010, A Corp. distributed dividends in the aggregate amount of $100,000 from money earned that year. That money was first subject to a corporate tax of as high as 35% and then subject to a tax as high as 15% in the individual shareholder's hands, for a total effective tax of 45%. If the $100,000 was instead paid out as interest on a corporate bond, it would only be subject to a 35% tax in the individual bondholder's hands because of the availability of the corporate deduction for interest payments.

(3) Losses on Debts

Ordinarily there is little difference between holding stock and debt if a loss is realized. The loss on stock is generally a capital loss (*see* Taxation of Individuals Summary for explanation of the restricted deductibility of capital losses). (*See*, however, *infra*, p. 84, for discussion of section 1244 stock.) The loss on corporate debt is also generally a capital loss because it is usually treated as a **nonbusiness bad debt**. [I.R.C. § 166(d)]

(a) Rationale

The rationale for treating the loss as a nonbusiness bad debt is that the creditor was making an investment when he acquired the debt. Only the corporation is treated as being in business—not the holder of its debt. Also, the shareholder is assumed not to be in the business of making such loans. [**Whipple v. Commissioner,** 373 U.S. 193 (1963)]

STOCK VS. DEBT—ADVANTAGES OF EACH | **GILBERT**

ADVANTAGES OF DEBT

A corporation may **deduct the interest** that it pays from its gross income, while dividends are nondeductible.

The shareholder being repaid **does not recognize gain** except to the extent repayment exceeds his basis in the loan.

The corporation may **accumulate a reasonable amount of assets** to repay the debt without incurring accumulated earnings tax liability.

Shareholders holding debt will **share with outside creditors** if the corporation becomes insolvent.

ADVANTAGES OF STOCK

If the shareholder is a corporation, interest on debt would be taxable as ordinary income; income in the form of **dividends is partially deductible**.

If the taxpayer is an individual, dividends received from most domestic corporations are **taxed at the capital gains rate**.

If the stock is section 1244 stock (stock in a domestic corporation that was issued for money or other property; corporation has active income and less than $1 million in paid-in capital initially), losses on its sale or worthlessness are treated as **ordinary** rather than capital.

If the taxpayer is not a corporation, it can **exclude from income 50% of the gain** from the sale of qualified small business stock (*see infra*, p. 85).

(b) Exception

In rare cases it is possible to show that the creditor was holding the debt in connection with an active trade or business. For example, if the creditor was compelled to loan money to the corporation in order to keep his position as a corporate employee, the debt would be a business bad debt, which qualifies for ordinary loss. [**Trent v. Commissioner,** 291 F.2d 669 (2d Cir. 1961)]

(4) Losses on Section 1244 Stock

If stock is section 1244 stock, losses on the sale or worthlessness of the stock are *ordinary*, rather than capital losses, up to a ceiling amount. This means that it is preferable to have stock rather than debt if a loss is incurred and the stock is section 1244 stock.

(a) Ceiling

Loss on sale or worthlessness of section 1244 stock is ordinary up to $50,000 per year. (If the taxpayer files a joint return, the figure is $100,000 per year.) Losses in excess of those amounts are capital losses. [I.R.C. § 1244(b)]

(b) Requirements

For stock to be section 1244 stock, the following requirements must be met:

1) The stock must be in a *domestic corporation* (but it can be common or preferred stock). [I.R.C. § 1244(c)(1)]

2) The stock must have been *issued for money or other property*—but not issued in exchange for stock or securities. [I.R.C. § 1244(c)(1)(B)]

3) During the period (up to five years) ending before the date of the loss, the corporation must have been *primarily an active trade or business*, rather than deriving mainly passive income. Thus it must not have derived more than 50% of its gross receipts from royalties, rents, dividends, interest, annuities, or gains from the exchange of stock or securities. [I.R.C. § 1244(c)(1)(C), (c)(2)]

4) At the time of issuance of the stock in question, the total amount paid in for stock (and as contributions to capital) cannot exceed *$1 million*. [I.R.C. § 1244(c)(1)(A), (c)(3)]

(5) Gains on Small Business Stock

(a) General Rule

A taxpayer (other than a corporation) can exclude from income 50% of the gain on the sale of qualified small business stock acquired before February 17, 2009. The exclusion is 75% for stock acquired after February 17, 2009 and before September 27, 2010 and 100% for stock acquired after September 27, 2010. In all cases, the stock must have been held for at least five years to obtain the exclusion. [I.R.C. § 1202(a)].

1) Note

This exclusion was enacted in 1993, before Congress reduced the capital gains rate to 20%. The amount of gain not subject to exclusion is taxed at 28% [I.R.C. §§ 1(h)(4), (7)] Since taxpayers may not claim both the exclusion and the lower rate on capital gains, the effective rate on gains on small business stock is 14%. Therefore, for taxpayers eligible for less than the 100% exclusion, the benefit of the exclusion may be lessened considerably. Moreover, the excluded gain is treated as a tax preference under the alternative minimum tax for sales of stock acquired before September 27, 2010. [I.R.C. § 57(a)(7)]

(b) Limit

The amount of gain subject to the 50% (or 75% or 100%) exclusion may not exceed the *greater* of:

(i) $10 million (in the taxable year and prior taxable years); or

(ii) Ten times the adjusted basis of the stock being disposed of. [I.R.C. § 1202(b)(1)]

> **e.g.** **Example:** Ted has a basis of $4 million for his Q Co. stock that he acquired before February 17, 2009. The stock is qualified small business stock. He sells the stock for $28 million. Ted can exclude $12 million from income (50% of the total gain). Although the gain exceeded $10 million, it did not exceed 10 times the adjusted basis of the Q stock.

(c) Qualified Small Business Stock

To qualify for this treatment, the stock must have been issued after August 1993; the taxpayer must have been the original purchaser of the stock from the corporation; and the corporation must conduct an active business (excluding most service and real estate businesses) and its assets after the time of stock issuance must not have exceeded $50 million. [I.R.C. § 1202(c)–(d), (e)]

2. Statutory Guidelines

I.R.C. section 385 provides guidelines for determining whether an interest should be classified as debt or equity. It gives the IRS power to adopt regulations to make these guidelines precise. Unfortunately, although several elaborate sets of regulations were proposed, all have been withdrawn. Consequently, section 385 has little current importance, although the factors given are similar to those relied on under case law. The factors that section 385 indicate should be considered are:

a. *The form of the instrument* (whether it is a written unconditional promise to pay on demand, or specified date, a sum certain in money, with a fixed rate of interest);

b. *Whether there is subordination to other debts*;

c. *The ratio of debt to equity*;

d. *Whether the item is convertible*; and

e. *The relationship between holdings of stock in the corporation and holdings of the interest in question.*

3. Case Law

In the absence of section 385 regulations, it is necessary to resort to the vast body of case law, which balances multiple factors, in assessing whether in substance a particular interest is really equity rather than debt. Some cases phrase the test as being whether an investment was placed "at the risk of the business." An investment placed at the risk of the business is equity rather than debt. [**Slappey Drive Industrial Park v. United States,** 561 F.2d 572 (5th Cir. 1977)]

a. Factors to Consider

The most important factors are:

(1) Form of Debt

Unless the form of the debt closely resembles a typical debt (such as a bond, promissory note, or debenture), it has little chance of being classified as debt for tax purposes. Thus, the debt should have a fixed repayment date, a reasonable and fixed rate of interest, and appropriate security.

(2) Ratio of Debt to Equity

It is necessary to measure the ratio of the debt to the corporate equity. "Equity," for this purpose, means the difference between the value of the assets and the liabilities. If the ratio is excessive (meaning that it would not be satisfactory to an independent creditor because the loan would be too risky), the loan is likely to be classified as equity. Ratios greater than about 3:1 are quite risky.

e.g. **Example:** When C Corp. is formed, the value of its assets is $50,000. Its liabilities to outside creditors total $30,000. In addition, C Corp. owes a debt to its shareholders of $15,000. C Corp.'s equity is $5,000 (assets less liabilities). Its debts total $45,000. Thus, the ratio of debt to equity is 9:1, which is quite high. Probably, an outside creditor would find this ratio excessive and would refuse to make the $15,000 loan. Consequently, that loan is likely to be treated as equity.

(3) Proportionality

If the distribution of debt among shareholders is the same as the distribution of stock, the debt is likely to be treated as equity. *Rationale:* When the holdings are perfectly proportional, it makes little difference to the shareholders how much of their investment is characterized as debt and how much as stock. [**Fin Hay Realty Corp. v. United States,** 398 F.2d 694 (3d Cir. 1968)]

e.g. **Example:** Alex owns 75% of C Corp. stock. Becky owns 25%. Each of them owns 50% of the debt. The holdings are not proportional. The debts are likely to be treated as debts, not as equity.

(4) Other Factors

If the corporation does not pay interest or principal when it is due, and the creditor takes no action to enforce payment, the debt is likely to be treated as equity. [**Slappey Drive Industrial Park v. United States,** *supra*] Also, some cases view with suspicion debts that are issued as part of the incorporation process to acquire the "basic assets of the business." These courts assert that such assets should be acquired in exchange for stock.

b. Economic Reality Test

Some courts have rejected the laundry list approach in favor of one core variable—whether an unrelated outside lender would lend money on similar terms to those agreed to by the holder of the instrument. In other words, an instrument is considered equity if it is far more speculative than what an outside lender would normally undertake. This test does not avoid some of the problems of the individual factors, but it does boil down the list to its essential component. [*See, e.g.,* **Scriptomatic, Inc. v. United States,** 555 F.2d 364 (3d Cir. 1977)]

4. Guarantees

Suppose a bank loans money to a corporation, and its shareholder guarantees the debt. The corporation becomes insolvent and the shareholder must honor the guarantee. It has been held that the shareholder then becomes a corporate creditor through the process of subrogation. Because the corporation is insolvent, the shareholder has a bad debt. Under the usual rule of *Whipple, supra,* p. 83, it would be a nonbusiness bad debt and thus a capital loss. [**Putnam v. Commissioner,** 352 U.S. 82 (1956)]

a. Distinguish

Suppose the corporation did not become insolvent. Instead, it paid interest to the bank. There is authority that the IRS can reclassify the transaction—treating it as if the bank loaned money *to the shareholder* who then invested it in the corporation. The interest payment would be treated as having been made to the shareholder (and in turn paid by the shareholder to the bank). If the shareholder's "investment" in the corporation was treated as equity, not debt, that payment could be treated as a dividend. For the IRS to prevail, it would have to show that the bank looked primarily to the shareholder as the main credit risk, not the corporation. [*See* **Santa Anita Consolidated, Inc. v. Commissioner,** 50 T.C. 536 (1968); **Plantation Patterns, Inc. v. Commissioner,** 462 F.2d 712 (5th Cir. 1972)]

Chapter Three

Corporate Taxation— Distributions

CONTENTS

PAGE

Key Exam Issues

Probably the majority of corporate tax exam questions contain distribution issues. Always examine both the shareholder level and the corporate level when asked to discuss the consequences of a distribution.

1. **Consequences to Shareholder—Distributions Not in Exchange for Stock**

   Here the main issue will be to calculate both current and accumulated earnings and profits to see whether they will turn a distribution into a dividend (as opposed to recovery of capital). If accumulated or current earnings and profits are present, the distribution is a dividend.

   a. Watch for the ***dividends-received deduction***. If the shareholder is itself a corporation, it can deduct 70% (or in some cases 80% or 100%) of the dividend.

   b. Many exam questions will include ***disguised dividends***, such as bargain sales of corporate assets to shareholders, unreasonable compensation, interest that is really a dividend because it is paid on equity rather than debt, or corporate payment of shareholder personal expenses. Be sure to reach the substance behind the form.

2. **Consequences to Shareholder—Liquidating Distributions**

   The usual rule is that liquidating distributions are taxable as capital gain to shareholders under section 331 (with stepped-up basis for assets received). When working on a problem with a liquidating distribution, watch for:

   a. The possibility of ***liquidation-reincorporation***, which would turn the distribution into a dividend;

   b. Attempts to ***shift the gain to a charity or related party***, which will be ignored if done after the liquidation period begins; and

   c. ***A corporate shareholder with 80% control*** of the corporation. Analyze liquidation under section 332, which provides that when one corporation controls another, no gain or loss is recognized to the parent.

3. **Consequences to Shareholder—Redemptions and Partial Liquidations**

   Here section 302 is your bible—the distribution must pass the section 302 screens or be treated as a dividend. Always be sure to apply the attribution rules.

   a. Your analysis should start with ***complete termination*** (corporation purchases all of the shareholder's stock). [I.R.C. § 302(b)(3)] Consider the difficulties in achieving complete termination when the attribution rules are applied, but recall that family attribution may be waived if certain requirements are met.

   b. Next you should consider whether the rule for ***substantially disproportionate redemptions*** [I.R.C. § 302(b)(2)] applies.

   c. Then a shareholder who is not a corporation may attempt to qualify the distribution as a ***partial liquidation*** [I.R.C. § 302(b)(4)], which is treated as a redemption.

   d. If a ***shareholder dies and the stock totals 35% or more of the estate***, the repurchase of shares will be treated as a redemption rather than a dividend. [I.R.C. § 303(a) and (b)(2)]

   e. Finally, if none of the above provisions applies, the distribution may still be treated as a redemption if it is "***not essentially equivalent to a dividend***." [I.R.C. § 302(b)(1)]

f. Remember that if the distribution is a dividend, not a redemption, there is **no basis recovery**. This is probably the most significant difference between a dividend and a redemption now that dividends are considered net capital gain.

g. Don't forget to analyze the impact of the redemption on corporate **earnings and profits**. Redemptions reduce earnings and profits by a ratable amount.

h. Watch for special rules under **section 304** when there are several corporations involved (*e.g.,* parent-subsidiary or brother-sister corporation transactions).

4. Impact of Distributions on Corporation

The general rule is that a corporation realizes gain (but not loss) on a nonliquidating distribution of property. It realizes gain and loss on a liquidating distribution (unless it is a section 332 liquidation). Taxpayers will try many schemes to avoid the double tax on liquidations, so it is important to penetrate through form to substance.

5. Distributions—Stock Dividends and Recapitalizations

When a corporation distributes its own stock to shareholders, start with the assumption that it is a dividend unless it falls within a specific exception in section 305 or it is a recapitalization. In these situations, the biggest issue is the preferred stock bailout under section 306. Therefore, when you see a tax-free distribution of preferred stock with respect to common stock, assume that it is section 306 stock, and be prepared to track through the results when the stock is either sold or redeemed.

A. Consequences to Shareholders of Corporate Distributions of Cash and Property

1. Distributions by the Going Concern

a. Earnings and Profits

(1) Needed for Dividend

A corporate distribution to shareholders is a dividend if the corporation has either *current* or *accumulated earnings and profits*. [I.R.C. § 316(a)]

(2) Definition

Earnings and profits are computed by starting with taxable income and subtracting income tax and previous dividends. This figure is *reduced* by many other items not deductible for tax purposes (such as unreasonable compensation, income taxes, or capital losses). It is *increased* by items that are not taxable income (such as interest on municipal bonds). It is also increased by items that are deductible for purposes of computing taxable income but not for computing earnings and profits. For example, earnings and profits are increased by the corporate dividends-received deduction under section 243. [Treas. Reg. § 1.312–6]

(a) Depreciation

Earnings and profits are reduced only by straight-line depreciation, even though a corporation uses accelerated depreciation for purposes of computing taxable income. In addition, in computing depreciation for earnings and profits purposes, the property has a much longer life than that permitted for purposes of computing depreciation. [I.R.C. § 312(k), referring to § 168(g)]

(b) Charitable Contribution

Earnings and profits are reduced by the full market value of a charitable contribution—not the adjusted basis of the donated property—whether or not deductible by the corporation. [**Kaplan v. Commissioner,** 43 T.C. 580 (1965); *contra,* Rev. Rul. 78–123, 1978–1 C.B. 87]

(c) Adjustments for Installment Method

A corporation that sells property and uses the installment method of reporting gain on the transaction [*see* I.R.C. § 453, discussed in Taxation of Individuals Summary] must increase earnings and profits in the year of the sale by the entire amount of recognized gain. [I.R.C. § 312(n)(6)]

(3) Accumulated and Current

It is necessary to maintain *two* earnings and profits accounts—one for all previous years ("accumulated earnings and profits") and one for the current year. If either account has a positive balance, a distribution is taxable as a dividend to the extent of that balance.

> **e.g.** **Example:** X Corp. was formed in 2000. During the years 2000 to 2015, X Corp.'s losses totaled $200,000 (*i.e.,* its deductions exceeded its income by that amount). In addition, it paid $15,000 of "interest" during those years on corporate "debts" which have been determined to be equity. Although nondeductible for tax purposes, these payments decrease earnings and profits. Hence, the accumulated earnings and profits account shows a deficit of $215,000. In 2015, X Corp. has taxable income of $75,000. It pays no income tax due to its net operating loss carryforward from prior years. Nonetheless, if X Corp. pays $5,000 in "interest" on its "debts" to shareholders (which have been reclassified as equity) during 2015, these will be taxable as dividends because there are *current* earnings and profits in excess of the distribution.

> **e.g.** **Example:** Assume that in the previous example X Corp. made no distributions in 2015. As of 2016, its accumulated earnings and profits would show a deficit of $140,000 (*i.e.,* $215,000 deficit reduced by the $75,000 2015 profit). Assume that in 2016, its taxable income is zero and it makes a $5,000 distribution to shareholders. The distribution would not be taxed as a dividend because there are neither current nor accumulated earnings and profits.

(a) Note

If there is a deficit in current earnings and profits and there are accumulated earnings and profits, the taxable status of the distribution is determined based on the earnings and profits available on the date of distribution. The current deficit must be prorated to the period before and after the distribution. [Rev. Rul. 74–164, 1974–1 C.B. 74]

Example: Y Corp. had accumulated earnings and profits of $40,000. In 2016, it had a deficit of $99,000. On April 30, 2016, it distributed $15,000 to its sole shareholder. Y Corp. had no current earnings and profits in 2016. Its deficit from 2016 reduced accumulated earnings and profits. Because the distribution occurred exactly one-third of the way through 2016, only $33,000 of the deficit reduced accumulated earnings and profits on April 30. Therefore, accumulated earnings and profits on April 30 were $7,000, and $7,000 of the distribution is taxable as a dividend.

b. Effect of Distribution

If accumulated or current earnings and profits are present, a distribution of cash or property is taxed as a dividend to the shareholders.

(1) Individual Shareholders

Formerly, a dividend was includible as ordinary income. However, as of January 1, 2003, "qualified dividend income" is fully includible as *net capital gain*, which means that it is taxed as the long-term capital gains rates of 20%. [I.R.C. § 1(h)(11)]

(a) Eligible Payors

"Qualified dividend income" means dividends received during the taxable year from the following:

(i) *Domestic corporations;*

(ii) *Foreign corporations* that are incorporated in a possession of the United States or are deemed by the IRS to be eligible for the benefits of a comprehensive tax treaty that includes an exchange of information program. A foreign corporation may also be treated as a qualified foreign corporation if the stock on which the dividend is paid is readily tradable on an established securities market in the United States. Note that a foreign corporation will not qualify if it is classified as a foreign personal holding company, a foreign investment company, or a passive foreign investment company in the taxable year in which the dividend was paid. [I.R.C. § 1(h)(11)(B)(i)]

(b) Holding Period

Stock must be held for more than 60 days during the 120-day period beginning 60 days before the ex-dividend date (*i.e.*, the date for determining to whom a dividend will be paid) in order for dividends paid on the stock to be eligible for the capital gains rate. [I.R.C. § 1(h)(11)(B)(iii)] This effectively extends the holding period requirement for intracorporate dividends (*see infra*, p. 95) to all dividends, while lengthening the period in which the stock must be held.

(c) Limitations

Dividends from corporations that are either not taxed or are eligible for a deduction on the payment of a dividend are not considered qualified dividend income for purposes of receiving the capital gains rate. [I.R.C. § 1(h)(11)(B)(ii)] Additionally, if the taxpayer includes the dividend as investment income for purposes of claiming a deduction of investment interest [*see* I.R.C. § 163(d)(4)(B)], the dividend is ineligible for the capital gains rate. This prevents a taxpayer (who has borrowed money to finance the acquisition of stock) from deducting interest payments against ordinary income (and thus saving as much as 35%) while only including a dividend in income at capital gains rates (with rates reaching only as high as 15%).

Be sure to remember that while formerly dividends received by individuals were treated as ordinary income, that is no longer the case. Dividends from domestic corporations and many foreign corporations are taxed at *long-term capital gains rates* (15% or 5%, depending on the recipient's income) as long as the recipient held the stock on which the dividend is being paid for *more than 60 days* in the 120-day period beginning 60 days before the ex-dividend date.

(2) Corporate Shareholders

A corporation receiving a dividend from another domestic corporation is allowed to *deduct at least 70% of the dividend* from income. [I.R.C. § 243(a)] If the two corporations are part of a chain of corporations in which the parent owns at least 80% of the stock of the subsidiary and an appropriate election is filed, the dividend exclusion is 100%. [I.R.C. § 243(b)] If the shareholder corporation owns 20% or more of the stock of the dividend-paying corporation, however, the dividends-paid deduction is 80%. [I.R.C. § 243(c)]

TAXATION OF DIVIDENDS TO CORPORATIONS	GILBERT
RECEIVING CORPORATION'S OWNERSHIP OF PAYING CORPORATION	**PERCENTAGE DEDUCTIBLE**
LESS THAN 20%	70%
AT LEAST 20% BUT LESS THAN 80%	80%
80% OR MORE	100%

(a) Limitations on Deduction

The dividends-received deduction must be reduced to the extent that the corporation purchased the stock with *borrowed money*. [I.R.C. § 246A] Also, if a corporate shareholder receives an "extraordinary dividend" and sells the stock before holding it for more than two years, its basis in the stock must be reduced by the untaxed portion of the extraordinary dividend. [I.R.C. § 1059] A corporate shareholder must hold stock for at least *46 days* to qualify for the dividends-received deduction (*91 days* for preferred stock). [I.R.C. § 246(c)]

(b) Business Purpose

There is a split of authority on the issue of whether a "business purpose" is needed for the parent to take advantage of the intercorporate dividend deduction. The problem arises when the parent wishes to sell the stock of the subsidiary. The sale will produce a large capital gain. However, if the subsidiary first distributes surplus assets to the parent as a dividend, the parent can exclude most or all of the distribution as an intercorporate dividend. Then when it sells the stock, its capital gain will be much less (because the assets of the subsidiary have been greatly reduced). [*See* **TSN Liquidating Corp. v. United States,** 624 F.2d 1328 (5th Cir. 1980)—deduction allowed; **Basic Inc. v. United States,** 549 F.2d 740 (Ct. Cl. 1977)—deduction disallowed, stock sale treated as if distribution had not occurred]

(3) Distributions in Excess of Earnings and Profits

If a corporation makes a distribution that exceeds its earnings and profits, the excess is not taxable as a dividend; instead, it reduces the shareholder's basis for his stock. After the basis is reduced to zero, the distribution is taxable as capital gain. [I.R.C. § 301(c)]

Example: X Corp. has current earnings and profits of $20,000 and no accumulated earnings and profits. It makes a distribution of $45,000 to Sonja, its sole shareholder. Of this amount, $20,000 is taxed as a dividend. If Sonja's basis for her stock in X Corp. was $8,000, the next $8,000 of the distribution is treated as a nontaxable recovery of basis. The last $17,000 would be taxed as capital gain.

---

c. Distributions of Property

If a corporation distributes property other than money as a dividend, the shareholder includes the fair market value of the property in income. The value of the property becomes its basis in the hands of the shareholder. [I.R.C. § 301(b), (d)] For the extent to which the distribution is treated as a dividend, *see supra,* p. 94.

(1) Property Subject to Liabilities

The amount of a dividend is reduced (but not below zero) to the extent that the property received is subject to a liability. [I.R.C. § 301(a)(2)] Suppose Alex (an individual shareholder) receives Blackacre as a dividend. It is worth $50,000 but is subject to a $30,000 mortgage. The dividend is $20,000. The basis of Blackacre in Alex's hands is $50,000.

(2) Effect on Earnings and Profits

On a distribution of appreciated property, the corporation increases corporate earnings and profits by the amount of the recognized gain on the distribution and reduces earnings and profits by the fair market value of the property. [I.R.C. § 312(a), (b)] If the distributed property has gone down in value but the loss is not recognized [I.R.C. § 311(a), (b)], earnings and profits are reduced by the adjusted basis of the distributed property. [I.R.C. § 312(a)(3)]

d. Disguised Dividends

In many cases, a dividend is taxable to shareholders even though it is camouflaged. For example, the following are treated as dividends.

(1) Unreasonable Compensation for Services

Unreasonable compensation for services is a dividend to the extent of the unreasonable portion. This is of less consequence to the shareholder now that compensation is taxed at ordinary income rates and dividends are taxed at capital gains rates. Employee-shareholders may also prefer dividends because they do not give rise to payroll taxes. This suggests the problem of disguised compensation. Nevertheless, paying unreasonable compensation still may be advantageous from the perspective of the corporate tax because compensation is deductible and dividends are not. [**Mulcahy, Pauritsch, Salvador & Co., Ltd. v. Commissioner**, 680 F.3d 867 (7th Cir. 2012—consulting fees paid to the founding shareholders for accounting services held to be non-deductible dividends]

(2) Sale of Property to Shareholder for Less than True Value

The sale of corporate property to a shareholder for less than its true value is a dividend to the extent of the bargain element. This means that there is no basis recovery with respect to the portion of the sale disguised as a dividend.

e.g. **Example:** X Corp. sells Blackacre to Sarah, a shareholder, for $1,000. Blackacre's actual value is $1,500. X Corp.'s basis is $300. Sarah has a dividend of $500. X Corp. recognizes the entire $1,200 gain.

(3) Use of Corporate Property Without Paying Fair Rental

A shareholder's use of corporate property without paying a fair rental is a dividend to the extent of the rental value.

e.g. **Example:** Resenhoeft owns the voting stock of Nichols Co. James, Resenhoeft's son, owns nonvoting stock. Nichols Co. buys a 52-foot yacht ("Pea Picker III") which is used 25% for business and 75% for James's pleasure. Because Resenhoeft made the decision to buy the yacht, 75% of its rental value is a constructive dividend to Resenhoeft. Under assignment of income principles, Resenhoeft rather than James is taxed on the dividend. [**Nichols, North, Buse & Co. v. Commissioner,** 56 T.C. 1225 (1971)]

(4) Loans to Shareholder Without the Expectation of Repayment

Similarly, a loan to a shareholder by a corporation without an expectation of repayment is a dividend.

(5) Expenses Incurred by Corporation That Actually Benefit Shareholder

When expenses benefit the shareholder rather than the corporation (such as paying for the shareholder's personal entertainment), these payments are dividends and are not deductible by the corporation.

(6) Corporate Discharge of Shareholder's Obligation to Buy Stock

Suppose shareholder Ali is unconditionally obligated to buy shareholder Bahar's stock in X Corp. Instead, X Corp. redeems Bahar's stock. This is treated as if X Corp. paid a dividend to Ali and he used the money to buy Bahar's stock. [*See* **Wall v. United States,** 164 F.2d 462 (4th Cir. 1947); Rev. Rul. 69–608, 1969–2 C.B. 42] However, the mere fact that X Corp. redeems Bahar's stock when Ali is under no obligation to do so, thus making Ali the sole shareholder, does not mean that the repurchase will be treated as a constructive dividend to Ali. [**Holsey v. Commissioner,** 258 F.2d 865 (3d Cir. 1958)]

(7) Intercorporate Transfers

Suppose Ken owns the stock of two corporations (A Corp. and B Corp.). A Corp. transfers money to B Corp. This can be treated as a dividend to Ken if the transfer is found to be primarily for his benefit instead of for A Corp.'s benefit. [**Stinnett's Pontiac Service, Inc. v. Commissioner,** 730 F.2d 634 (11th Cir. 1984)—advance by A Corp. needed to protect Ken's investment in B Corp.]

(8) Interest-Free Loans

If a corporation makes a loan to a shareholder and fails to charge interest at least equal to the rate the government must pay to borrow money (a rate readjusted frequently by the IRS), the interest element of the loan is a dividend to the shareholder. [I.R.C. § 7872; *and see* Taxation of Individuals Summary]

(a) Demand Loan

If the loan is a demand loan, the amount of forgone interest is treated as a dividend each year. In addition, this amount is treated as if it were paid by the shareholder back to the corporation as interest. This gives the shareholder a potential interest deduction and gives the corporation interest income.

(b) Term Loan

If the loan is a fixed term loan, the entire difference between the amount of the loan and the present value of the payments is a dividend in the year the loan is made. Each year the loan remains outstanding, this amount will be prorated and treated as interest income to the corporation and interest payment (potentially deductible) to the shareholder.

(c) De Minimis Exception

If the loan is for less than *$10,000*, interest will not be imputed— *unless* tax avoidance was one of the principal purposes of the loan.

(d) Disallowance of Deduction

Under many circumstances, the shareholder will be denied an interest deduction for the annual payment of imputed interest back to the corporation. For example, if the shareholder used the loan proceeds for personal consumption or to buy tax-exempt securities, no interest deduction is available. [I.R.C. §§ 163(h), 265(2)] (For discussion of interest deductions, *see* Taxation of Individuals Summary.)

CHECKLIST OF "DISGUISED" DIVIDENDS—EXAMPLES

THE FOLLOWING WILL BE TREATED AS A DIVIDEND (TAXABLE TO THE DISTRIBUTEE SHAREHOLDER AND NOT DEDUCTIBLE BY THE CORPORATION):

☑ *Unreasonable compensation* for the shareholder's services

☑ A *sale of property to a shareholder for less than the property's true value* (the "discount" is treated as a dividend)

☑ *Use of corporate property without paying fair rental* (the unpaid rental is treated as a dividend)

☑ *Loans to shareholders made without an expectation of repayment*

☑ *Expenses incurred by a corporation on a shareholder's behalf* (*e.g.,* paying a shareholder's personal expenses)

☑ *The corporation's discharge of a shareholder's obligation to buy stock*

☑ An *intercorporate transfer made primarily for the benefit of a shareholder*

☑ *Interest-free loans* from the corporation to the shareholder (imputed interest is treated as a dividend)

(9) Note—Dividend Can Be Taxable Even If Not Paid Pro Rata

Even if a distribution is not paid pro rata to the shareholders (*e.g.,* shareholder A receives a $500 dividend for his 100 shares, but no other shareholders of the same class receive any dividend), it is still taxable as a dividend. Note that such a distribution would violate state corporate law (requiring pro rata payment of dividends).

e. Dividends to Purchasers of Stock

It makes no difference that a profit was earned before a shareholder purchased her stock. A dividend is taxable to the shareholder even if the corporation's earnings and profits accumulated before the shareholder purchased her stock.

Example: Suppose X Corp. has accumulated earnings and profits of $200,000, but is losing money steadily at the time Althea buys X Corp. stock. X Corp. continues to lose money after Althea buys her stock. Nevertheless, if X Corp. makes a distribution to Althea, the distribution will be treated as a dividend even though the investment has been a losing venture for Althea.

2. Distributions in Complete Liquidation

a. General Rule Under Section 331

In most cases, distributions to shareholders in complete liquidation of the corporation are treated as being *in exchange* for their shares. Thus, the amount of money plus the value of property received in the liquidation, less the basis of the stock, gives rise to an immediate capital gain. If basis exceeds the amount realized, there is a capital loss. [I.R.C. § 331(a)]

(1) Capital Gain vs. Ordinary Income

An *individual's* long-term capital gain is taxed at a lower rate than ordinary income. Although ordinary income can be taxed at rates up to 35%, capital gain is taxed at the lower maximum rate of 15%. [I.R.C. § 1(h)] *Corporate* capital gain, however, is taxed at a maximum rate of 35%, which for most corporations is at or above the top marginal rate. [I.R.C. § 1201(a)]

(a) Capital Loss

The deduction of capital losses is restricted. [I.R.C. § 1211(b)] For an individual shareholder, capital losses are deductible only to the extent of capital gain plus $3,000 per year; ordinary losses are deductible without limit.

(2) Earnings and Profits

It is often better to remove liquid assets in a corporation by liquidating the corporation than by paying a dividend. A liquidation produces capital gain regardless of whether the corporation has earnings and profits; the earnings and profits simply disappear at the time of liquidation. A payment of the earnings and profits as a dividend, on the other hand, is fully taxable as a dividend. Although both the dividend and the liquidating distribution give rise to capital gain, there is *no basis recovery* when a dividend is paid.

e.g. **Example:** Sue's basis in her C Corp. stock is $100. C Corp. has cash of $160 and earnings and profits of $160. If C Corp. pays out its cash as a dividend, Sue has a capital gain of $160. If C Corp. is completely liquidated, Sue has a capital gain of only $60.

(3) Basis

The basis of the assets received in a section 331 liquidation is their fair market value at the time of the liquidation. [I.R.C. § 334(a)]

(4) Deferral or Shifting of the Gain

A complete liquidation can trigger a large capital gain, and if the assets received are not liquid, it may be difficult to pay the tax. Had the stock been sold to an outsider (rather than exchanged for the assets of the corporation), the shareholder could use the installment method of section 453 to defer tax. Similarly, she could have given away the stock to a charity or a relative and avoided tax on the capital gain. (For discussion of the installment method, which allows taxpayers to defer tax until they collect installment payments, *see* Taxation of Individuals Summary.)

(a) Use of Installment Method on Liquidation

If a corporation sells its assets in exchange for deferred payments, the shareholder is allowed to use the installment method to account for the collection of those deferred payments. Thus, the shareholder does not include the value of the installment obligation in income at the time of the liquidation. [I.R.C. § 453(h)]

(b) Rules

To use the installment method after a complete liquidation to account for payments received from a buyer of corporate assets, the corporation must have sold its assets during the 12-month period beginning on the date a plan of complete liquidation was adopted, and the liquidation must be completed during that 12-month period. If the obligation arose from the sale of inventory, the inventory must have been sold in bulk to a single person. [I.R.C. § 453(h)(1)(A), (B)]

(c) Shifting

Once the liquidation period has begun, it is too late to shift income by giving away the stock. [**Kinsey v. Commissioner,** 477 F.2d 1058 (2d Cir. 1973)— taxpayer gave stock to children or to charity during the liquidation period]

(d) Assets with Unascertainable Value

In a typical section 331 complete liquidation, the value of the assets received from the corporation, minus the liabilities to which they are subject, will determine the shareholder's amount realized and thus his capital gain or loss. In unusual cases, however, assets will be received that have no *ascertainable fair market value*. [*See* **Commissioner v. Carter,** 170 F.2d 911 (2d Cir. 1948)] In this situation, the transaction is *held open* until the assets are finally realized upon. The money that ultimately comes in will be applied against the basis of the stock. If it exceeds the basis, the excess will be in capital gain. If the basis never is recovered, there will ultimately be a capital loss. However, the IRS prefers to value all assets at the time of liquidation. [*See* **Waring v. Commissioner,** 412 F.2d 800 (3d Cir. 1969)]

b.   Section 332 Liquidations

A second provision for corporate liquidations applies when *one corporation controls a second. No gain or loss is recognized* to the parent at all. [I.R.C. § 332]

(1) "Control" [§ 391]

"Control" is defined as ownership by the parent corporation of at least 80% of the *voting power* and 80% of the total value of all stock. The parent must own the stock on the date of the adoption of the plan of liquidation and at all times until the receipt of the property from the subsidiary. [I.R.C. §§ 332(b)(1), 1504(a)(2)]

(a) When Is Plan Adopted?

Normally, the date of adoption of the plan of liquidation occurs when the parent corporation completes the appropriate steps to authorize the liquidation under state corporate law, not at earlier times when the possibility of liquidation is being contemplated. [**George L. Riggs, Inc. v. Commissioner,** 64 T.C. 474 (1975)—liquidation tax-free where parent corporation obtained 80% control before formally adopting plan of liquidation]

(b) Avoiding Control

Similarly, if the parent corporation wants to avoid section 332 (in order to recognize a loss), it might sell or give away enough of the subsidiary's shares, before adopting the plan of liquidation, to reduce its ownership to less than 80% of the voting stock. If the sale or gift represents a bona fide transfer, section 332 is inapplicable. [**Granite Trust Co. v. United States,** 238 F.2d 670 (1st Cir. 1956)]

(2) Timing

The distributions by subsidiary to parent must either be completed within a single taxable year of the parent or, if a series of distributions is made, they must be completed within three years after the first distribution is made.[I.R.C. § 332(b)(2), (3); Rev. Rul. 71–326, 1971–2 C.B. 177]

(3) Basis of Assets Received

The basis of property received by the controlling corporate parent on a section 332 liquidation is the *same as the basis that the assets had in the hands of the subsidiary*. [I.R.C. § 334(b)(1), (2)]

(a) Note

The basis of the assets in the subsidiary's hands may have been increased earlier if the parent made an election under section 338 (*see infra,* p. 125 *et seq.*).

(b) Other Shareholders

If the subsidiary had shareholders other than the controlling corporate parent, the liquidation is treated as a taxable *section 331* liquidation to the *other shareholders*. The basis of the assets received will be equal to their fair market value on the date of the liquidation. [I.R.C. § 334(a), (b)(3)]

(4) Treatment of Liquidated Subsidiary

Generally, a subsidiary does not recognize gain or loss on the transfer of its assets to its parent in a section 332 liquidation [I.R.C. § 337(a)]; and it does not recapture depreciation on depreciable assets it transfers to its parent [I.R.C. §§ 1245(b)(3), 1250(d)(3)]. Similarly, the subsidiary is not required to accelerate gain on installment obligations arising from asset sales it made before liquidation. [I.R.C. § 453B(d)(1)]

(a) Exception—Tax-Exempt Parent Corporation

If the parent corporation is a tax-exempt organization, the subsidiary is required to recognize gain on the transfer of its assets to its parent in a section 332 liquidation. [I.R.C. § 337(b)(2)] However, if the tax-exempt organization will use the property in an unrelated trade or business (*i.e.,* one subject to tax on its operations), the subsidiary need *not* recognize gain on the distribution.

(b) Distributions to Minority Shareholders

If the subsidiary distributes property to minority shareholders (*i.e.,* those holding, in the aggregate, less than 20% of the stock), it recognizes gain but not loss on those transfers. [I.R.C. § 336(d)(3)]

(c) Distributions with Respect to Debts

Suppose the subsidiary owes money to its parent. At the time of the section 332 liquidation, it distributes appreciated property to the parent in satisfaction of the debt. It does not recognize gain with respect to this transfer. [I.R.C. § 337(b)(1)]

3. Stock Redemptions

a. Overview

A stock redemption is a repurchase of some of a company's own stock from one or more of its shareholders. If the corporation redeems some of its own stock pro rata from each shareholder, the economic effect is the same as if a dividend had been paid. Elaborate tests have been devised to differentiate such a repurchase (which should be treated as a dividend that is fully includible in income at capital gains rates) from redemptions (which are treated as sales giving rise to capital gain to the extent that they exceed basis). Unless the distribution meets one of the four tests of section 302(b), or the test of section 303, it will be a dividend. This means that the *entire* amount distributed will be taxable (to the extent of earnings and profits)—without even allowing the distributee any recovery of basis.

(1) Recovery of Basis

If the distribution is treated as a dividend, the recipient is allowed no basis recovery. If it is treated as a redemption, the recipient is allowed to recover basis.

Example: C Corp. repurchases 50 of Sue's 100 shares for $50,000. Sue has a basis of $41,000 for the redeemed shares. If the distribution is taxed as a dividend, Sue has $50,000 of capital gain (assuming that C Corp. has at least $50,000 in earnings and profits). If it is taxed as a redemption, Sue has only $9,000 of capital gain.

(2) Capital Loss

If a redeemed shareholder has capital loss in the same year as the redemption, it is advantageous to treat the repurchase as a redemption. Because a dividend is deemed to be "net capital gain," and not the gain from the sale or exchange of a capital asset, *a dividend cannot be used to offset capital losses*. Redemptions, by contrast, give rise to capital gain from the sale or exchange of a capital asset, which may be used to offset capital losses. [I.R.C. § 1211(b)]

Example: Assume that in the previous example Sue has a capital loss from an unrelated transaction of $24,000 and no other capital gain. If the redemption is taxed as a dividend, Sue cannot offset the capital loss against the dividend. She can deduct only $3,000 of the capital loss (the balance is carried forward to future years). If the transaction is taxed as a redemption, the $9,000 capital gain can be offset against $9,000 of the capital loss. Therefore, Sue can deduct $12,000 of her capital loss (*i.e.,* her capital gain of $9,000 plus $3,000).

b. Redemptions Are Not Treated as Dividends

There are several safe harbor provisions for distinguishing redemptions from dividends. There is also one residual facts and circumstances test for repurchases that fail to qualify for any of the safe harbors.

(1) Complete Terminations—Section 302(b)(3)

Under I.R.C. section 302(b)(3), a transaction qualifies as a redemption if the corporation purchases *all of the stock owned by the shareholder* (a "complete termination").

(a) Attribution

However, in determining if *all* of a shareholder's stock is purchased, the Code requires consideration both of stock owned actually and stock owned by *attribution* from close relatives or related entities. If any stock is *attributed* to the shareholder, a purchase only of the stock *actually* owned would *not* be treated as a complete termination.

(b) Attribution Rules

I.R.C. section 318 sets out the rules of attribution.

1) Family Attribution

The shareholder is deemed to own the stock owned by members of his family—his spouse, children, grandchildren, and parents. [I.R.C. § 318(a)(1)] However, double family attribution is not permitted. Thus, if P is the parent of H, who is married to WP's stock would be attributed to H but not reattributed to W. [I.R.C. § 318(a)(5)(B)]

2) Attribution from Entities

If an individual is the beneficiary of an estate or trust, a percentage of the stock owned by the estate or trust is attributed to the individual. For example, if T's beneficial interest in a trust is 25%, then 25% of the stock owned by the trust is attributed to T. Similarly, the appropriate percentage of stock owned by a partnership or an S corporation is attributed to the partners or stockholders. And if an individual owns (directly or indirectly) at least 50% of the stock of a C corporation, the appropriate percentage of any stock owned by that corporation is attributed to him. [I.R.C. § 318(a)(2)]

3) Attribution to Entities

If the redeemed shareholder is a partnership, trust, or estate, any stock owned by its partners or beneficiaries is attributed to it. If the redeemed shareholder is a corporation, stock is attributed to it from its shareholders if they own 50% or more of its stock. [I.R.C. § 318(a)(3)]

4) Sideways Attribution

Although double attributions are generally permissible under section 318, the IRS cannot attribute stock *to an entity* from some of its partners, beneficiaries, or shareholders, and then *reattribute* that stock to other partners, beneficiaries, or shareholders. [I.R.C. § 318(a)(5)(C)]

a) And Note

Similarly, the same stock cannot be attributed to the same person twice. [Treas. Reg. § 1.318–1(b)(2)]

5) Options

If a person owns an option to purchase stock, he is treated as the owner of the stock. [I.R.C. § 318(a)(4); **Patterson Trust v. United States,** 729 F.2d 1089 (6th Cir. 1984)—rule applied to favor taxpayer]

6) Result

In closely held family corporations, it is often very difficult to arrange a complete termination because stock will be attributed to each shareholder from many other shareholders who are somehow related to him.

Example: X Corp., which has earnings and profits of $2,000, has three shareholders: Joe (25 shares), Betsy (25 shares), and the Smith Trust (50 shares). Joe is Betsy's father. Betsy has a 40% beneficial interest in the Smith Trust. X Corp. redeems all of Joe's stock for $2,300 but Joe remains as president of the company. Joe's basis for his stock was $100. By reason of section 318, Joe is considered to own all of Betsy's shares. Betsy owns 25 shares directly and 40% of the Trust's shares—or an additional 20 shares. Thus, Joe owns his own 25 shares and also 45 shares attributed from Betsy. Therefore, the distribution is not a complete termination. Because it does not fall under either section 302(c)(2) (*infra,* pp. 105–106) or section 302(b)(2) (*infra,* p. 106), and probably not under section 302(b)(1) (*infra,* pp. 107, 108), it is taxed as a dividend. Because earnings and profits were $2,000, the distribution gives rise to $100 of basis recovery, $2,000 in net capital gain, and $200 in capital gain from the sale or exchange of a capital asset (Joe's stock).

(c) Relief from Family Attribution

Some relief from the strict attribution rules is provided by I.R.C. section 302(c)(2). There will be no *family attribution* to the redeemed shareholder if certain requirements are met. This "waiver of attribution" provision applies only to a *complete termination under I.R.C. section 302(b)(3)*—not to I.R.C. section 302(b)(2) or (b)(1).

1) No Interest After Redemption

After the redemption, the shareholder being redeemed may have *no interest* in the corporation as an employee, officer, director, or otherwise. [I.R.C. § 302(c)(2)(A)(i)] In the previous example, Joe remained president of the company; thus, he could not use section 302(c)(2).

a) Interest as Creditor or Independent Contractor

A redeemed shareholder is permitted to retain an interest as a creditor of the corporation (as long as the corporate "debt" is not reclassified as "equity"). However, the redeemed shareholder is not permitted to work for the corporation *as an employee.* [**Cerone v. Commissioner,** 87 T.C. 1 (1986)] On the other hand, some cases permit the redeemed shareholder to work for the corporation *as an independent contractor* if the shareholder retains neither a financial stake in the corporation nor any ability to control or manage it. [**Estate of Lennard v. Commissioner,** 61 T.C. 554 (1974)] However, in the view of other cases, a redeemed shareholder cannot render any services, even as an independent contractor. [**Lynch v. Commissioner,** 801 F.2d 1176 (9th Cir. 1986)]

b) Agent of Shareholder

Neither the shareholder nor an agent of the shareholder (such as her lawyer) may serve as a director of the corporation after the redemption. [Rev. Rul. 59–119, 1959–1 C.B. 68]

2) Ten-Year Period

The shareholder may not acquire any such interest within 10 years, and must file an agreement to notify the IRS if he ever does acquire any such interest. [I.R.C. § 302(c)(2)(A)(ii)] The agreement should be filed with the tax return for the year in which the redemption occurs (but extensions can be granted for reasonable cause). [Treas. Reg. § 1.302–4(a)] However, the courts accept agreements filed late if the failure to file earlier was inadvertent. [**Niedermeyer v. Commissioner,** 62 T.C. 280, *aff'd,* 535 F.2d 500 (9th Cir. 1976)]

3) No Transfers Within Family to Avoid Tax

Furthermore, the waiver of attribution will **not** apply if any portion of the stock redeemed was **acquired** within a 10-year period from another family member. Also, it will **not** apply if the shareholder being redeemed **transferred** any of his shares within 10 years to another family member. But such transfers within 10 years to or from the redeemed shareholder will not disqualify the waiver of attribution if they did not have as one of their principal purposes the **avoidance of federal income tax**.

a) Comment

If the transferor retains no practical or legal control over the transferred shares, it is likely that tax avoidance is not present. [Rev. Rul. 77–293, 1977–2 C.B. 91]

4) Applies Only to Family Attribution

Note that the "waiver of attribution" provision of section 302(c)(2) only breaks the chain of family attribution [I.R.C. § 318(a)(1)], not attribution to or from entities [I.R.C. § 318(a)(2), (3)]. However, section 302(c)(2) can still be employed in certain cases of redemptions from entities, such as trusts, decedent's estates, corporations, or partnerships.

e.g. Example: Corp. A wishes to redeem stock held by Trust X. One of the beneficiaries of Trust X is Roy, who also owns Corp. A stock. The redemption from Trust X cannot be a complete termination because Roy's stock is attributed to the trust. [I.R.C. § 318(a)(3)(B)] The waiver provision of section 302(c)(2) cannot be used because the attribution provision involved is not family attribution (it is attribution to entities).

e.g. Example: Assume, however, that Roy is a beneficiary of Trust X but does not own any Corp. A stock. However, Roy's mother, Mary, does own Corp. A stock. Mary is not a beneficiary of Trust X. Again, the redemption is not a complete termination because the trust is deemed to own Mary's stock. This occurs because a two-step attribution is required: from Mary to Roy [I.R.C. § 318(a)(1)], and from Roy to Trust X [I.R.C. § 318(a)(3)(B)]. However, in this situation, the waiver of attribution provision does apply; it breaks the link in the chain between Mary and Roy. To take advantage of section 302(c)(2), both Roy and Trust X may have no interest in Corp. A; neither can acquire an interest for 10 years after the distribution; and both Roy and Trust X must file an agreement to notify the IRS if they do acquire such an interest during the 10-year period. [I.R.C. § 302(c)(2)(C)]

(2) Substantially Disproportionate Redemptions—Section 302(b)(2)

Even if the redemption is not a complete termination, it may be "substantially disproportionate" under I.R.C. section 302(b)(2). If so, it will be a redemption, not a dividend.

(a) Requirements

I.R.C. section 302(b)(2) is complied with if the ratio of the voting stock owned after the redemption is **less than 80%** of the ratio owned before the redemption.

Furthermore, the redeemed shareholder must have *less than 50%* of the voting power.

> **e.g.** **Example:** C Corp. has 100 shares outstanding. A owns 70 shares. C Corp. redeems 20 of A's shares. Thus, after the redemption there are 80 shares outstanding and A owns 50 of them. This is not a substantially disproportionate redemption and therefore may be treated as a dividend. Prior to the redemption, A owned 70% of the stock; afterwards, A owns 62.5% of the stock (50 out of 80). But to qualify, the fraction of stock owned afterwards must be less than 80% of the fraction owned before the redemption. This means that to meet the 80% test, A's interest would have to be reduced below 56% of the stock (80% of 70%), which did not occur. In addition, A would have to meet the 50% test; his interest must be below 50% after the redemption. Of course, A failed this test also.

(b) Attribution

As in the case of complete terminations, the attribution rules of I.R.C. section 318 are applicable in computing how much stock A owns before and after the redemption. Moreover, the provision waiving family attribution discussed above, section 302(c)(2), does *not* apply; it applies only to attempted complete terminations, not to substantially disproportionate redemptions.

(c) Series of Redemptions

In determining whether a redemption meets the substantially disproportionate test, it is necessary to take into account other redemption transactions that have also occurred or will occur and are pursuant to a plan. Taking the whole series of redemptions together, the distributions may not be disproportionate. [I.R.C. § 302(b)(2)(D)]

> **e.g.** **Example:** Alex has 1,000 shares of X Corp. stock. Becky, Cindy, and Dee each have 200 shares. All parties are unrelated. Becky plans to retire, and X Corp. plans to redeem Becky's shares. First, however, X Corp. redeems 600 of Alex's shares. By itself, this would be a substantially disproportionate redemption; Alex now has only 400 of the 1,000 shares, so he has less than 50% of the stock. Moreover, the reduction from 62.5% to 40% meets the 80% requirement. In the second redemption, which occurs two weeks later, X Corp. redeems all of Becky's shares. Taking the two planned redemptions together, as required by section 302(b)(2)(D), Alex reduced his interest only from 62.5% to 50%. Because section 302(c)(2)(B) requires a reduction to *less than* 50% of the stock, and to *less than* 80% of the former holding, Alex meets neither test. [Rev. Rul. 85–14, 1985–1 C.B. 83] However, the redemptions might qualify under section 302(b)(1). (*See infra*, p. 108.)

(3) Equivalence to Dividend—Section 302(b)(1)

Finally, even if the tests of I.R.C. section 302(b)(3) or (b)(2) cannot be met, the redemption will not be treated as a dividend if it is "not essentially equivalent to a dividend." [I.R.C. § 302(b)(1)] This provision has been very difficult to interpret. Under section 302(b)(1), the test is whether there has been a "meaningful reduction" in the shareholder's stock interest—directly and by attribution. [**United States v. Davis,** 397 U.S. 301 (1970)] The presence or absence of a business purpose for the redemption is immaterial. *Davis* held that if there is only one shareholder (directly or by attribution), a redemption will always be essentially equivalent to a dividend.

(a) What Is "Meaningful"?

Just how much of a reduction is "meaningful" has not been established by the case law. [*See* **Wright v. United States,** 482 F.2d 600 (8th Cir. 1973)—a reduction from 85% to 61% is meaningful enough where state law required a two-thirds vote for important corporate changes; *but see* Rev. Rul. 78–401, 1978–2 C.B. 127]

(b) IRS Position

The IRS has ruled that several redemptions passed the section 302(b)(1) test even though they narrowly missed passing the section 302(b)(2) test. In these rulings, it appears to be critical that the redeemed shareholder is not in control after the redemption. [Rev. Rul. 75–502, 1975–2 C.B. 111; 75–512, 1975–2 C.B. 112; 76–364, 1976–2 C.B. 91] In addition, the shareholder's ability to form coalitions with other shareholders must be significantly reduced. [Rev. Rul. 85–106, 1985–2 C.B. 116]

e.g. **Example:** Corporation redeems all shares held by a decedent's estate. The estate actually owned 14% of the shares but constructively owned 57%. After the redemption, it constructively owned exactly 50%. Because it no longer had absolute control of the corporation, the reduction in its interest was "meaningful," and thus, it qualified under section 302(b)(1). Note that section 302(b)(2) requires that the interest be reduced *below* 50% in order to be "substantially disproportionate." [Rev. Rul. 75–502, *supra*]

(c) Attribution Rules Relaxed

There is authority that the section 318 attribution rules will not be rigidly applied in a section 302(b)(1) situation. If family members are in fact completely alienated from one another, their stock will not be attributed to the distributee. [**Haft Trust v. Commissioner,** 510 F.2d 43 (1st Cir. 1975); *but see* **Metzger Trust v. Commissioner,** 693 F.2d 459 (5th Cir. 1982); *and* **Cerone v. Commissioner,** 87 T.C. 1 (1986)—*contra*]

(4) Partial Liquidations

A partial liquidation is treated as a redemption. [I.R.C. § 302(b)(4)] A partial liquidation entails a substantial change at the level of the distributing corporation (whereas redemptions qualifying under section 302(b)(1), (2), or (3) all involve substantial changes at the shareholder level).

(a) Who May Take Advantage of Partial Liquidation?

Only a shareholder who is *not a corporation* can take advantage of partial liquidation treatment. [I.R.C. § 302(b)(4)(A)]

(b) Timing

The distribution must be pursuant to a "plan" and occur within the year the plan is adopted or the next year. [I.R.C. § 302(e)(1)(B)]

(c) "Contraction" of Corporation's Business

Under prior law, partial liquidation was a provision separate from section 302. Most cases that considered whether a distribution qualified as a partial liquidation looked to see whether the distributing corporation had undergone a "contraction" of its trade or business. Presumably, this same test will continue to be followed under section 302(b)(4).

Example: The top two stories of A Corp.'s building were damaged by fire. Thus A Corp.'s business had to be contracted, and part of its assets became superfluous. A Corp. distributed these assets to the shareholders. This is a classic "contraction." The shareholders had capital gain, not a dividend. [**Imler v. Commissioner,** 11 T.C. 836 (1948)]

REDEMPTION VS. DIVIDEND—A SUMMARY OF TESTS	⬛GILBERT
COMPLETE TERMINATION OF INTEREST	If a repurchase **completely terminates a shareholder's interest** in the corporation, the transaction will be treated as a redemption, not a dividend. But stock owned by the distributee's close family members and entities in which the distributee has an interest may be attributed to the distributee so that a redemption will not be found.
SUBSTANTIALLY DISPROPORTIONATE REDEMPTION	If after repurchase: (i) the ratio of the shares owned by the shareholder to the total shares outstanding is **less than 80% of the ratio owned before** the repurchase, and (ii) the shareholder owns less than 50% of the voting power, the repurchase will be treated as a redemption.
NOT ESSENTIALLY EQUIVALENT TO A DIVIDEND	If there has been a **meaningful reduction in the shareholder's stock interest** (*e.g.,* if the shareholder loses voting control), the repurchase may be treated as a redemption rather than a dividend.
REDEMPTION ON DEATH	If a shareholder's stock is repurchased on his death and his stock makes up **more than 35% of his gross estate** (less estate tax deductions for expenses, claims against the estate, and losses incurred by the estate), the repurchase may be treated as a redemption rather than a dividend to the extent of the **state and federal death taxes** and **funeral and administrative costs**.

1) Note

A partial liquidation can include not only the assets (or proceeds from a sale of the assets) but also the working capital attributable to the discontinued activity. [Rev. Rul. 60–232, 1960–2 C.B. 115]

(d) Code Test

The Code also provides a mechanical test that qualifies a distribution as a partial liquidation. If the corporation distributed the assets of a business carried on for at least five years, and continues to operate a second business also carried on for five years, the distribution is a partial liquidation. [I.R.C. § 302(e)(2), (3); *see* **Blaschka v. United States,** 393 F.2d 983 (Ct. Cl. 1968)] To meet this test, the corporation must have operated both businesses itself—not through a subsidiary corporation. [Rev. Rul. 79–184, 1979–1 C.B. 143] This test is similar to one provided for a divisive reorganization under section 355 (*infra,* p. 135 *et seq.*).

(5) Section 303 Redemptions

An additional method by which a redemption can avoid being treated as a dividend is provided by I.R.C. section 303. If a shareholder dies, a redemption of her shares can be treated as a redemption, not a dividend, to the extent of the state and federal *death taxes* and *costs of administration and funerals*. However, section 303 applies only if the shares totaled more than 35% of the decedent's gross estate (less her estate tax deductions for expenses, claims against the estate, and losses incurred by the estate). [I.R.C. § 303(b)(2)]

(6) Collateral Consequences of Redemptions

In considering the tax consequences of a redemption, it is necessary to consider the effect on the recipient's basis and on the corporation's earnings and profits.

(a) Effect on Basis

When a redemption is treated as a dividend, the recipient must include the entire amount received (to the extent of the corporation's earnings and profits) as income (taxable at capital gains rates). If the entire amount is a dividend, no basis recovery is allowed. If the recipient has any shares remaining, the basis of the redeemed shares is added to the basis of the remaining shares. If the recipient has no shares remaining, the basis of the redeemed shares is added to the basis of stock owned by the remaining shareholders from whom stock was attributed to the distributee. [Treas. Reg. § 1.302–2(c)]

Example: Bea and Art each owned 50% of the stock of X Corp. X Corp. buys all of Bea's stock for $2,000 when its earnings and profits are $3,000. Bea is Art's mother. Bea remains as president of the company. Bea's basis for her stock was $1,000. The entire $2,000 received by Bea is a dividend. Her $1,000 basis is added to and increases Art's basis for his shares.

(b) Effect of a Redemption on Earnings and Profits

A distribution that is treated as a redemption reduces earnings and profits by a "ratable" amount. [I.R.C. § 312(n)(7)]

Example: When X Corp.'s earnings and profits were $50,000, it redeemed 10 shares owned by Theo for $75,000. X Corp. had 100 shares of stock outstanding. X Corp. is permitted to reduce its earnings and profits by only $5,000 (because Theo owned 10% of the stock, his ratable share of earnings and profits is 10%).

1) Limitation

The reduction in earnings and profits cannot exceed the amount distributed.

Example: Suppose in the preceding example that X Corp. bought Theo's shares for only $3,000. Earnings and profits would be reduced by only $3,000.

2) Redemption Taxed as Dividend

In the example above, if the redemption of Theo's stock was taxed as a dividend to him rather than a redemption (*see supra,* p. 103 *et seq.*), earnings and profits would be reduced by $75,000.

(c) Deductibility of Redemption Costs

No deduction is allowed for any amount paid or incurred by a corporation in connection with redemption of its stock. [I.R.C. § 162(k)(1)]

1) Exceptions

A corporation can deduct interest on debt incurred to repurchase its stock. Also, if the redemption is taxed as a dividend to the recipient stockholder, the corporation can deduct the dividend for purposes of the accumulated earnings tax or the personal holding company tax. [I.R.C. § 162(k)(2); *and see supra*, pp. 62–68]

2) Application

This section was sometimes applied strictly, precluding a corporation from amortizing costs (other than interest) of obtaining debt financing for the redemption. [*See, e.g.*, **Fort Howard Corp. v. Commissioner,** 103 T.C. 345 (1994)] However, section 162(k) has since been amended to allow amortization of the costs and fees associated with a redemption as well as the interest paid. [*See* **Fort Howard Corp. v. Commissioner,** 107 T.C. 187 (1996)]

(7) Tax Planning in Redemptions

Several useful planning techniques for redemptions have been developed. These include the bootstrap sale and the gift-redemption combinations.

(a) Bootstrap Purchases

Suppose Art wants to purchase the stock of X Corp. from Bea but does not have enough money. Art wants to use money that is in X Corp. This can be managed without adverse tax consequences if it is done correctly. Bea should sell some of her shares to Art, following which X Corp. will redeem the balance of Bea's shares. Because this is a complete termination of Bea's interest, Bea would be entitled to treat the distribution as a redemption, not a dividend. [**Zenz v. Quinlivan,** 213 F.2d 914 (6th Cir. 1954); Rev. Rul. 75–447, 1975–2 C.B. 113]

EXAM TIP   **GILBERT**

If an exam question asks you how to structure a takeover of a small corporation when the buyer does not have enough money to purchase the corporation outright, remember the **bootstrap strategy**. The seller can sell some of his shares to the buyer and then have the corporation repurchase the rest of the seller's shares. Because this is a complete termination of the seller's interest, the repurchase is treated as a redemption rather than a dividend, so that amounts received go first to reduce the seller's basis to zero and only the excess is taxed at capital gains rates. A similar strategy can be used by spouses who own a corporation in order to transfer the corporation to one spouse upon divorce, but if the transfer occurs before the divorce decree, a waiver of family attribution must be obtained (*see* discussion below).

(b) Redemptions and Divorce

A common problem in divorce tax planning concerns stock in closely held corporations. Assume H and W are married and own stock in X Corp. Assume further that the stock is in W's name and that W is the manager of X Corp.

along with other members of her family. H is inactive in the business. H and W now intend that H will be bought out and W will remain as a shareholder of X Corp. Under state law (either community property or equitable distribution), the X stock is marital property and H has property rights in it.

1) Spousal Sale

If H simply transfers his stock to W in exchange for cash or a promissory note, H's gain is not recognized and W takes over H's basis for his stock. [I.R.C. § 1041]

2) Redemption

H and W may wish to use X Corp.'s cash to purchase H's interest in X Corp. Thus, W might transfer half of her X Corp. stock to H, and X Corp. will then redeem H's stock. Assume the transaction is taxed in accordance with its form. In that case, the sale of H's stock to X Corp. would qualify as a complete termination if it occurs after H and W are divorced; H would have capital gain or loss on the exchange. [I.R.C. § 302(b)(3), *and see supra*, pp. 103–104] Even if the redemption occurs before divorce (or if the children of H and W will remain as shareholders), H should be able to qualify for waiver of family attribution. [I.R.C. § 302(c)(2); *and see supra*, pp. 105–106]

3) Redemption from Whom—Primary Obligation

Assume that W was unconditionally obligated to purchase H's stock. Then the parties change their minds, and X Corp. purchases H's stock instead. In this situation, X Corp. has discharged W's personal liability. The distribution is treated as a dividend to W. [**Hayes v. Commissioner**, 101 T.C. 593 (1993); Rev. Rul. 69–608, 1969–2 C.B. 42; *and see supra*, p. 97]

4) Redemption from Whom—No Primary Obligation

Now assume that W was never primarily obligated to purchase H's stock. The redemption deal is between H and X Corp. Nevertheless, under the Ninth Circuit view, this transaction is still viewed as if X Corp. redeemed stock from W, not from H, because W benefited from the transaction. This results in a dividend to W because the distribution does not meet any of the tests for a redemption set forth in I.R.C. section 302(b). [**Arnes v. United States**, 981 F.2d 456 (9th Cir. 1992)] However, the Tax Court does not agree with the Ninth Circuit's view and taxes the transaction in accordance with its form—a redemption from H, not from W. [**Arnes v. Commissioner**, 102 T.C. 522 (1994); **Blatt v. Commissioner**, 102 T.C. 77 (1994)]

(c) Gift and Redemption

A taxpayer might seek to avoid the capital gain on a redemption and also seek a charitable contribution deduction. Thus, suppose T gives his stock in X Corp. to charity, and the stock is then redeemed by X Corp. T deducts the value of the stock as a charitable contribution. He argues that he should not be taxed on the gain from the redemption because he did not own the stock when it was redeemed. Taxpayers have won these cases, provided that no binding agreement existed at the time of the gift that required the redemption to occur.

[**Grove v. Commissioner,** 490 F.2d 241 (2d Cir. 1973); Rev. Rul. 78–197, 1978–1 C.B. 83]

c. Multicorporate Redemptions

The Code provides explicitly that a sale by a shareholder of the stock of a corporation she controls to another corporation she controls will be treated as a redemption, not as a sale of stock. The "redemption" is often taxed as a dividend. [I.R.C. § 304] Control for this purpose means 50% of the stock. Attribution is used to determine stock ownership. [I.R.C. § 304(c); **Niedermeyer v. Commissioner,** *supra*, p. 105]

(1) Brother-Sister Corporations

Assume that Ariel controls both X Corp. and Y Corp. She sells part of her X Corp. stock to Y Corp. This is treated as a redemption by Y Corp. Unless the change in Ariel's voting stock position in X Corp. meets the requirements of section 302(b) or 303, the fictitious redemption is treated as a dividend by Y Corp. to the extent of the earnings and profits of both X Corp. and Y Corp. [I.R.C. § 304(a)(1), (b)(2)(A)]

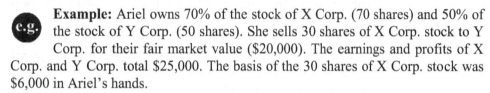 **Example:** Ariel owns 70% of the stock of X Corp. (70 shares) and 50% of the stock of Y Corp. (50 shares). She sells 30 shares of X Corp. stock to Y Corp. for their fair market value ($20,000). The earnings and profits of X Corp. and Y Corp. total $25,000. The basis of the 30 shares of X Corp. stock was $6,000 in Ariel's hands.

1) Mechanically, this transaction is treated as if Ariel had contributed her 30 shares of X Corp. stock to Y Corp. Thus, Y Corp. has a basis of $6,000 for its 30 X Corp. shares. Ariel is entitled to add $6,000 to her basis for her 50 shares in Y Corp. [Treas. Reg. § 1.304–2(a)]

2) It is necessary to analyze the change in Ariel's position in X Corp. Before the transaction, she owned 70% of the stock of X Corp. After the transaction, she owns 40 shares directly and 15 shares indirectly. She owns 15 shares indirectly because she owns 50% of the stock of Y Corp., and Y Corp. owns 30 shares of X Corp. [*See* I.R.C. §§ 318(a)(2)(C)—which for this purpose is applied *without* the 50% limitation, 304(c)(2)]

3) Ariel fails the tests of section 302(b). The reduction in voting control of X Corp. from 70% to 55% does not meet the test of section 302(b)(2). Consequently, this transaction is treated as a distribution from Y Corp. of $20,000; because the earnings and profits of X Corp. and Y Corp. exceeded $20,000, the entire amount received is a dividend.

(a) Conflict with Section 351

Assume in the example above that Y Corp. issued new Y Corp. shares plus $5,000 in cash for the X Corp. shares. Assume further that as a result of the issuance of Y Corp. shares, Ariel now has at least 80% of the stock of Y Corp. Thus, the transaction is explicitly covered by both section 351 and section 304(a). Under section 304(a), the $5,000 would be a dividend from Y Corp. But under section 351, the $5,000 would be treated as boot under section 351(b) and would be taxed as capital gain. The Code provides that section 304 controls; hence, the $5,000 is a dividend. [I.R.C. § 304(b)(3)]

(2) Parent-Subsidiary Redemptions

Assume that Alex controls P Corp. and P Corp. controls S Corp. (a parent-subsidiary relationship). S Corp. buys P Corp. shares from Alex. This is treated as a distribution by P Corp. to Alex and, depending on the change in Alex's voting stock position in P Corp., may be treated as a dividend from P Corp. (to the extent of P Corp.'s earnings and profits). [I.R.C. § 304(a)(2)]

Example: Alex owns 60% of the stock of P Corp. (60 shares). The remaining 40% is owned by unrelated persons. P Corp. owns 100% of the stock of S Corp. Alex sells all 60 shares of P stock to S Corp. for $50,000 (their value). The basis for these shares was $18,000. The earnings and profits of P Corp. (prior to this transaction) were $10,000.

1) Mechanically, this transaction is treated by section 304(a)(2) as if S Corp. first paid a dividend of $50,000 to P Corp. Then P Corp. is treated as if it redeemed its own shares from Alex.

2) The $50,000 "dividend" increases P Corp.'s earnings and profits to $60,000. Thus, P Corp. will have sufficient earnings and profits to tax the $50,000 distribution to Alex as a dividend if the fictitious redemption by P Corp. fails to meet the tests of section 302(b) or 303. However, the $50,000 fictitious dividend is not actually taxed to P Corp.; it is treated as a dividend solely for the purpose of increasing P Corp.'s earnings and profits for purposes of section 304. [**Broadview Lumber Co. v. United States,** 561 F.2d 698 (7th Cir. 1977)]

3) Next, it is necessary to apply section 302 standards to see whether the fictitious redemption by P Corp. of its own shares should be treated as a dividend. Prior to the transaction, Alex owned 60% of P Corp.'s shares. Afterwards, Alex owns no shares of P Corp.—either directly or by attribution. Consequently, Alex meets the tests of section 302(b)(3) and is entitled to a $32,000 capital gain on the transfer. [Treas. Reg. § 1.304–3(b)]

4) S Corp.'s basis for its P Corp. shares is its purchase price—$50,000. [**Broadview Lumber Co. v. United States,** *supra*]

B. Distributions of Property in Kind—Impact on the Corporation

1. General Rule

Traditionally, a corporation did not recognize gain or loss when it distributed its property to shareholders. [**General Utilities & Operating Co. v. Helvering,** 296 U.S. 200 (1935)] The *General Utilities* rule was a major source of corporate tax avoidance and complexity and was frequently criticized. In the Tax Reform Act of 1986, Congress overturned the *General Utilities* rule once and for all. The general rule now is that a corporation *must recognize gain* when it distributes property to its shareholders, whether it does so as a dividend, redemption, or partial or complete liquidation. (Thus, former I.R.C. sections 311 and 336 were repealed.) Note, however, that a corporation recognizes *loss* only when it distributes property in complete liquidation; it does not recognize loss when it distributes property as a dividend, redemption, or partial liquidation. [I.R.C. § 311(b)]

a. Sale of Assets in Liquidation

Under prior law, a corporation did not recognize gain or loss when it sold its assets to an outsider as part of a plan of liquidation. [Former I.R.C. § 337] This provision was also repealed. Thus, a corporation must recognize gain or loss when it sells its assets as part of the liquidation process.

Example: Assume the stock of A Corp. is worth $100,000. All of the stock is owned by Terrance, who has owned it for 10 years. A Corp. has only one asset—raw land with a basis of $2,000 and a value of $100,000. Terrance's basis for his stock is $30,000. Suppose that A Corp. is completely liquidated. It distributes the land to Terrance. Terrance has a capital gain of $70,000. [I.R.C. § 331] A Corp. must recognize its $98,000 gain on the transfer of the land to Terrance; thus there is a *double tax*—to Terrance and to A Corp.

Compare: Suppose in the previous example that A Corp. sells the land to Blair for $100,000 and distributes the proceeds to Terrance. Terrance has a $70,000 capital gain. Moreover, A Corp. must recognize its $98,000 gain on the sale to Blair.

b. Value of Gain

The value of the gain is measured as if the corporation sold the entire property to an unrelated buyer in an arm's-length transaction, rather than as if it sold just the recipient shareholder's portion of the property.

Example: C Corp. held a large parcel of land with a fair market value of $100,000. It contributed the land to a publicly held partnership in exchange for interests in the partnership and then distributed those interests to its five individual shareholders. Each shareholder's interest in the partnership was trading on a public exchange for $15,000 immediately after the transaction. Thus, while the land was worth $100,000 while held by a single party, it was worth only $75,000 when owned by a number of individual partners. For purposes of section 311, the value of the land while in the corporation's hands is the figure used to calculate gain. [**Pope & Talbot v. Commissioner,** 104 T.C. 574 (1995)]

2. Additional Rules Relating to Treatment of Corporation on Distributions

a. Liquidation of Subsidiary by Parent

If a parent corporation liquidates an 80%-owned subsidiary corporation under I.R.C. section 332, the subsidiary does not recognize gain or loss on the distribution of assets to the parent. However, the subsidiary recognizes gain (but not loss) if it distributes property to minority shareholders as part of a section 332 liquidation. (*See supra,* p. 102.)

b. Corporate Reorganization

In many corporate reorganizations, the acquired corporation receives stock of the acquiring corporation, which it distributes to its shareholders in complete liquidation. (*See infra,* pp. 142–146.) The acquired corporation does not recognize gain or loss on the distribution. [I.R.C. § 336(c)]

c. Recognition of Loss

A corporation is generally entitled to recognize loss when it distributes assets to its shareholders in complete liquidation. However, there are some exceptions to this rule:

(1) Related Persons

If a corporation distributes property to a shareholder owning more than 50% of the stock, and the distribution of assets is not pro rata to all shareholders, the corporation cannot recognize loss on this transfer. [I.R.C. § 336(d)(1)(A)(i)] Similarly, the corporation cannot recognize loss on a distribution to a shareholder owning more than 50% of the stock if the property was acquired in a transaction to which section 351 applies (or as a contribution to capital) during the preceding five years. [I.R.C. § 336(d)(1)(A)(ii)]

(2) Carryover Basis

The loss deduction must be scaled down by the amount of built-in loss in the case of certain tax avoidance schemes. [I.R.C. § 336(d)(2)]

(a) Built-In Loss

A built-in loss is the excess of the basis of the property over its value at the time that the corporation acquired the property.

(b) Property Affected

This provision affects property that was acquired (i) in a transaction to which section 351 applied or (ii) as a contribution to capital, and the acquisition was part of a plan, a principal purpose of which was to recognize loss on the liquidation.

Example: A Corp. owns raw land with a value of $100,000 and a basis of $2,000. It has two equal shareholders, Terrance and Vinnie. A Corp. is about to be liquidated and will have a $98,000 capital gain when it distributes the property to Terrance and Vinnie. Terrance and Vinnie also own AT&T stock as tenants in common, which they purchased for $220,000 and is worth only $130,000. They contribute it to A Corp. A Corp., therefore, has a basis of $220,000 for the AT&T stock. [I.R.C. § 362(a)] A Corp. then distributes both the land and stock to Terrance and Vinnie in complete liquidation. A Corp. wants to deduct the $90,000 loss on the stock to offset the $98,000 gain on the land. The related party rule discussed above does not apply because neither Terrance nor Vinnie owned *more than 50%* of the stock. However, the built-in loss rule applies, and A Corp. will not be permitted to deduct the loss. The stock was received as a contribution to capital and was part of a tax-avoidance scheme. There was a built-in loss of $90,000 on the stock. Therefore, its basis is reduced by $90,000 to $130,000, and A Corp. has no loss to recognize.

3. Prior Law—*Court Holding* Doctrine

When *General Utilities* was the rule, an important line of cases developed to thwart certain kinds of tax avoidance schemes. Strictly speaking, these cases (*Court Holding Co.* and *Cumberland Public Service*) are no longer relevant because of the repeal of *General Utilities*. Nevertheless, their reasoning applies in countless other situations throughout corporate taxation (and indeed the entire income tax). Therefore, they will continue to be covered in many tax classes.

a. The Problem

Suppose A Corp. has appreciated land that it wants to sell to Becky. Prior to the enactment of former I.R.C. section 337, it had a dilemma. If it sold the land and distributed the proceeds to Tyler, its sole shareholder, there was a double tax—on A Corp. and again on Tyler. But if it distributed the land to Tyler first, then Tyler sold it to Becky, there would be only a single tax. Tyler would be taxed when he received the land from A Corp. [I.R.C. § 331] but not when he sold the land to Becky because the liquidation gave him a stepped-up basis [I.R.C. § 334(a)]. Under *General Utilities,* A Corp. was not taxed when it distributed the property to Tyler. [Former I.R.C. § 336]

b. Pre-1986 Solution

This dilemma was solved in the 1954 Code by I.R.C. section 337, which provided that A Corp. did not recognize gain when it sold the property to Becky as part of the liquidation process.

c. Present Law

Under present law, A Corp. is taxed no matter how it disposes of the land. It is taxed on the capital gain whether it sells the property to Becky or whether it distributes the property to Tyler. There is going to be a double tax no matter how the deal is structured.

d. *Court Holding Co.* Case

But now go back to the pre-1954 era when the double tax could be avoided if the property were distributed to Tyler first, then Tyler sold it to Becky. Suppose that substantial negotiations concerning the sale price occur between Becky and Tyler, negotiating for A Corp. Just before the deal is finalized, however, A Corp. distributes the property to Tyler. Tyler then proceeds to finalize the deal and sell the property to Becky. The sale is deemed to have been made by A Corp., not by Tyler; A Corp. is deemed to have distributed the sale proceeds to Tyler. Thus, there is a double tax—to A Corp. on the deemed sale and to Tyler on the deemed cash distribution. [**Commissioner v. Court Holding Co.,** 324 U.S. 331 (1945)]

e. Distinguish—*Cumberland* Case

On the other hand, if there was never any real agreement on the terms of the sale at the corporate level, and the agreement is reached by Tyler and Becky after the property is distributed to Tyler, A Corp. would not be taxed on the sale made by Tyler. [**United States v. Cumberland Public Service Co.,** 338 U.S. 451 (1950)] As a result, under the *General Utilities* rule, there was only a single tax—to Tyler but not to A Corp.

f. Principle of *Court Holding* is Often Applied

If, in substance, a sale was made by one person, it cannot be attributed to someone else. More broadly, *Court Holding Co.* is an example of the doctrine that a transaction will be taxed according to its substance, not necessarily according to its form.

g. Nonliquidating Distributions

Court Holding Co. has been applied, for example, to a nonliquidating distribution of property (*e.g.,* a dividend), followed by a sale of the property by shareholders, particularly where the corporation participates in the sale (*e.g.,* through the use of its facilities). [*See* **Hines v. United States,** 477 F.2d 1063 (5th Cir. 1973)]

C. Stock Dividends

1. General Rule

A stock dividend is a distribution of *stock with respect to existing stock*, and as a general rule is tax-free to the recipient. [I.R.C. § 305(a)] This general rule covers distributions of common stock on existing common stock as well as distributions of preferred stock pro rata to the holders of common stock.

a. Basis

When a nontaxable stock dividend is received, the shareholder prorates her existing basis over both the new and old stock by the respective fair market values of each. [I.R.C. § 307]

Example: Audrey's basis for her common stock is $6,000. At a time when her common stock is worth $7,500, she receives a dividend of preferred stock worth $2,500. Her old basis is split up as follows: $4,500 to old common (*i.e.,* three-fourths of the total basis) and $1,500 to the new preferred (*i.e.,* one-fourth of basis).

b. Constitutional Rule

The Supreme Court held that a stock dividend of common stock on common stock is constitutionally immune to income tax because there is no realization of income at the time of the distribution. [**Eisner v. Macomber,** 252 U.S. 189 (1920)] It seems unlikely that this decision would be followed today; however, the point does not arise because stock dividends of the type described in *Macomber* are excluded from income as a result of section 305(a).

(1) Distinguish

A dividend that alters the shareholder's proportionate interest in the corporation is constitutionally taxable. [**Koshland v. Helvering,** 298 U.S. 441 (1936)—dividend of common stock on preferred stock]

2. Exceptions

The following distributions are taxable to the recipient of the stock dividend.

a. *If any shareholder can choose to receive a distribution either in stock or in property*, and chooses the stock dividend, all shareholders who receive stock dividends must treat them as a dividend. This means they are includible in income and taxed at capital gains rates to the extent of corporate earnings and profits. [I.R.C. § 305(b)(1); Treas. Reg. § 1.305–2(a)]

b. *If the distribution (or a series of distributions) gives property to some shareholders and increases the interest of others* in the assets or income, the distribution of stock is taxable. For example, if the corporation has two classes of common stock, one paying cash dividends and the other paying stock dividends, both the stock dividends and the cash dividends are taxable. [I.R.C. § 305(b)(2)]

c. *If the distribution gives preferred stock to some common shareholders* and common stock to other common shareholders, both distributions of stock are taxable. [I.R.C. § 305(b)(3)]

d. *Any stock dividend on existing preferred* stock is taxable. [I.R.C. § 305(b)(4)]

e. ***Distributions of convertible preferred stock*** are taxable ***unless*** it is established to the IRS's satisfaction that the distribution will not have the effect of distributing property to some shareholders while increasing the proportionate interest of others. [I.R.C. § 305(b)(5)]

f. ***Other transactions*** that can be used to achieve the results proscribed by sections 305(b)(1) through (b)(5) are also treated as taxable stock dividends. These may include transactions such as a change in a conversion ratio, a change in a redemption price, a difference between the redemption price and the issuance price, or a redemption treated as a dividend to which section 301 applies. [I.R.C. § 305(c)]

> **e.g.** **Example:** Corp. A distributes a dividend of preferred stock on common stock. Ordinarily this would be a tax-free distribution under section 305(a). Assume, however, that each share of preferred (worth $100) can be redeemed by the corporation for $250 in five years. The difference between the issue price ($100) and the redemption price ($250) is treated as an additional distribution of preferred stock with respect to preferred stock (prorated over five years). Because dividends of preferred on preferred are taxable stock dividends, under I.R.C. section 305(b)(4), the $150 difference between issue price and redemption price is a taxable stock dividend (of $30 per year for each of the five years). [Treas. Reg. § 1.305–5(b)]

3. Basis Where Stock Dividend Taxable

If a stock dividend is taxable, the new stock will have a basis equal to its value at the date of the distribution. The basis of the old stock will stay the same.

4. Section 306 Stock—Preferred Stock Bailouts

a. Background

Prior to the 1954 Code, a favorite method of tax avoidance was a stock dividend of preferred stock on existing common stock. This is a nontaxable stock dividend both under previous and present law. [I.R.C. § 305(a), *supra,* p. 118] The shareholders would sell the preferred stock to an outsider for cash, claiming capital gain. The corporation would then redeem the preferred stock held by the outsiders. The result would be that corporate funds were extracted, but the funds were taxed as a capital gain rather than as a dividend (which, at the time, was subject to ordinary income rates); and the shareholder would not lose any portion of his control of the corporation. This scheme was approved by one court. [**Chamberlin v. Commissioner,** 207 F.2d 462 (6th Cir. 1953)] The Tax Court, however, disagreed. It found that the sale should be taxed as a dividend. [**Rosenberg v. Commissioner,** 36 T.C. 716 (1961)]

b. Approach of Section 306

This loophole was blocked through the enactment of I.R.C. section 306. If a shareholder has ***section 306 stock*** and it is redeemed, the redemption is automatically treated as a dividend to the extent of current earnings and profits. If the section 306 stock is ***sold,*** part of the sale price equal to the seller's share of the earnings and profits at the time of the earlier stock dividend is taxable as if it were a dividend. When dividends were taxed as ordinary income, both a redemption or sale of section 306 stock would give rise to tax at a much higher rate than a redemption or sale of non-section 306 stock (which would only give rise to tax at capital gains rates). Under current rules, the difference in treatment is less stark because both a sale of section 306 stock and a sale of non-section 306 stock give rise to tax at capital gains rates. Nevertheless, a difference remains. In a redemption or sale of section 306 stock, the ***entire recovery***, rather than merely the amount in excess of basis, is taxable. Furthermore, capital gain from the sale of non-section 306 stock may be offset by capital losses. Capital gain from the sale of section 306 stock, on the other hand, is "net capital gain" rather than gain from the sale or exchange of a capital asset and, therefore, may not be offset by capital losses. [I.R.C. § 306(a)(1)(D)]

c. Definition

"Section 306 stock" is defined as stock received in **any stock dividend** (other than common stock on common stock) that was **tax free under section 305(a)**. [I.R.C. § 306(c)(1)] Typically, this covers tax-free distributions of preferred stock on common stock. Section 306 stock also includes preferred stock received in a tax-free reorganization if the effect of the transaction was substantially the same as receipt of a stock dividend. [I.R.C. § 306(c)(1)(B)(ii); *see* Rev. Rul. 66–332, 1966–2 C.B. 108]

(1) "Common Stock"

Whether stock issued in a stock dividend is "common stock" (and thus cannot be section 306 stock) depends on whether it could be used to effect a bailout like the one in the *Chamberlin* case, *supra.* [Rev. Rul. 76–387, 1976–2 C.B. 96] Thus, if the stock is limited either as to dividends or in liquidation, it is not "common stock." [Rev. Rul. 79–163, 1979–1 C.B. 131]

e.g. **Example:** Stock that had dividend and liquidation preferences, but also was **voting stock** and could receive **more than the preference** amount of dividends or on liquidation, was not section 306 stock. [Rev. Rul. 81–91, 1981–1 C.B. 123]

(2) Preferred Stock in Section 351 Exchange

Ordinarily, preferred stock received in an exchange qualifying under section 351 (*see supra,* p. 68 *et seq.*) is not section 306 stock. However, suppose the section 351 exchange involves an existing, rather than a new, corporation. Assume further that if money, rather than preferred stock, has been distributed, it would have been treated as a distribution taxable as a dividend under section 304 (*see supra,* p. 113). In that narrow situation, the preferred stock will be treated as section 306 stock. [I.R.C. § 306(c)(3)]

d. Exceptions

(1) Complete Terminations

The unfavorable treatment given to section 306 stock will not apply if the shareholder **sells her entire stock interest**. [I.R.C. § 306(b)(1)] However, for this purpose, the attribution rules of section 318 apply. Thus, if any stock from other family members or related entities is attributed to the shareholder, she has not completely disposed of her stock. If the disposition is by a redemption, section 306 will not apply if section 302(b)(3) (*supra,* p. 103) applies to the redemption. [I.R.C. § 306(b)(1)(B)]

(2) Nonrecognizing Transactions

Transactions in which gain or loss is not recognized (such as gifts) do not trigger ordinary income under section 306. [I.R.C. § 306(b)(3)] However, the gifted stock retains its section 306 "taint" in the hands of the donee.

(3) Liquidations

If the stock is redeemed as part of a partial or complete liquidation, section 306(a) is not applied. [I.R.C. § 306(b)(2)]

(4) Purpose Not Tax Avoidance

In any other transaction, if the IRS is satisfied that tax avoidance was not one of the principal purposes, the unfavorable consequences of section 306 will not occur. [I.R.C. § 306(b)(4); *see* **Fireoved v. United States,** 462 F.2d 1281 (3d Cir. 1972); **Bialo v. Commissioner,** 88 T.C. 1132 (1987)—§ 306 stock donated to charity; tax avoidance found, and deduction reduced under § 170(e)]

Example: X Corp. has two equal shareholders, Ann and Bernie. At a time when the earnings and profits are $40,000, X Corp. distributes a tax-free stock dividend of preferred stock on common stock. It is, by definition, section 306 stock. The fair market value of Ann's preferred stock is $50,000. Assume that the basis of Ann's new preferred stock is $5,000. Ann sells the preferred stock for $50,000. The first $20,000 received is fully includible at capital gains rates, because that was Ann's pro rata part of earnings and profits at the time of the distribution. The next $5,000 is tax-free recovery of basis, and the remaining $25,000 is capital gain. X Corp.'s earnings and profits are not reduced.

Example: Suppose in the previous example that Ann's preferred stock was *redeemed* by X Corp. for $50,000. At the same time, part of Ann's common stock was also redeemed in a substantially disproportionate redemption that qualified for capital gain under section 302(b)(2). At the time of the redemption, earnings and profits of X Corp. were $55,000. The entire $50,000 received for the preferred stock is taxed as a dividend; redemptions of section 306 stock are fully includible based on all available earnings and profits at the time of the redemption. Ann's $5,000 basis for the preferred is reapplied to her common stock, so it will not be wasted. It is possible that the Commissioner would rule that tax avoidance was not one of the principal purposes and allow capital gain on redemption of the preferred, particularly if Ann clearly does not have control of X after the redemptions. [I.R.C. § 306(b)(4)] If, in this example, the redemption of common stock had been a *complete termination* of all of Ann's interest, the redemption of preferred stock would have fallen under an exception to section 306 and would be capital gain to the extent that it exceeds basis. [I.R.C. § 306(b)(1)(B); *see* Rev. Rul. 75–247, 1975–1 C.B. 104]

Chapter Four

Corporate Taxation— Parent's Purchase of Subsidiary's Stock and Adjustment to Basis of Assets

CONTENTS	PAGE

Key Exam Issues

This chapter details the tax consequences of a parent company's purchase of the stock and assets of a subsidiary corporation. Generally, when one company purchases another's stock, the seller has gain, but the basis of the assets of the corporation remains the same. If the buyer wants a stepped-up basis for the assets, it can make an election under section 338. But this election will result not only in a stepped-up basis, but also in taxable gain on the appreciation of the assets. When working on an exam question involving this type of transaction, watch for an *unintentional* section 338 election. In the absence of a carry-over basis election, a section 338 election is deemed to be made if the purchasing corporation made certain asset purchases from the target corporation during the "consistency period" (approximately three years, beginning one year prior to the first acquisition purchase of stock).

A. Background

1. Stepped-Up Basis for Purchased Assets

Suppose that Purchaser Corp. ("P") wishes to acquire Target Corp. ("T"). If P buys T's *assets*, the basis of those assets in P's hands will be equal to their purchase price— which often considerably exceeds their former basis in T's hands. Of course, T will recognize gain on its sale of those assets.

2. Stepped-Up Basis for Assets on Stock Purchase

If P decides instead to buy T's *stock*, the basis of T's assets would not be affected. However, section 338 allows P to achieve a stepped-up basis for T's assets without liquidating T. [I.R.C. § 338] However, because the election requires T to pay tax on the appreciation of its assets, now that the *General Utilities* rule is no longer followed (*see supra,* p. 114), relatively few purchasers find the election desirable. However, the election is still valuable in the context of sales by consolidated groups (*see infra,* p. 127).

B. Election by Parent

1. General Requirements

If P wishes to obtain a stepped-up basis for T's assets, it must make a "qualified stock purchase" of T stock and make an election within nine months and 15 days after the "acquisition date." [I.R.C. § 338(g)] The election is irrevocable.

a. "Qualified Stock Purchase"

A "qualified stock purchase" is a transaction, or series of transactions, by which P acquires "control" of T. "Control" means at least 80% of the voting stock of T and at least 80% of the nonvoting stock of T (except for nonvoting preferred stock). [I.R.C. § 338(d)(3)]

b. "Twelve-Month Acquisition Period"

The acquisition must occur during the "12-month acquisition period," which means the 12-month period beginning with the date of the first acquisition by purchase. [I.R.C. § 338(h)(1)]

c. "Acquisition Date"

The "acquisition date" is the first day on which P has the requisite 80% controlling interest in T. [I.R.C. § 338(h)(2)]

d. "Purchase"

For this purpose, a "purchase" is essentially a transaction in which P's basis for its T stock is not determined by reference to the transferor's basis. Most "purchases," therefore, are straightforward taxable exchanges of P's cash for the T stock.

e.g. **Example:** An acquisition of stock through a "B" reorganization (*see infra*, p. 144) would *not* be treated as a "purchase." Similarly, an acquisition of stock through a section 351 exchange would not count (*see supra*, p. 68 *et seq.*). Neither would an acquisition from any person whose ownership of the stock would be attributed to P under section 318 (*see supra*, pp. 103–106).

cf. **Compare:** But a "purchase" does include the following transaction: P purchases the stock of T, which already owns a controlling interest in the stock of Z Corp. P wishes to obtain a stepped-up basis for the assets of Z Corp. P is treated as if it purchased the Z Corp. stock directly. Consequently, a section 338 election can be made with respect to both T and Z. [I.R.C. § 338(h)(3)(B)]

2. Effect of Election

If P makes the election, T is treated as if it had *sold its assets* on the "acquisition date" to a single purchaser—and then *bought them back*. [I.R.C. § 338(a)] For purposes of measuring the amount taxed to T Corp. on the deemed sale of its assets, the assets will be considered to have been sold for their fair market value. Thus the price at which the assets are deemed "sold" is not the same as the price for which they are deemed "repurchased." The "repurchase" price is discussed below (*see infra*, p. 126). The election and the fictitious sale would have the following consequences:

a. *T would recognize gain or loss on the deemed sale of its assets.*

b. *T's earnings and profits and loss carryforwards would be wiped out.*

3. Price of the Purchase

The price at which the fictitious "repurchase" of T's assets occurs is, in general, the same as the price that P paid for its T stock. Any tax T paid on its fictitious sale of assets is also added to the price. [Treas. Reg. § 1.338–4(d)(1)] However, the following modifications must be made [I.R.C. § 338(b)]:

(i) T's liabilities should be added to the price. [I.R.C. § 338(b)(2)]

(ii) The price should be increased ("grossed up" is the phrase used in the Code) in the event that P acquired less than 100% of the T stock. [I.R.C. § 338(b)(1), (4)]

a. Gross-Up Formula in General

The gross-up formula is as follows: multiply P's purchase price by a fraction, which has a numerator of 100 and a denominator of the percentage of T's stock (by value) held by P on the acquisition date.

e.g. **Example:** P purchases 90% of the stock of T for $90,000. Multiply $90,000 by 100/90. The grossed-up basis is $100,000. If T had liabilities of $30,000, the price at which the assets are deemed repurchased is $130,000. The basis of T's assets after the election is $130,000.

b. Formula Adjustment for Old Stock

There is a distinction between P's stock in T that is "recently" purchased and "nonrecently" purchased. "Recently" purchased stock is stock that was acquired during the 12-month acquisition period (*supra,* p. 125). "Nonrecently" purchased stock is stock that was acquired before the 12-month acquisition period. Only "recently" purchased stock is "grossed up." The numerator of the gross-up fraction is 100 less the percentage of "nonrecently" purchased stock. The denominator is the percentage of T's stock that was "recently" purchased. Thus the price at which T's assets are deemed repurchased is equal to the gross-up price paid for recently purchased stock plus the actual price paid for nonrecently purchased stock plus T's liabilities. (An election is provided by which the nonrecently purchased stock can also be grossed up if P elects to recognize gain in the process.) [I.R.C. § 338(b)(3), (4), (6)]

e.g. **Example:** For several years, P owned 8% of the stock of T. Its basis for this stock was $800. During a 12-month period it bought an additional 80% of T's stock for $20,000. Assume that T has no liabilities and a section 338 election is made. For purposes of measuring the deemed purchase price of T's assets, only the $20,000 figure is grossed up. The fraction is:

$$\frac{100 - \text{nonrecently purchased stock}}{\text{percentage of T's stock recently purchased}} = \frac{100 - 8}{80} = \frac{92}{80}$$

Thus, the grossed-up value of the recently purchased stock is 92/80 × $20,000, or $23,000. The basis of the nonrecently purchased stock ($800) is added to the grossed-up basis of the recently purchased stock ($23,000), so that the price at which the assets are deemed repurchased is $23,800. (P can elect to gross up the nonrecently purchased stock if it is willing to recognize gain with respect to that stock.)

4. Consistency Requirement

Even if P makes no section 338 election, an election is *deemed to be made* if P has made certain *asset purchases* from T during the "consistency period." This is a period that begins one year *before* the beginning of the 12-month acquisition period, continues through the 12-month acquisition period, and also includes the one-year period beginning on the day after the acquisition date. [I.R.C. § 338(e), (h)(4)] The consistency provision is not triggered by asset acquisitions in the ordinary course of business. [I.R.C. § 338(e)(2)(A)] P could avoid the deemed section 338 elections by filing a "carryover basis election." This election would preclude P from taking a stepped-up basis for its asset purchases during the consistency period. Also, if P buys stock of several affiliated corporations, it must make a section 338 election for all or none. [I.R.C. § 338(f)]

C. Consolidated Groups

1. Introduction

Suppose that T Corp. is part of an affiliated group (meaning that at least 80% of its stock is owned by X Corp.). In that situation, T and X can file a consolidated return on which transactions between members of the group will cancel each other out. (*See supra,* p. 102.)

2. Election Under Section 338

Suppose further that P Corp. acquires the stock of T Corp. from X Corp. and makes a section 338 election, which steps up the basis of T's assets. Of course, this election results in a deemed sale of assets by T Corp., which is taxable to T Corp. (T Corp. pays this tax on a separate return—not a consolidated return, either with X or with P). [I.R.C. § 338(h)(9)]

3. Special Election

X Corp. can elect to take the gain on the deemed sale of T's assets into income and correspondingly step up the basis of its T stock by the amount of that gain. Thus, X Corp. will have much less tax to pay on its sale of stock to P. [I.R.C. § 338(h)(10)] *Rationale:* X could have liquidated T in a section 332 liquidation and taken over its assets without any tax; then it could have sold those assets to P Corp. with only a single tax. The election under section 338(h)(10) treats X as if it had first liquidated T Corp., then sold its assets.

Chapter Five

Corporate Taxation— Reorganizations

CONTENTS	PAGE

Key Exam Issues

This chapter considers both divisive and combining reorganizations and recapitalizations, and examines the tax consequences of each.

1. **Divisive Reorganizations**

   If you have an exam question in which one corporation divides into two or more, you must work through each requirement of *section 355* to see whether the division qualifies as a *tax-free reorganization*. Remember that to qualify:

   a. The reorganization must have a *business* purpose.

   b. The reorganization *cannot* be used principally as a *device for the distribution of earnings and profits* of either corporation.

   c. *Control* (at least 80% of the voting stock) of the subsidiary *must be distributed* to the shareholders of the original corporation.

   d. Both corporations must carry on an *active trade or business* after the reorganization, and that business must have been carried on by the corporation for *at least five years prior* to the reorganization.

2. **Combining Reorganizations**

   Transactions in which one corporation (L Corp.) combines with another (Target Co.) by acquiring stock or assets may also qualify as tax-free reorganizations if they meet the requirements of *section 368*. "A," "B," and "C" reorganizations qualify for this treatment.

   a. An *"A" reorganization* is a statutory merger or consolidation. For a merger or consolidation to qualify as a tax-free "A" reorganization:

      (i) There must be a *continuity of interest*; *i.e.*, a substantial number of Target Co. shareholders must continue as shareholders of L Corp. Otherwise, the transaction is treated as a taxable sale of stock or assets; and

      (ii) The *business* of the acquired corporation *must be continued*.

      In an "A" reorganization there may be *boot*. Remember that if the boot has the effect of a dividend, although it will be taxed at capital gain rates, basis will not be offset. Note that boot destroys "B" reorganizations and is limited in "C" reorganizations to the value of 20% of Target Co.'s assets.

   b. A *"B" reorganization* is a *stock-for-stock* exchange; *i.e.*, Target Co. shareholders exchange their shares for L Corp. shares. In addition to the *continuity of interest* and the *continuity of business* requirements, a "B" reorganization requires that the acquiring corporation (i) obtain *80% of the voting and nonvoting stock*, and (ii) *exchange only voting stock* for shares (anything else disqualifies the entire transaction). Note that an issue may arise as to stock bought for cash in a separate prior transaction. It will not disqualify the reorganization if the stock is *"old and cold."*

   c. In a *"C" reorganization*, Target Co. conveys its assets to L Corp. in exchange for L Corp. stock. Again *continuity of interest and business* are required. Like a "B" reorganization, generally *only voting stock* may be exchanged by L Corp. However, other consideration (including Target Co.'s liabilities) may be used—up to 20% of the value of Target Co.'s assets. Lastly, L Corp. must acquire *"substantially all"* of Target Co.'s assets.

3. Single Corporation Reorganizations

Some transactions involve a single corporation, but they also may qualify as taxfree reorganizations if they constitute mere changes in the capital structure ("E" reorganizations) or the identity, form, or place of organization of a corporation ("F" reorganizations).

4. Carry-Over of Tax Attributes

Many tax attributes (including net operating loss carryforwards) of the acquired corporation carry over to the acquiring corporation. But be aware of statutory obstacles. Under section 269, if the principal purpose of acquiring control of a corporation is tax avoidance, the tax benefit is disallowed. Section 382 limits the post-acquisition earnings against which a loss carryforward can be applied.

A. Divisive Reorganizations

1. Techniques

Quite frequently, there is a need to divide one corporation into two, so that the shareholders will hold the stock of two corporations rather than one. If this transaction meets the tightly drawn statutory criteria, it will be a tax-free reorganization. [I.R.C. §§ 355, 368(a)(1)(D)] It is often called a " 'D' reorganization qualifying under section 355." This means that neither the corporations nor the shareholders will recognize gain or loss on any part of the transaction. A tax-free corporate division can occur in one of three different forms:

a. Spin-Off

A "spin-off" ordinarily occurs when Parent ("P") Corp. forms Subsidiary ("S") Corp. and places part of its assets in S Corp. in return for all of the S Corp. stock. P Corp. then distributes the S Corp. stock *pro rata* to the P Corp. shareholders so that the P Corp. shareholders now own all of the stock of both P Corp. and S Corp. S Corp. need not be newly formed: P Corp. could also distribute stock of an existing subsidiary.

b. Split-Off

In a "split-off," the same steps occur as in a spin-off. However, P Corp. distributes the S Corp. stock to only *some* of the P Corp. shareholders, *who turn in their P Corp. stock*. In other words, P Corp. *redeems* part of its stock using S Corp. stock as the medium of exchange. After the split-off, some of the former P Corp. shareholders own S Corp. stock and some shareholders still own P Corp. stock. The result is that the two groups of shareholders can now go their separate ways.

c. Split-Up

In a "split-up," P Corp. forms two new corporations, S1 and S2, and puts all of its assets into the two corporations in return for their stock. It then distributes the stock of S1 and S2 to the former P Corp. shareholders in exchange for *all of their P Corp. stock*. Usually some former P Corp. shareholders get S1 stock and others get S2 stock. The result is that P Corp. no longer exists and the former P Corp. shareholders are divided into S1 and S2 shareholders.

2. Business Purpose Requirement

For a corporate division or any other reorganization to achieve nonrecognition status, it must be carried out for a corporate business purpose. "The principal reason for this business purpose requirement is to provide nonrecognition treatment only to distributions that are incident to readjustments of corporate structures required by business exigencies and that effect only readjustments of continuing interests in property under modified corporate forms." [Treas. Reg. § 1.355–1(b)(1)]

a. *Gregory* Case

This requirement was established in the famous case of **Gregory v. Helvering,** 293 U.S. 465 (1935).

(1) Facts

In *Gregory,* the taxpayer owned all of the stock of P Corp., which held some valuable securities. The taxpayer wanted the securities sold, and she wanted to receive the proceeds of the sale personally. Of course if she had merely distributed the securities (or the proceeds from their sale) to herself, it would have been a taxable dividend (taxed as ordinary income at the time). Instead, P Corp. formed a new S Corp. and transferred the securities to S Corp. Then there was a *spin-off* so that the taxpayer owned all the stock of P and S Corps. She claimed that the distribution of S stock was tax-free to her as a corporate reorganization. She then completely liquidated S Corp., claiming that this transaction gave rise to capital gain to her under a complete liquidation. [I.R.C. § 331] Now she had the securities in hand, with their basis equal to fair market value [I.R.C. § 334(a)], and she sold them.

(2) Holding

The Supreme Court held that the transaction did not qualify as a reorganization. Therefore, the distribution of the S Corp. stock to the taxpayer was a *dividend* from P Corp. The Court held that the concept of "reorganization" implied that the two corporations would *continue* in business and that the division have some *business purpose*. Here the division had no business purpose at all; it was merely designed to convey the securities to the taxpayer without being taxed as a dividend. The Court declared that, generally speaking, a tax avoidance purpose makes no difference, but if the *particular statutory benefit claimed* is one that requires a business purpose, the benefit would not be available without one. The reorganization provisions were held to have such a requirement.

b. Other Applications

The rule of the *Gregory* case has enormous scope. It certainly applies to all reorganizations, not just divisive ones. [Treas. Reg. § 1.368–1(b)] It has also been applied to many other sections of the Code. For example, it has been held that an interest deduction is not available if the transaction giving rise to the loan has no business purpose other than the creation of deductions. [**Goldstein v. Commissioner,** 364 F.2d 734 (2d Cir. 1966)]

c. Corporate vs. Shareholder Business Purpose

The business purpose must be "germane to the business of the distributing corporation, the controlled corporation, or the affiliated group . . . to which the distributing corporation belongs. . . ." [Treas. Reg. § 1.355–1(b)(2)] A *shareholder* purpose (such as personal planning) does not qualify as a corporate business purpose. However, a shareholder purpose may be so nearly coextensive with a corporate business purpose as to preclude any distinction between them, in which case the corporate business purpose requirement is satisfied. [*Id.*; see § 1.355–1(b)(3), example 2]

Example: P Corp. spun off the stock of S Corp. because S Corp. was losing money and would have interfered with P Corp.'s ability to borrow. This was a valid business purpose. [Rev. Rul. 85–122, 1985–2 C.B. 119]

Example: P Corp. spun off S Corp. because S Corp. wanted to hire a key employee who wanted to invest in shares of S Corp., but only if S Corp. became independent of P Corp. This also was a valid business purpose. [Rev. Rul. 88–34, 1988–1 C.B. 115]

Example: A distribution motivated by the need to resolve administrative, management, financial, systemic, or other problems resulting from the operation of two or more businesses by a single corporation is an acceptable business reason. [Rev. Proc. 96–30, Appendix A, § 2.05]

Example: P Corp. spun off S Corp. to enhance stock value. While this would benefit shareholders, it would also (i) enhance the value of employee compensation, and (ii) allow the corporation to undertake future acquisitions with stock-based consideration. These were both considered valid business purposes. [Rev. Rul. 2004–23, 2004–1 C.B. 585]

d. Ruling Requests

Taxpayers often seek private rulings that a proposed corporate division will satisfy IRS standards. The IRS regularly used to grant such requests if the taxpayer provided a detailed explanation and documentation to establish that a corporate purpose significantly motivated the distribution. [Rev. Proc. 96–30, 96–1 C.B. 36] However, recently, the IRS announced that it would no longer issue such rulings to determine whether the distribution is carried out for a business purpose, whether the transaction is principally used as a device for the distribution of earnings and profits (*see infra,* p. 135), or whether the distribution and a subsequent acquisition is part of a plan within the meaning of section 355(e) (*see infra,* p. 137). [Rev. Proc. 2003–48] Instead, the IRS has promised to issue revenue rulings to provide guidance on common issues of concern. [*See, e.g.*, Rev. Ruls. 2003–74, –75—both on "fit and focus" business purposes]

3. Tax Consequences of a Corporate Division

If the divisive transaction meets the statutory requirements (discussed below), the tax consequences are as follows:

a. ***S Corp. takes its new assets at the same basis*** P Corp. formerly had. [I.R.C. § 362(b)]

b. ***P Corp. recognizes no gain or loss*** on the transfer of assets to S Corp. in return for its stock. [I.R.C. § 361(a)]

c. ***The shareholders of P Corp. recognize no gain or loss*** on their receipt of S Corp. shares. [I.R.C. § 355(a)]

d. ***The shareholders of P Corp. retain the same basis*** in their stock as they had before. If they now have both P and S Corps.' stock (as in a spin-off), they divide their old basis between the two. [I.R.C. § 358(a)]

e. ***If the transaction involves any boot***—i.e., if anything other than S Corp. stock is distributed—gain is recognized. [I.R.C. § 356(a), (b)] The consequences are discussed in detail in connection with "combining reorganizations" (see infra, pp. 157–158).

4. Requirements for a Tax-Free Corporate Division

The statutory requirements for a tax-free corporate division are very strict. [I.R.C. § 355]

a. "Device" Rule

The transaction cannot be used principally as a *device* for the *distribution of the earnings and profits* of either P Corp. or S Corp. Pro rata distributions (spin-offs) are more likely to flunk the "device" test than distributions that are not pro rata (*i.e.,* split-offs). As with the section 306 protection against preferred stock bailouts (*see supra,* p. 119 *et seq.*), this rule may be less important now that dividends are subject to capital gains rates as well, albeit without the basis recovery permitted in a sale. The fact that the P or S Corp. shares are *sold or exchanged* shortly after the reorganization is evidence that it was used as such a device, particularly if this disposition was planned before the reorganization (pre-negotiation of a disposition is "substantial evidence" of a device). [I.R.C. § 355(a)(1)(B); Treas. Reg. § 1.355–2(d)(2)(iii)] This provision is designed as a statutory embodiment of the *Gregory* case. Generally the "device" rule would compel the same conclusion as the "business purpose" requirement of *Gregory*. The facts in *Gregory* are a good example of a reorganization that obviously was used principally as a device to distribute the earnings and profits of the parent corporation. However, if a split-off would meet the test under I.R.C. section 302 or 303 for a redemption rather than a dividend, the distribution would not ordinarily be treated as a device. [Treas. Reg. § 1.355–2(d)(5)(iv); *see supra,* p. 102 *et seq.*]

Example: Rafferty owns the stock of RSB Steel Corp. ("RSB"), which processes steel. RSB owns the stock of Teragram Realty Corp. ("Teragram"). Teragram owns a steel mill that it leases to RSB. RSB spins off Teragram to Rafferty. The stated business reason was that Rafferty intended to make gifts of the RSB stock to his daughters to assist in the family's estate planning. Because this scheme looked like a bailout (it would be easy to sell the Teragram stock or liquidate Teragram), the court held that the taxpayers failed to carry their burden of proof to disprove the Commissioner's finding that the spin-off was a device to distribute the earnings and profits of Teragram. [**Rafferty v. Commissioner,** 452 F.2d 767 (1st Cir. 1971)]

b. Continuity of Interest

The continuity of interest requirement, more commonly applied to combining reorganizations, must also be satisfied in the case of divisive reorganizations. (*See infra,* p. 146 *et seq.* for discussion of continuity of interest.)

c. Distribution of Control

P Corp. must distribute *all* of the stock in S Corp. to the P Corp. shareholders. If it does not distribute all of the stock, it must distribute *at least 80%* of the voting stock and show to the satisfaction of the IRS that the reason for retaining some of the stock was not tax avoidance. [I.R.C. § 355(a)(1)(D)] In one case, P Corp. distributed more than 80% control after a long period of time. As a result of failing promptly to distribute at least 80%, a spin-off was not entitled to tax-free status. [**Commissioner v. Gordon,** 391 U.S. 83 (1968)]

d. Five-Year Active Business

Both P Corp. and S Corp. must carry on an *active trade or business* after the reorganization, and those businesses must have been carried on for at least *five years* prior to the reorganization. [I.R.C. § 355(b); Treas. Reg. § 1.355–3]

(1) Ownership Requirement

P Corp. or S Corp. must not have acquired the trade or business within the five-year period in a transaction in which gain or loss was recognized. [I.R.C. § 355(b)(2)(C)]

(2) Active Business

The concept of active conduct of a trade or business excludes merely *passive* income-producing activities. Thus, where a factory takes in a small amount of income from renting out a small part of its space, without any active effort at promoting rentals and without separate records, rental is not an active trade or business. [**Bonsall v. Commissioner,** 317 F.2d 61 (2d Cir. 1963)] An active trade or business requires substantial management and operational functions. [Treas. Reg. § 1.355–3(b)(2)]

(3) Horizontal Division

If P Corp. was engaged in *only one business* but it was *divided into parts*, so that both P Corp. and S Corp. actively engaged in the same kind of business (each of which contained all of the elements of making a profit), the active trade or business requirement is met.

Example: P Corp. has been in the construction business for five years. Its two shareholders (A and B) wish to separate the business and go their separate ways. P Corp. inserts some of its current construction jobs into S Corp. but keeps the others. The construction machinery is divided between P Corp. and S Corp. Then the stock of S Corp. is distributed to A in exchange for all of his P Corp. stock (a "split-off"). The distribution of S Corp. stock to A is tax free because the transaction qualifies as a reorganization. The single construction business—divided into two parts—fits the requirement after the reorganization that each corporation be actively conducting a business previously operated for at least five years. [**Coady v. Commissioner,** 289 F.2d 490 (6th Cir. 1961); Treas. Reg. § 1.355–3(c), example (5)]

Example: P Corp. has been operating a farming business for five years. Two years ago, it bought a new farm. The new farm is placed into S Corp. and spun off. Because the new farm was part of the farming business and the farming business has been operating for more than five years, the spin-off is tax free. [**Estate of Lockwood v. Commissioner,** 350 F.2d 712 (8th Cir. 1965); Treas. Reg. § 1.355–3(c), examples (7)–(8)]

Example: P Corp. has been operating X car dealership for more than five years. P Corp. acquires Y car dealership and operates it for two years before it is placed into S Corp. and spun off. Although the two businesses involved different types of cars, they were both car dealerships and, therefore, P Corp.'s operation of the Y car dealership is considered an extension of its operation of the X car dealership for over five years. Thus the spin-off is tax free. [Rev. Rul. 2003–18]

Example: P Corp. has operated a "bricks and mortar" shoe store for more than five years. In Year 6, P Corp. launches a website to sell shoes. In Year 8, P Corp. places the website operation into S Corp. and spins off the S Corp. stock. Although the website required different know-how than the retail shoe store, it still involved the sale of shoes and, therefore, is considered an extension of the operation of the shoe store. [Rev. Rul. 2003–38]

(4) Vertical Division

Apparently, P Corp. may be divided along vertical lines. In other words, it may be divided into two corporations, one of which sells products to the second one. However, a vertical division can be evidence of a device for the distribution of earnings and profits. [Treas. Reg. § 1.355–2(d)(2)(iv)(C)]

e.g. **Example:** B Corp. owns all of the stock of C Corp. and D Corp. C Corp. makes food products, which it sells only to D Corp. D Corp. buys only from C Corp. and sells to outsiders. B Corp. distributed the stock of both C Corp. and D Corp. to its shareholders (a "split-up"). The food business carried on by C Corp. and D Corp. had been conducted for more than five years. *Held:* The five-year test was satisfied. The split-up was a tax-free reorganization. [Treas. Reg. § 1.355–3(c), examples (9)–(12); Rev. Rul. 75–160, 1975–1 C.B. 112]

(5) Feeder Business

The IRS has ruled on the situation in which P Corp. has two separate businesses that have been operating for five years but there has been a large increase in the scope of one of them *within* the five-year period. If *this increase* was financed by the profits generated by the other business, there has been a failure to meet the five-year active business rule. [Rev. Rul. 59–400, 1959–2 C.B. 114]

(6) Affiliated Group of Corporations

If at least one member of an affiliated group (as defined in the consolidated return rules in section 1504(a)) is actively engaged in the conduct of a trade or business within the five-year period, all members of the group will be considered to have been actively engaged in the conduct of a trade or business during the five-year period. [I.R.C. § 355(b)(3)]

GILBERT

CHECKLIST OF REQUIREMENTS FOR A TAX-FREE CORPORATE DIVISION

A CORPORATE DIVISION WILL BE TAX FREE IF THE FOLLOWING REQUIREMENTS ARE MET:

☑ The division serves a *corporate purpose* (as opposed to a shareholder purpose)

☑ The division is *not a device* to distribute earnings and profits

☑ There is a *continuity of interest* after the division (*i.e.,* a substantial number of the shareholders must continue to be shareholders of one of the corporations involved)

☑ There is a *distribution of control* of the subsidiary corporation (the parent corporation must distribute all of its subsidiary stock or at least 80% of the voting stock)

☑ Both the parent and subsidiary corporations have carried on an *active trade or business for at least five years*

---

5. Use of Divisive Reorganizations as Part of Acquisitive Transactions

a. Divisive Reorganization Plus Acquisition

A divisive reorganization is disqualified if the distribution is part of a plan whereby one or more persons acquire a 50% or greater interest in the stock or assets of either the distributing or the controlled corporation. The existence of such a plan is presumed if such an acquisition occurs during the four-year period beginning on a date two years before the date of the distribution. If the divisive reorganization is disqualified under this provision, a corporate level tax is imposed (as if the distributing corporation had sold the controlled corporation). [I.R.C. § 355(e)] This provision was enacted to overrule a case that allowed a spin-off to be followed by a merger of one of the corporations into an unrelated corporation. [**Commissioner v. Morris Trust**, 367 F.2d 794 (4th Cir. 1966)]

EXAM TIP GILBERT

Be sure to remember that the tax-free status of a corporate division hinges not only on events before the division; *events after the division* can also affect it. For example, if one or more persons acquire a 50% or greater interest in either corporation within two years after the division, the parent corporation may incur tax liability for selling control of the relevant corporation.

---

(1) Safe Harbors

The Treasury Department has identified nine specific types of transactions that will not be considered part of a plan whereby one or more persons acquire a 50% or greater interest in the stock or assets of either the distributing or controlled corporation. [Treas. Reg. § 1.355–7(d)] They can be roughly grouped as follows:

(a) Post-Distribution Acquisitions

1) *Safe Harbor I* provides that a distribution motivated by a separate corporate business purpose will not be considered part of a plan if the acquisition takes place more than six months after the distribution and there have been no discussions related to the acquisition during the period that begins one year before the distribution and ends six months after. [Treas. Reg. § 1.355–7(d)(1)]

2) *Safe Harbor II* is the same as I, except that the distribution merely must not have been motivated by the acquisition (rather than having a corporate business purpose) as long as no more than 25% of the stock of the acquired corporation was acquired or the subject of discussions during the period beginning one year prior to the distribution and ending six months after. [Treas. Reg. § 1.355–7(d)(2)]

3) Under *Safe Harbor III*, a post-distribution acquisition is not part of a plan as long as there were no discussions related to the acquisition at the time of the distribution and within one year after. [Treas. Reg. § 1.355–7(d)(3)]

(b) Pre-Distribution Acquisitions

1) If an acquisition occurs prior to the first public disclosure of the distribution, it will not be considered part of a plan under *Safe Harbor IV* as long as the acquiring corporation is not a controlling shareholder or a 10% holder of the distributing or controlled corporations during the period between the acquisition and the distribution, and as long as no more than 20% of the vote or value of the distributing or controlled corporations is acquired in the acquisition. [Treas. Reg. § 1.355–7(d)(4)]

2) Under *Safe Harbor V*, an acquisition prior to a pro rata distribution is not part of a plan if it occurs after the public announcement of the distribution and there were no discussions prior to the public announcement. [Treas. Reg. § 1.355–7(d)(5)]

3) A pre-distribution acquisition involving a public offering will not be part of a plan under *Safe Harbor VI* if it occurs prior to the first disclosure of the distribution (in the case of stock that is not listed on a public exchange after the distribution) or prior to the first public announcement of the distribution (in the case of stock that is listed on a public exchange). [Treas. Reg. § 1.355–7(d)(6)

(c) Open Market Acquisitions

1) *Safe Harbor VII* provides that an acquisition of distributing or controlled corporation stock in an open market acquisition from a listed exchange will not be considered part of a plan, unless it is acquired by the distributing or controlled corporations, a corporation controlled by one of those corporations or a member of its affiliated group, or by a controlling or more than 10% shareholder of the distributing or controlled corporations. [Treas. Reg. § 1.355–7(d)(7)]

(d) Employee Benefit Acquisitions

1) *Safe Harbor VIII* and *Safe Harbor IX* provide, respectively, that acquisitions of stock by employees or directors as part of their compensation or by retirement plans of the distributing or controlled corporations will not be considered part of a plan so long as in each case the stock acquired does not represent more than 10% of the vote or value of the acquired stock. [Treas. Regs. § 1.355–7(d)(8)–(9)]

(2) Factors and Circumstances

The Treasury Department has also described several factors that are used to determine whether a distribution is part of a plan whereby one or more persons acquire a 50% or greater interest in the stock or assets of either the distributing or controlled corporation where one of the safe harbors does **not** apply. [Treas. Reg. § 1.355–7(b)]:

(a) Plan Factors

The regulations identify a number of factors that tend to demonstrate the existence of a plan. These focus on the presence of substantial discussions with a third party regarding the acquisition or public offering before the distribution took place or other evidence that the distribution was motivated by a business purpose to facilitate the subsequent acquisition. [Treas. Reg. § 1.355–7(b)(3)(i)–(v)]

(b) Non-Plan Factors

The regulations also identify a number of factors that tend to disprove the existence of a plan. These tend to be the opposite of the plan factors, such as the absence of substantial discussions with a third party regarding the subsequent acquisition or public offering prior to the distribution [Treas. Reg. § 1.355–7(b)(4)(i)–(iii)], or evidence of some alternative explanation for the subsequent transaction, such as a corporate business purpose or a change in market or business conditions [Treas. Reg. § 1.355–7(b)(4)(iv)–(vi)]. [*See* Rev. Rul. 2005–65, 2005–2 C.B. 684—finding that a distribution was not part of a plan to effect an acquisition because the distribution had an independent business purpose, it would have taken place in the absence of the acquisition, and there were no discussions regarding the acquisition prior to the public announcement of the distribution, although there were such discussions prior to the distribution itself]

b. Taxable Purchases of Stock Followed by "D" Reorganization

A number of recent amendments to I.R.C. section 355 are intended to block schemes arising out of a combination of a taxable purchase of stock followed by a "D" reorganization. These schemes were generally intended to get around the repeal of *General Utilities* and the resulting corporate-level tax on distribution of assets. (*See supra*, p. 114 *et seq.*)

(1) Purchase of Control Followed by Division

Suppose P Corp. purchases at least 80% of the stock of T Corp. in a taxable transaction but does not make a section 338 election (*see supra*, p. 125 *et seq.*). Assume that both T Corp. and its subsidiary S Corp. have engaged in an active trade or business for at least five years. Following the purchase, T Corp. spins off S Corp. to P Corp. P Corp. then sells the stock of S Corp. to outsiders. The spin-off does not qualify as a D reorganization unless P Corp. holds the T Corp. stock for at least five years prior to the spin-off. [I.R.C. § 355(b)(2)(D)]

(2) Purchase of Stock Interest Followed by Division

Suppose P (an individual or a corporation) purchased stock of T Corp. in a taxable transaction. Within five years, T Corp. distributes the stock of S Corp. to P in a tax-free "D" reorganization. After the distribution, P holds 50% or more of the stock of T Corp. The distribution is taxable to T Corp. (as if it had sold rather than distributed the stock of S Corp.). The distribution of S Corp. stock is tax free to P. [I.R.C. § 355(d)]

c. Purchase of Stock Followed by Division in Which Purchaser Has at Least 50% of Controlled Corporation

Suppose that P (an individual or corporation) purchased stock of T Corp. in a taxable transaction. Within five years, T Corp. distributes the stock of S Corp. to P in a tax-free "D" reorganization. P now has at least 50% of the stock of S Corp. Again, the distribution is taxable to T Corp. (as if it had sold rather than distributed the stock of S Corp.). The distribution of S Corp. stock remains tax free to P. [I.R.C. § 355(d)]

d. Cash-Rich Split-Offs

Recently, Congress became concerned with the use of the split-off to effectively sell appreciated portfolio investment assets in a tax-favorable manner. For example, a parent corporation (P) holds a non-controlling interest in a subsidiary corporation (S). If P sold the S stock back to S for cash, it would give rise to full taxation on the gains. Instead, S contributes cash, plus a small amount of assets in an active trade or business (which allows it to satisfy the requirements under section 355) to a new corporation (S1) in exchange for stock in the new subsidiary. S then distributes the S1 stock to P in exchange for its S stock. In effect, a taxable redemption was converted into a non-taxable split-off and reorganization. To shut down this transaction, Congress enacted section 355(g). This provision denies section 355 treatment if either the distributing or controlled corporation is a "disqualified investment corporation" and there is a change in the majority ownership of that corporation. A disqualified investment corporation is defined as one in which at least two-thirds of the fair market value of its assets consist of investment assets. [I.R.C. § 355(g)]

B. Liquidation and Reincorporation

1. Fact Situation—Shareholder Scheme to Extract Unneeded Liquid Assets

Suppose A Corp. has a large amount of unneeded liquid assets and large earnings and profits. The shareholders would like to extract the assets but are not willing to pay tax on the full amount of the dividend. Furthermore, they want to continue operating the business in corporate form so they cannot simply sell the stock or liquidate the corporation. However, they might go through a complete liquidation of A Corp. and then put the *operating assets into a newly formed B Corp.*, retaining the unneeded liquid assets for themselves. The shareholders would claim that under section 331, the complete liquidation is taxed as a capital gain to them only to the extent that it exceeds the basis in their stocks. [I.R.C. § 334(a)]

2. IRS Attack

The IRS attempts to attack this sort of transaction by disregarding it as a sham, on the argument that nothing has really happened except the payment of a dividend; B Corp. is treated as the same entity as A Corp. [Rev. Rul. 61–156, 1961–2 C.B. 62] Alternatively, the IRS argues that it is a reorganization. Under either theory, the assets retained by the shareholders would be taxed as a dividend, and there would be no new basis for the assets inserted into B Corp. The IRS has not had much success with its theory that the liquidation and reincorporation was a sham. In certain cases, however, the IRS has successfully argued that it was a reorganization.

a. "D" Reorganization

The IRS has had most success with the argument that the transaction is a "D" reorganization qualifying under I.R.C. section 354.

(1) Definition

To be a "D" reorganization, the transaction must be a transfer by a corporation of "all or part of its assets to another corporation if immediately after the transfer the transferor, or one or more of its shareholders . . . is in control of the corporation to which the assets are transferred; but only if, in pursuance of the plan, stock or securities of the corporation to which the assets are transferred are distributed in a transaction which qualifies under section 354. . . ." [I.R.C. § 368(a)(1)(D)]

(2) Section 354(b)

The transaction described above (p. 135) fits the definition of a "D" reorganization, but in addition it must meet the requirements set forth in section 354(b). Section 354(b) requires that B Corp. acquire "substantially all" of the assets of A Corp. However, the courts have held that when the operating assets go over to the new corporation and the liquid assets are kept by the shareholders, there has been a transfer of "substantially all." [**James Armour, Inc. v. Commissioner,** 43 T.C. 295 (1964)]

(3) Control

Furthermore, the shareholders of A Corp. must be "in control" of B Corp. For this purpose, control is defined as 50% of the voting stock or 50% of the total value of all the stock. Therefore, if the shareholders of B Corp. (who were not shareholders of A Corp.) have more than half of the stock of B Corp., the transfer cannot be a "D" reorganization. Moreover, the constructive ownership rules of I.R.C. section 318 (*see supra,* p. 103 *et seq.*) apply for the purpose of measuring control. [I.R.C. § 368(a)(2)(H)— incorporating the definition of "control" in I.R.C. § 304(c)]

(4) Caution

The "D" reorganization discussed here is entirely different from the "D" reorganization discussed in connection with divisive reorganizations (*supra,* p. 140). A "D" reorganization that qualifies **under section 354** is a weapon used by the IRS to attack liquidation-reincorporation, but a "D" reorganization that qualifies **under section 355** is used by taxpayers to avoid recognition of gain in divisive reorganizations.

b. "E" reorganization

The transaction could also be attacked as an "E" reorganization (a recapitalization discussed *infra,* p. 155). [I.R.C. § 368(a)(1)(E)] The IRS has had little success using this theory, especially if there are any new shareholders in B Corp. [**Commissioner v. Berghash,** 361 F.2d 257 (2d Cir. 1966)] However, one circuit has accepted this theory. [*See* **Reef Corp. v. Commissioner,** 368 F.2d 125 (5th Cir. 1966)]

C. Combining Reorganizations

1. Techniques

When the shareholders of one corporation ("L Corp.") wish to combine with another company ("Target Co."), they will often seek to do so by means of a tax-free reorganization. There are three different ways by which L Corp. can "acquire" Target Co.

a. Statutory Merger or Consolidation

State laws provide that upon appropriate director and shareholder approval and the filing of a certificate with the secretary of state, a corporation and another business entity can "merge"—*i.e.,* become one. When Target Co. is **merged** into L Corp., all of the assets and liabilities of Target Co. are automatically conveyed to L Corp. The stock of Target Co. is converted into L Corp. stock in accordance with the merger plan. This exchange is **tax free** to the Target Co. owners. [I.R.C. § 354(a)(1)] It is called an *"A" reorganization* because it is described in I.R.C. section 368(a)(1)(A). A **consolidation** is the same as a merger except that a new corporation, New Corp., is formed, and both L Corp. and Target Co. disappear into it. L Corp. and Target Co. stock is converted into New Corp. stock.

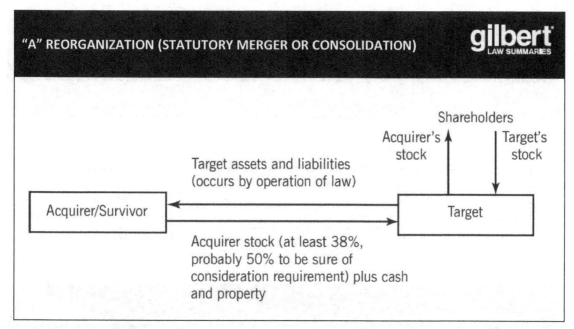

(1) Caution

Although merger authorized and effected pursuant to some statute (whether state, federal, or foreign) is a necessary condition to qualify a merger as an "A" reorganization, it is not a sufficient condition. As part of the merger, all of the assets and liabilities of Target Co. must become the assets and liabilities of L Corp., and Target Co. must cease its separate legal existence. [Treas. Reg. § 1.368–2(b)(1)(ii)] Thus, although a merger pursuant to a state statute that permitted both parties to survive would be a "statutory merger," as that phrase is commonly understood, it would not qualify as an "A" reorganization. [Rev. Rul. 2000–5, 2000–1 C.B. 436]

(2) Disregarded Entity Mergers

Sometimes, the merger that occurs under state law is not the same merger for tax purposes. One such example is the "disregarded entity merger." As discussed previously (*see supra*, p. 6), when the Treasury Department adopted the check-the-box regulations, it permitted single-owner entities, such as a single-member LLC, to be disregarded as an entity separate from its owners. Thus, a merger under state law between an LLC whose only member is a corporation and another corporation may be viewed as a merger between the two corporations for tax purposes. Not all disregarded entity mergers, however, will qualify as "A" reorganizations. A merger of a target company into a single-member LLC of L Corp. would qualify because all of the assets and liabilities of Target Co. become the assets and liabilities of L Corp. and Target Co. then goes out of existence. [Treas. Reg. § 1.368–2(b)(1)(ii), (iv), example 2] By contrast, a merger of Target Co.'s single-member LLC into L Corp. would not qualify because only the assets of Target Co.'s held in the LLC would be transferred to L Corp. in the merger and Target Co. would remain in existence. [Treas. Reg. § 1.368–2(b)(1)(ii) and (iv), example 6]

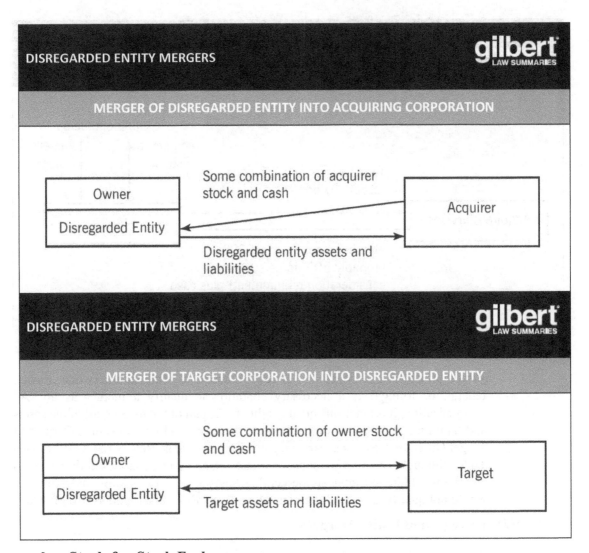

DISREGARDED ENTITY MERGERS

MERGER OF DISREGARDED ENTITY INTO ACQUIRING CORPORATION

Owner / Disregarded Entity → Acquirer

Some combination of acquirer stock and cash

Disregarded entity assets and liabilities

DISREGARDED ENTITY MERGERS

MERGER OF TARGET CORPORATION INTO DISREGARDED ENTITY

Owner / Disregarded Entity → Target

Some combination of owner stock and cash

Target assets and liabilities

b. Stock-for-Stock Exchange

A second method is to have the owners of Target Co. *exchange their ownership interests* for newly issued shares of L Corp. If all of the Target Co. owners make the exchange, the result is that Target Co. will be a wholly owned *subsidiary* of L Corp. If not all of the owners make the exchange, Target Co. will be a partially owned subsidiary of L Corp. If the transaction meets the statutory requirements, the exchange is a tax-free reorganization referred to as a *"B" reorganization*. [I.R.C. §§ 368(a)(1)(B), 354(a)(1)]

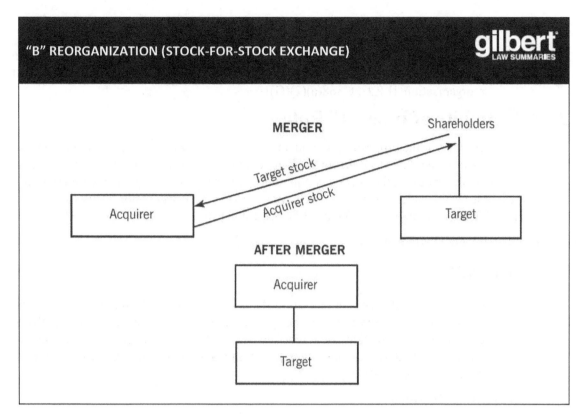

(1) Eighty Percent Limitation

The transaction will not qualify unless L Corp. holds at least 80% of the voting stock of Target Co., as well as 80% of all other classes of stock immediately after the acquisition. [I.R.C. § 368(a)(1)(B), (c)]

c. Stock for Assets

A third method to reorganize is to have Target Co. *convey its assets* to L Corp. *in return for L Corp. stock*. Target Co. is then completely liquidated, its shareholders taking the L Corp. stock in exchange for their Target Co. ownership interests. If the reorganization meets statutory requirements, it is also a tax-free reorganization and is described as a *"C" reorganization*. Both the sale of assets by Target Co. and the exchange of the Target Co. ownership interests for L Corp. stock are tax free. [I.R.C. §§ 368(a)(1)(C), 354(a)(1)]

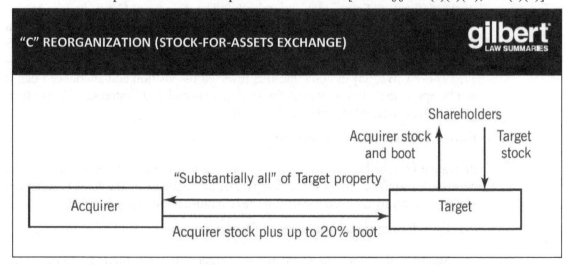

(1) Liquidation

Target Co. must distribute all of its assets (including the consideration received in connection with the reorganization) to its owners in pursuance of the plan of reorganization. [I.R.C. § 368(a)(2)(G)]

2. "Continuity of Interest" Rule

Case law established the proposition that in a tax-free reorganization, a substantial number of the Target Co. owners must *continue* as shareholders of L Corp. If the Target Co. owners disappear as shareholders, the necessary continuity of interest is lacking and the transaction is treated as a taxable sale of stock or assets, not a tax-free reorganization. This rule is now discussed in the regulations. [*See* Treas. Reg. § 1.368–1(e)]

a. Case Law Development

(1) Origin

One early case denied reorganization status to a sale of assets in return for cash and short-term promissory notes. Although the statute at that time appeared literally to treat such a transaction as a reorganization, the court added a requirement of continuity of interest to the statute. [**Cortland Specialty Co. v. Commissioner,** 60 F.2d 937 (2d Cir. 1932)]

(2) Must Be Stock

The Supreme Court held that a sale of assets in return for long-term corporate bonds would not supply sufficient continuity of interest. Instead, there must be a proprietary interest—a substantial amount of stock must be received by the owners of the acquired entity. [**Le Tulle v. Scofield,** 308 U.S. 415 (1940)]

(3) Long-Term Debt

Even 100-year bonds could not be treated as stock for this purpose. [**Roebling v. Commissioner,** 143 F.2d 810 (3d Cir. 1944)]

(4) Quantitative Requirements

Prior to 2005, the continuity of interest requirement only indicated that a "substantial" amount of the consideration be in the form of acquiring corporation stock, without defining that numerically. The Supreme Court had approved transactions in which as low as 38% of the consideration was stock. [**John A. Nelson Co. v. Helvering,** 296 U.S. 374 (1935)] For ruling purposes, however, the IRS insisted on 50% of the consideration in acquiring corporation stock. [Rev. Proc. 77–37, 1977–2 C.B. 568] In 2005, the IRS reversed its position and announced that it would apply the 40% standard for testing continuity of interest. [Treas. Reg. § 1.368–1(e); T.D. 9225, 2005–2 C.B. 739]

(5) Entire Transaction Considered

In evaluating whether the continuity of interest test is met, the entire transaction must be scrutinized, not just the reorganization segment of the total transaction. However, recently adopted regulations have modified the case law rules.

(a) Post-Reorganization Sales of Stock

Suppose that the shareholders of Target Co. sell their L Corp. stock immediately after the merger of Target Co. into L Corp. Under the case law, the merger is not a tax-free reorganization because the post-merger sale defeats the continuity of interest requirement. However, Treasury regulations have reversed the case law. The merger qualifies even though some or all of the shareholders of Target Co. sell their stock to persons unrelated to L Corp. In fact, the merger qualifies even if the sale of the L Corp. stock was planned before the merger, or even if the sale was required by a binding contract. [Treas. Reg. § 1.368–1(e)(1), (8), examples (1), (3)] The merger would not qualify, though, if the shareholders of Target Co. sold their L Corp. stock to L Corp. or a related party, under the theory that the acquiring corporation had directly or indirectly supplied cash consideration for the Target Co. stock. Thus, a redemption would defeat the continuity of interest requirement [Treas. Reg. § 1.368–1(e)(8), example (4)], although the IRS has suggested that a sale to the acquiring corporation as part of an open market stock repurchase program may not threaten continuity of interest [Rev. Rul. 99–58].

1) Prior Law—*McDonald's* Case

Prior law disqualified a tax-free reorganization if the shareholders of Target Co. sold a high percentage of their L Corp. stock soon after the merger pursuant to a plan formed before the merger. [**McDonald's Restaurants of Illinois v. Commissioner,** 688 F.2d 520 (7th Cir. 1982); *but see* **Penrod v. Commissioner,** 88 T.C. 415 (1987)—nine-month holding period passed the continuity of interest test because Target Co. shareholders formed their plan to sell after the merger]

(b) Pre-Reorganization Sales of Stock

Assume that L Corp. first purchases a substantial part of Target Co. stock for cash. Then L Corp. acquires Target Co. (now a partially owned subsidiary) in exchange for L Corp. stock in a statutory merger. The result differs depending on whether L Corp. could have made a section 338 election.

1) Acquisition of Eighty Percent

If L Corp. acquires 80% of Target Co. stock for cash within a 12-month period, L Corp. can make a section 338 election. The effect of the election would be to treat L Corp. as if it had purchased the assets rather than the stock of Target Co. (*See supra,* p. 125 *et seq.* for discussion of section 338 elections.) If L Corp. does not make a section 338 election, but instead merges Target Co. into itself, the merger is treated as a reorganization, despite the fact that most of the historic shareholders received cash rather than stock. [Treas. Reg. § 1.338–2(c)(3)]

2) Case Law

Suppose L Corp. acquires more than 50% but less than 80% of Target Co. for cash. L Corp. could not make a section 338 election in this situation. Hence Treasury Regulation section 1.338–2(c)(3) is inapplicable.

a) Reorganization Disqualified

Suppose L Corp. purchases 78% of Target Co. for cash and immediately merges Target Co. into itself. Alex, a holder of 2% of Target Co. stock, receives L Corp. stock. *Held:* The transaction fails to satisfy the continuity of interest test and thus is taxable to Alex. The Tax Court held that it was required to apply the continuity of interest test by looking to Target Co.'s shareholders as they were before L Corp.'s cash purchase (the "historic shareholder" doctrine). Under that method of applying the continuity of interest test, L Corp. acquired only 22% of Target Co. for stock. This is not a high enough percentage to satisfy the continuity of interest requirement. [*See* **Kass v. Commissioner,** 60 T.C. 218 (1973); **Yoc Heating Co. v. Commissioner,** 61 T.C. 168 (1973)—cash purchase of stock followed by cash-out merger not a reorganization; L Corp. has stepped up basis for Target's assets]

1/ "Old and Cold Stock"

Under the facts above, assume that L Corp. had purchased the stock of Target Co. for cash long before the subsequent merger (*i.e.,* Target Co. stock was "old and cold"). In that situation, according to *Kass*, the merger would have qualified as a reorganization because L Corp. would be a "historic shareholder." However, in *Kass* the cash purchase was part of the same transaction as the reorganization. Therefore, it failed the continuity of interest test.

b) Reorganization Qualified—Sales of Stock Prior to Merger

Assume that a large percentage of the shareholders of the acquired corporation sell their shares for cash immediately before the merger. However, these sales are *not made to the acquiring corporation or to any party related to the acquiring corporation.* Under the regulations, the continuity of interest test is satisfied even though a large number of the "historic shareholders" of the acquired corporation received cash rather than stock. [Treas. Reg. § 1.368–1(e)(1)] However, if the cash sale is made to the acquiring corporation (or parties related to it), the continuity of interest test may not be satisfied, as discussed *supra,* p. 147. [Treas. Reg. § 1.368–1(e)(1), (8), examples (4)(ii), (4)(iii)]

1/ Prior Case Law

The regulations are consistent with some prior case law. Assume that HostileCorp purchases 32% of Target Co. stock for cash as part of an attempt to acquire Target Co. through a hostile takeover. To defeat HostileCorp's bid, L Corp. acquires 46% of Target Co. stock for cash. Members of the public hold the remaining 22% of Target Co. stock. L Corp. merges Target Co. into L Corp. and issues L Corp. stock to HostileCorp and the public. HostileCorp seeks to deduct a loss on the transaction, arguing that the merger is not a reorganization because it fails the continuity of interest test. HostileCorp argues that only 22% of "historic" Target Co. shareholders received L Corp. stock. The Tax Court held that L Corp.'s acquisition of Target Co. qualified as a reorganization. The court held that the historic shareholder doctrine was unmanageable when applied to public companies in which large numbers of shares are constantly being traded. Therefore, HostileCorp would be treated like any other public shareholder, even though it had recently purchased its shares for cash. Therefore, 54% of Target Co. shareholders received L Corp. stock, and the continuity of interest test was satisfied. [**J.E. Seagram Corp. v. Commissioner,** 104 T.C. 75 (1995)]

2/ Effect of Regulations on Case Law

It appears that the regulations endorse the result in *Seagram.* The sale from the public to HostileCorp would be disregarded for continuity of interest purposes because HostileCorp is not related to Target Co. or L Corp.

CONTINUITY OF INTEREST REQUIREMENT—SALES AFFECTING TAX-FREE STATUS	GILBERT
SALES DEFEATING TAX-FREE STATUS	**SALES NOT DEFEATING TAX-FREE STATUS**
After merger Target Co. shareholders sell their *L Corp.* shares to L Corp.	*After merger* Target Co. shareholders sell their *Target Co.* shares to L Corp.
Before merger L Corp. acquires stock from Target Co. shareholders for cash	*After merger* Target Co. shareholders sell their L Corp. shares to a person unrelated to L Corp.
	Before merger L Corp. purchases at least 80% of Target Co. shares for cash and does not make a section 338 election
	Before merger Target Co. shareholders sell their Target Co. shares to a party unrelated to L Corp.

b. Statutory Requirements

The continuity of interest requirement is embodied in strict *statutory standards in "B" and "C" reorganizations*.

(1) "B" Reorganizations

In a "B" reorganization, the transaction does not qualify unless L Corp. uses "solely voting stock" in exchange for Target Co. stock. Any other form of consideration, such as debt or *even nonvoting stock*, will disqualify the *entire transaction*. [**Turnbow v. Commissioner,** 368 U.S. 337 (1961)—the sole shareholder of Target Co. received a mixture of stock and cash]

(a) Old and Cold Rule

If L Corp. purchased some Target Co. stock for cash, and in a separate and subsequent transaction acquired additional shares in exchange for voting stock, the second transaction can be treated as a "B" reorganization (assuming that L Corp. has control of Target Co.). However, the earlier cash transaction must not be part of the same plan as the later stock transaction (*i.e.,* the stock bought for cash must be "old and cold"). [Treas. Reg. § 1.368–2(c)—involving a 16-year time gap]

(b) Mixed Consideration

Even if L Corp. acquired more than 80% of the stock of Target Co. in exchange for L Corp. voting stock, if it acquired any stock for cash as part of the same transaction, the stock-for-stock exchanges are taxable. [**Heverly v. Commissioner,** 621 F.2d 1227 (3d Cir. 1980); **Chapman v. Commissioner,** 618 F.2d 856 (1st Cir. 1980)]

EXAM TIP   **GILBERT**

You must carefully scrutinize the facts in a "B" reorganization to ensure that L Corp. did **not exchange anything but its voting stock** for Target Co. shares. If it did, the transaction will not qualify as a tax-free reorganization unless the nonvoting stock exchange was not part of the merger plan (*i.e.,* it was "old and cold").

---

(2) "C" Reorganizations

In a "C" reorganization, again L Corp. can use *only voting stock* in exchange for the Target Co. assets. The use of any other form of consideration disqualifies the whole transaction.

(a) Exception

Under one narrow exception applicable to "C" reorganizations, L Corp. *can* use consideration other than voting stock. However, the amount cannot be more than 20% of the fair market value of Target Co.'s assets. And for this purpose only, the liabilities of Target Co. (if taken over by L Corp.) count as consideration other than voting stock. [I.R.C. § 368(a)(2)(B)]

e.g. **Example:** Target Co.'s assets are worth $100,000. Its liabilities total $25,000. L Corp. acquires all the assets of Target Co., subject to all liabilities, for $70,000 worth of voting stock and $5,000 worth of nonvoting stock. The transaction is not a "C" reorganization and will be treated as a taxable sale of assets. Because L Corp. is using consideration other than voting stock (the $5,000 of nonvoting stock), the transaction can be a "C" reorganization only if it qualifies under the rule of I.R.C. section 368(a)(2)(B)—but it does not. The liabilities count as boot for this purpose; so L Corp. has furnished voting stock for only 70% of the value of Target Co.'s assets and boot for 30%. Consequently, L Corp. has exceeded the 20% limit. Note that if no nonvoting stock had been used, the fact that L Corp. took over Target Co.'s liabilities would not have destroyed the "C" reorganization because they would not then be treated as boot. [I.R.C. § 357(a)]

(b) Prior Stock Purchase

Suppose L Corp. purchased some shares of Target Co. for cash. Then it acquired the assets of Target Co. in exchange for voting stock. Obviously, it would receive back some of its voting stock in exchange for the Target Co. shares that it bought for cash. For many years, this prior stock purchase was held to disqualify the subsequent transaction from receiving "C" reorganization treatment because L Corp. acquired some of the assets in exchange for the Target Co. shares that it owned rather than for L Corp. voting stock. [**Bausch & Lomb Optical Co. v. Commissioner,** 267 F.2d 75 (1959)] Under recently issued regulations, however, prior ownership of Target Co. stock would not disqualify a "C" reorganization so long as the stock was not purchased as part of the reorganization. [Treas. Reg. § 1.368–2(d)(4)]

(3) "A" Reorganizations

There is *no* statutory continuity of interest rule for an "A" reorganization (a statutory merger or consolidation), although the common law rule has been adopted in the regulations. [Treas. Reg. § 1.368–1(e), *supra*, p. 146]

(4) Triangular Reorganizations

It is often difficult to structure an acquisition at the parent level because the acquiring corporation does not want to directly merge with or acquire the assets of the target due to liability concerns. Similarly, the target shareholders don't want to acquire stock of a subsidiary since it is typically illiquid, especially as compared with the stock of the public parent. Ideally, the target merges with or transfers assets to a subsidiary and the target shareholders receive stock in the parent as consideration. In two cases, however, the Supreme Court originally ruled that such an approach was not permitted. [*See* **Groman v. Commissioner**, 302 U.S. 82 (1937); **Helvering v. Bashford**, 302 U.S. 454 (1938)] There were two primary objections: (1) the parent corporation was not a "party to the reorganization," as required for nonrecognition treatment [I.R.C. §354(a)(1)]; (2) the result violated what came to be known as the "remote continuity of interest" doctrine, which provided that a proprietary interest in a corporation in control of the acquiring corporation was too remote to satisfy the continuity of interest doctrine. Subsequently, Congress enacted several provisions to overturn the Groman/Bashford line of cases. However, the advent of the disregarded entity merger (*see supra,* p. 143) may supplant these transactions in certain instances.

(a) Parenthetical "B" and "C" Reorganizations

In both the "B" and "C" reorganizations, the problem is alleviated by adding parenthetical clauses that permit the consideration to consist of voting stock of a corporation that is in control of the acquiring corporation. [I.R.C. §§ 368(a)(1)(B), (C)] The definition of "Party to a reorganization" was also revised to permit the term to include a corporation in control of the acquiring corporation. [I.R.C. § 368(b)]

1) Subsidiary Mergers

In the "A" reorganization, Congress enacted two provisions to permit mergers in which the parent company's subsidiary merges with the target company and the target shareholders receive parent company stock. However, the advent of the disregarded entity merger (*see supra* p. 143) may supplant these transactions in certain instances.

"(a)(2)(D)" REORGANIZATION (FORWARD SUBSIDIARY MERGER)

"(a)(2)(E)" REORGANIZATION (REVERSE SUBSIDIARY MERGER)

2) Reverse Subsidiary Merger

If L Sub merges into Target Co., the transaction will be tax free so long as Target Co. maintains ownership of "substantially all" of its assets and the assets of L Sub, and L Corp. acquires "control." The principal advantage of the reverse subsidiary merger over the forward subsidiary merger is that it permits up to 20% of the consideration to be boot. [I.R.C. § 368(a)(2)(E)]

(5) Post-Reorganization Transfers to Controlled Corporations

A transaction that otherwise meets the statutory or judicial continuity requirements to qualify as an "A," "B," or "C" reorganization will not be disqualified if all or part of the assets or stock acquired are transferred to a corporation controlled (within the meaning of section 368(c)) by the corporation that acquired the assets or stock. [I.R.C. § 368(a)(2)(C)] Even successive transfers of the assets or stock will not disqualify the transaction as long as the stock or assets remain in the corporate group and the continuity of business enterprise requirement (*see infra*, p. 153) is still satisfied. [Treas. Reg. § 1.368–2(k)]

c. Contingent Stock

The IRS will permit the use by L Corp. of a promise to issue additional stock in the future if certain contingencies materialize. For example, L Corp. might agree to issue additional voting stock after two years if Target Co. achieves a certain level of profitability after the acquisition. If the promise is to issue only ***more voting stock***, it will not destroy a "B" or "C" reorganization. However, the IRS requires that the promise extend for not more than five years and that at least 50% of the total stock that can ever be issued under the deal be issued immediately. [Rev. Proc. 84–42, 1984–1 C.B. 521]

d. Continuity of Business Enterprise

The business of the acquired corporation must be continued. Under the regulations, at least one of the historic businesses of the acquired corporation must be continued or at least a significant portion of its historic business assets must continue to be used. [Treas. Reg. § 1.368–1(d)] However, the requirement of continuity of business enterprise does not apply to the acquiring corporation, only to the acquired corporation. [Rev. Rul. 81–25, 1981–1 C.B. 132]

3. "Substantially All" Requirement in "C" Reorganizations

In a "C" reorganization, L Corp. must acquire "substantially all" of the assets of Target Co. Otherwise, the acquisition will be taxable. The IRS defines "substantially all" to mean at least 90% of the fair market value of the net assets and at least 70% of the fair market value of the gross assets. [Rev. Proc. 77–37, 1977–2 C.B. 568]

Example: Target Co. has assets worth $20,000 and liabilities worth $8,000. This means that its "net assets" are $12,000. L Corp. acquires Target Co. assets worth $14,500. Because this exceeds 90% of the net assets ($10,800) and 70% of the gross assets ($14,000), the IRS will treat it as a transfer of "substantially all." For this purpose, it does not matter whether or not L Corp. takes over the Target Co. liabilities.

"A," "B," AND "C" REORGANIZATIONS—A SUMMARY

	"A" REORGANIZATION	*"B" REORGANIZATION*	*"C" REORGANIZATION*
DESCRIPTION	**Statutory merger or consolidation:** All of Target Co.'s assets and liabilities are conveyed to L Corp. and *Target Co. disappears* (merger), or L Corp. and Target Co. convey their assets to a new corporation and both L Corp. and Target Co. disappear (consolidation).	**Stock for stock transfer:** Target Co. owners *exchange their ownership interests* for L Corp. voting stock. At least 80% of Target Co. voting stock and at least 80% of all other classes of Target Co. stock must go to L Corp. in order to qualify for tax-free status.	**Stock for assets transfer:** Target Co. *exchanges substantially all of its assets* (at least 90% fair market value of net assets and 70% fair market value of gross assets) for L Corp. voting stock and then is completely liquidated.
CONTINUITY OF INTEREST	There is *no statutory* continuity of shareholder interest requirement, but case law still requires *some continuity*. The Supreme Court has upheld tax-free status where Target Co. owners received only 38% of their former ownership interest in L Corp. stock, but Treasury Regulations require at least 40%.	Per statute, Target Co. owners must receive *only L Corp. voting stock (or voting stock of L Corp.'s parent company)*; if L Corp. exchanges anything but voting stock, the entire transaction will be disqualified from receiving tax-free status.	Per statute, L Corp. must use its own voting stock (or its parent corporation's voting stock) to purchase at least *80% of Target Co.'s assets*; up to 20% of the fair market value of the assets can be paid for with other consideration, and L Corp.'s assumption of Target Co. liabilities is *not* taxed as boot *if there is no other boot.*
CONTINUITY OF BUSINESS	At least *one of the historic businesses of Target Co. must continue* or a significant portion of its assets must be used.	At least *one of the historic businesses of Target Co. must continue* or a significant portion of its assets must be used.	At least *one of the historic businesses of Target Co. must continue* or a significant portion of its assets must be used.

a. Judicial Test

The tests applied by the courts focus on the *purpose* for retaining the assets—was it to pay claims, or to distribute to the shareholders? Or was it to go back into an active business? In the latter case, there would not be a transfer of "substantially all." [*See* Rev. Rul. 57–518, 1957–2 C.B. 253]

b. Entire Transaction Considered

It is necessary to consider related transactions when deciding whether the "substantially all" requirement has been met. If the related transactions indicate that the transaction was really a corporate division, or that significant assets have been retained, the transaction flunks the "substantially all" test.

(1) Corporate Division

Suppose Target Co. had a spin-off prior to a "C" reorganization for the purpose of removing assets that L Corp. did not want. The assets removed in contemplation of the reorganization have to be considered in deciding whether L Corp. acquired substantially all. [**Helvering v. Elkhorn Coal Co.**, 95 F.2d 732 (4th Cir. 1937)]

(2) Sale of Historic Assets for Cash

Suppose Target Co. sells to Beckco (an unrelated party) part of its historic assets for cash in a taxable transaction. Then L Corp. acquires the remaining assets of Target Co.—the balance of its historic assets plus the cash received from Beckco. Because Target Co. did not retain any assets and the transaction was not a concealed corporate division, the transaction qualifies as a "C" reorganization. [Rev. Rul. 88–48, 1988–1 C.B. 117]

D. Single Corporation Reorganizations

1. Recapitalizations

a. Definition

A recapitalization is defined as a reshuffling of the capital structure of an existing corporation. [**Helvering v. Southwest Consolidated Corp.**, 315 U.S. 194 (1942)] For example, the corporation might substitute a new class of preferred stock for an existing class of preferred stock to remove cumulative dividends in arrears. Or it might change an all common stock structure to a new one in which some shareholders have common stock and some have preferred stock. The distributions of stock and exchanges of stock that occur by reason of a recapitalization are tax free because the transaction is given nonrecognition treatment as a *corporate reorganization*. [I.R.C. §§ 368(a)(1)(E), 354] (The details of reorganization treatment are discussed *infra*.) Because it is defined in section 368(a)(1)(E), it is often called an "E" reorganization.

b. Exception

The Supreme Court has held that a transaction purporting to be a recapitalization could instead be treated merely as a dividend. The result would be that a distribution occurring as part of the recapitalization is taxable to the extent of earnings and profits. [**Bazley v. Commissioner,** 331 U.S. 737 (1947)]

Example: *Bazley* involved an exchange of existing common stock for new common stock plus bonds. (Under present law, the distribution of the bonds would be taxable under I.R.C. sections 354 and 356, *see infra,* p. 156 *et seq.*) The Court held that although this looked like a recapitalization, it was simply a disguised method of paying a dividend; and that if a transaction partakes, for all practical purposes, of the characteristics of a dividend rather than a recapitalization, it must be treated as a dividend.

2. "F" Reorganizations

An "F" reorganization is a "mere change in identity, form, or place of organization of one corporation, however effected." [I.R.C. § 368(a)(1)(F)] A common example of an "F" reorganization is a reincorporation of one corporation in another state. A transaction does not qualify as an "F" reorganization unless there is no change in existing shareholders or in the assets of the corporation. However, a transaction is not disqualified if fewer than 1% of the shareholders exercise their rights as dissenting shareholders and thus fail to participate. [Rev. Rul. 66–284, 1966–2 C.B. 115] In addition, an "F" reorganization qualifies as such even if it was a step in the transaction in which a corporation also issued stock to the public or carried on other corporate transactions, provided there was a valid business reason for the "F" reorganization. [Rev. Rul. 96–29, 1996–24 I.R.B. 5]

3. No Continuity of Interest or Continuity of Business Enterprise Requirement

Neither the continuity of shareholder interest nor the continuity of business enterprise requirements apply to an "E" or "F" reorganization. [Treas. Reg. 1.368–1(b)] Previously courts and the IRS had ruled that neither requirement applies in an "E" reorganization [*see* Rev. Rul. 82–34, 1982–1 C.B. 59; Rev. Rul. 77–415, 1977–2 C.B. 311], but that they would apply to an "F" reorganization.

E. Boot in Reorganizations

1. General Rules

No gain or loss is recognized if stock or securities in a corporation that is a party to a reorganization are, in pursuance of the plan of reorganization, exchanged *solely* for stock or securities in the corporation or another corporation that is a party to the reorganization. [I.R.C. § 354(a)(1)]

a. Treatment of Securities

"Securities" are generally long-term corporate debts. Under section 354, however, securities are treated much differently than under section 351. If the principal amount of securities received in a reorganization exceeds the principal amount of securities given up, the excess is treated the same as boot. [I.R.C. §§ 354(a)(2), 356(d)]

Example: L Corp. acquires Target Co. in an "A" reorganization. Shareholder Tyler surrenders Target Co. stock and other securities. The securities have a principal amount of $10,000. Tyler receives L Corp. securities, which also have a principal amount of $10,000. Under section 354, no gain or loss is recognized. However, if L Corp. provided securities with a principal amount of $14,000, Tyler would have

$4,000 of boot, and his realized gain would be recognized to the extent of $4,000. (*See infra,* p. 157, for treatment of boot.)

(1) Accrued Interest

Income must be recognized, despite section 354, when a taxpayer receives stock or securities in exchange for accrued interest on debts. [I.R.C. § 354(a)(2)(B)]

Example: L Corp. acquires Target Co. in an "A" reorganization. Shareholder Tyler surrenders Target Co. stock and other securities. The securities have a principal amount of $10,000. Tyler receives only L Corp. stock in exchange. However, $7,000 of interest had accrued on the securities while Tyler held them, but this interest had never been paid by Target Co. On the exchange, Tyler has $7,000 of interest income.

(a) Options

Options (or warrants) that provide rights to buy or sell the stock of the acquiring company are treated as boot. [**Estate of Smith v. Commissioner,** 63 T.C. 722 (1975)]

(b) Nonqualified Preferred Stock

Certain forms of preferred stock, which more closely resemble debt than stock, are treated as boot when distributed in a reorganization. (*See supra*, p. 74.)

2. Taxation of Boot in Reorganizations

a. Recognition of Gain

When boot is received in a reorganization, realized *gain is recognized* up to the amount of the boot. *No loss is recognized*. [I.R.C. § 356(a)]

(1) Caution

Any boot at all destroys a "B" reorganization and is permitted in a "C" reorganization only within the limits of section 368(a)(2)(B) (*see supra*, p. 150). Boot is freely permitted in "A" reorganizations. It is also permitted in "D" reorganizations (*see supra*, p. 132 *et seq.*). Remember also that if the shareholders of Target Co. receive *securities* of L Corp. in excess of the principal amount of securities given up, the excess is treated as boot.

Example: Tyler, a shareholder of Target Co., has a basis of $500 for his Target Co. stock. Target Co. is acquired by L Corp. by a statutory merger (a reorganization). Tyler receives L Corp. nonvoting stock worth $900 and a 20-year L Corp. bond worth $300. The nonvoting stock is not boot, but the bond is a security, which is treated as boot. Tyler's *realized* gain is $700, but his *recognized* gain is only $300 (the amount of the boot). Target Co. recognizes neither gain nor loss on the transfer of its assets to L Corp. even though L Corp. paid for the assets partially with boot, because all of the boot was distributed to the Target Co. shareholders. [I.R.C. § 361(b)]

Example: In the previous example, suppose Tyler's basis was $1,100 instead of $500. Then his *realized* gain would be $100. His *recognized gain* would also be limited to $100.

(2) Basis of New Stock

The basis of Target Co. shareholders in the new L Corp. stock is ***increased by gain recognized*** and ***decreased by boot received***. The boot has a basis equal to its fair market value. Thus, in the first example above, Tyler's new basis would be $300 for the bond and $500 for the L Corp. stock. In the second example above, Tyler's basis for the bond would again be $300, but the basis for the stock would be $900. [I.R.C. § 358]

(3) Basis of Assets

The basis of the acquired assets in the hands of L Corp. will be the same as the basis was in the hands of Target Co. It is not increased even though the Target Co. shareholders recognized gains by reason of boot furnished in the reorganization. However, if Target Co. (as distinguished from the Target Co. shareholders) recognized gain, L Corp. increases its basis by the amount of such gain. [I.R.C. § 362(b)]

b. Sale or Dividend

If the boot "has the effect of the distribution of a dividend," then the entire gain will be included in income as capital gain (to the extent of Target Co.'s earnings and profits), rather than just the amount in excess of basis. [I.R.C. § 356(a)(2)]

(1) How Decided

Although early authority suggested that the presence of boot in a reorganization was automatically a dividend [**Commissioner v. Estate of Bedford,** 325 U.S. 283 (1945)], later cases have been more lenient. Instead, the question is whether the receipt of the boot is essentially equivalent to a dividend—using the standards of section 302 (relating to redemptions—*see supra,* p. 102 *et seq.*). [**Commissioner v. Clark,** 489 U.S. 726 (1989)]

(a) Caution

Note that the boot can be treated as a dividend only to the extent of realized gain. If the taxpayer of the target company has no realized gain, the receipt of boot would not require any gain to be recognized. Moreover, note that the boot could be taxed as a dividend only to the extent of Target Co.'s earnings and profits. If it has no earnings and profits, the boot would not be a dividend.

(b) Applying Section 302 Standards

Section 302 is applied by considering whether the shareholder of Target Co. has materially changed his position vis-a-vis the other shareholders of L Corp. [**Commissioner v. Clark,** *supra*]

e.g. **Example:** Alex is the sole shareholder of Target Co. Target Co. is acquired by L Corp. in a statutory merger. Alex receives 1,000 shares of L Corp. stock (which is 1% of L Corp.'s total outstanding stock) in exchange for his Target Co. stock. The L Corp. stock is worth $10 per share. Alex also receives $20,000 in cash. This transaction is recast as if Alex received 3,000 shares of L Corp. (*i.e.,* 3% of the total). Then L Corp. redeemed 2,000 of the shares. This hypothetical redemption qualifies for capital gain treatment under I.R.C. section 302(b)(2) because Alex's percentage of L Corp. stock is less than 80% of his percentage ownership before the redemption (*i.e.,* he went from owning 3% of the stock to owning 1% of the stock), and also he owns less than 50% of L Corp. stock. [**Commissioner v. Clark,** *supra*]

1) Note

In applying section 302 standards, the attribution rules of section 318 (*supra,* p. 103 *et seq.*) must be applied. [I.R.C. § 356(a)(1)]

2) "D" Reorganizations

If any boot is used in a spin-off, it is treated as a dividend to the extent of the earnings and profits of the distributing corporation. [I.R.C. § 356(b)] In all other "D" reorganizations, including split-ups and split-offs, if boot is used, it is taxable only to the extent of recognized gain, and then will be capital gain unless it has the effect of the distribution of a dividend.

F. Carry-Over of Tax Attributes

1. Tax Attributes and Reorganizations

In an "A" or "C" reorganization, many of the "tax attributes" of the acquired corporation *carry over to the acquiring corporation*. These include its earnings and profits, capital loss carry-overs, methods of accounting, methods of computing depreciation, and many others. [I.R.C. § 381(c)]

a. Loss Carry-Overs

Among the most important of such attributes is the *net operating loss* ("NOL") carryforward of the acquired company. When a corporation has a loss (*i.e.,* its deductions exceed its income), it can *carry the loss back for two years and forward for 20 years*. [I.R.C. § 172—discussed in detail in Taxation of Individuals Summary] If the acquired corporation has a loss carryforward that it has not exhausted, the carryforward will pass with its assets to the acquiring corporation in an "A" or "C" reorganization. In a "B" reorganization, the assets of the acquired corporation are undisturbed; thus, the loss carryforward remains in the acquired corporation. The loss carryforward is a very valuable asset if it can be used to offset the profits of the *acquiring* corporation after the reorganization.

b. Loss Carryback

The acquiring corporation cannot *carryback* a loss incurred after the reorganization against the reacquisition profits of the acquired corporation, except in the case of an "F" reorganization. [I.R.C. § 381(b)(3); for discussion of "F" reorganizations *see supra*, p. 156]

2. Obstacles to Use of the Loss

There are a variety of statutory obstacles designed to prevent use of the carryforward in many cases.

c. Section 269

Under I.R.C. section 269(a)(1), if *control* of a corporation is acquired and the *principal purpose* is tax avoidance, the tax benefit sought is disallowed.

(1) *Control"* for this purpose means at least 50% of the voting power or of the total value of all the shares.

(2) *If the persons who acquire the stock have as their principal purpose* the acquisition of the loss carryforward, the carryforward is wiped out. This requires analysis of the *purposes* of the acquiring persons to see whether they were principally interested in buying a business or in obtaining a loss carryforward.

(3) *I.R.C. section 269(a)(1)* applies both to taxable purchases of stock and to "B" reorganizations.

(4) *I.R.C. section 269(a)(2)* applies the same principle to tax-free asset acquisitions ("A" or "C" reorganizations). There again, if the principal purpose is tax avoidance, the carryforward is wiped out.

(5) *I.R.C. section 269(b)* applies the same principle to a purchase of stock followed by a section 332 liquidation.

d. Section 382

Section 382 curtails the usefulness of a loss carryforward from an acquired corporation by limiting the post-acquisition *earnings* against which the carryforward can be applied. The annual limitation is equal to the product of a prescribed *rate of return* multiplied by the value of the loss corporation's equity immediately before the acquisition. In addition, the Act requires that the loss corporation meet a continuity of business enterprise test for two years after the acquisition.

(1) Rate of Return

The prescribed rate of return is equivalent to the current published rate of return on tax-exempt bonds.

(2) Change in Ownership

This provision applies after an ownership change of more than 50% or after a reorganization in which there is more than a 50% shift in ownership. An ownership change occurs if the holdings of persons holding at least 5% of the stock change (before or after the change) by more than 50%.

Example—Ownership Shift: Purchaser Corp. buys 100% of the stock of Target Co. for $50,000 (which is its value). (This is an ownership shift—purchaser is a more-than-5% shareholder after the purchase, and its holdings increased by more than 50%.) Target Co. has a $250,000 NOL carryforward. Assume the rate of return is 7%. The maximum amount of Target Co.'s post-acquisition earnings that can be offset by Target Co.'s NOL carryforward is 7% of $50,000, or $3,500 per year. Obviously, Target Co. is never going to be able to use up its $250,000 NOL carryforward.

Example—Equity Shift: The same analysis follows if Purchaser Corp. acquired Target Co. in an "A" or a "C" reorganization when Target was worth $50,000 (assuming that the former Target shareholders have less than 50% of the stock of Purchaser immediately after the acquisition).

G. Capitalization of Costs of Corporate Reorganization

1. Introduction

The costs of reorganizing a corporation must be capitalized, rather than deducted as an expense, because they produce significant long-term benefits. [**INDOPCO, Inc. v. Commissioner,** 503 U.S. 79 (1992)]

2. Friendly Takeovers

In *INDOPCO, supra,* a corporation incurred substantial costs in arranging to be taken over in a friendly corporate acquisition. This takeover was expected to produce important long-term benefits for the corporation because of the superior financial strength of the acquiring corporation. Another benefit is that the takeover got rid of 3,500 public shareholders; thus, it saved the corporation substantial expenses in dealing with the shareholders.

3. No Asset Created

In *INDOPCO,* the Supreme Court rejected the idea that an outlay had to produce some specific, identifiable asset in order to be capitalized rather than deducted. The costs of arranging the takeover did not produce any specific asset, but they did produce long-run benefits for the corporation that were more than "incidental." That was sufficient to require them to be capitalized.

4. Resisting a Hostile Takeover

The cost of unsuccessfully resisting a hostile takeover is deductible. Traditionally a business is permitted to deduct the cost of defending itself against attack; moreover, there are no long-term benefits to a corporation from resisting a hostile takeover. Consequently, INDOPCO is distinguishable. [**A.E. Staley Manufacturing v. Commissioner,** 119 F.3d 482 (7th Cir. 1997)]

Chapter Six

Corporate Taxation—S Corporations

CONTENTS

Key Exam Issues

There is an alternative scheme of corporate taxation for certain corporations with a small number of individual shareholders. In essence these corporations are taxed as partnerships.

1. **S Corporation Status**

    To determine whether a corporation qualifies for S corporation treatment, ask:

    a. Are there more than *100 shareholders*? If so, it is not an S corporation.

    b. Are all of the shareholders *individuals*? If not, it is probably not an S corporation. But note that there are several exceptions to this rule (*e.g.*, estates, certain trusts, charities).

    c. Is there more than *one class of stock*? If so, the corporation does not qualify.

    d. Did the corporation *properly elect* to be taxed under subchapter S, and if so, has the election been *terminated*? Note that the election may be *involuntarily terminated* if the corporation fails to meet the above *eligibility requirements* or fails the *passive income test*.

2. **Taxation of S Corporations**

    Once you have determined that a corporation is an S corporation, you must consider how the corporation and its shareholders are taxed. Generally, all items of income, deduction, and credit *"pass-thru"* (so spelled in the Code) to the shareholders, and the corporation pays *no tax*. But be aware of the exceptions for *built-in gain* and *passive income*. Also, when losses are passed to shareholders, watch for the possibility of running out of basis for the stock or debt.

A. Introduction

1. In General

Subchapter S of the Code sets forth an alternative scheme of corporate taxation. [I.R.C. §§ 1361–1379] In many cases, it is advantageous to be taxed as an "S corporation" rather than a "C corporation" (*i.e.*, a corporation taxed under the rules of subchapter C, previously summarized in Chapter Two). Roughly speaking, an S corporation is taxed much like a partnership; it pays no taxes, and its income and deductions pass through to the shareholders. In other respects, however, S corporations are taxed like C corporations.

2. Advantages

An S corporation can distribute its profits to shareholders with only a *single tax*, whereas a C corporation incurs a double tax because dividends are not deductible. The *losses* of an S corporation are currently *deductible by shareholders*; the losses of a C corporation cannot be deducted by shareholders. Also, many difficult problems of C corporations, such as reasonable compensation of employee-shareholders or reclassification of debt as equity, are not problems for S corporations.

3. Disadvantages

There are *many limitations* on S corporations, such as the requirement that it have only one class of stock. Moreover, it is difficult for an S corporation to reinvest its profits in the business because current profits are taxed to shareholders *whether or not they are distributed*.

B. S Corporation Status

1. Eligibility Requirements

An S corporation must meet a number of eligibility requirements.

a. Number of Shareholders

An S corporation *may not have more than 100 shareholders* with none of them being nonresident aliens. [I.R.C. § 1361(b)(1)(A)] All members of the same family, including spouses, are treated as a single shareholder. Members of the family include common ancestors (no more than six generations removed from the youngest shareholder), any lineal descendent of the common ancestor, and any spouse or former spouse of the common ancestor or a lineal descendent. [I.R.C. § 1361(c)(1)]

(1) Note

The 100 shareholder limitation can be avoided by the following scheme: Suppose 200 shareholders want to form an S corporation. They might form two separate S corporations, each having 100 shareholders; then the two corporations could form a partnership. Despite the tax avoidance motivation for this scheme, the IRS has approved it. [Rev. Rul. 94–43, 1994–2 C.B. 198]

EXAM TIP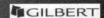

Be sure to remember that while S corporations are generally limited to 100 shareholders, they can get around this by forming a *partnership* between two or more S corporations. Because all members of the same family are counted as one shareholder, however, the partnership scheme may not be necessary in many cases.

---

b. Individuals Only

An S corporation may have only individuals as shareholders. However, there are a number of exceptions to this requirement. [I.R.C. § 1361(b)(1)(B)]

(1) Estates

A decedent's estate or the estate of an individual in bankruptcy may be a shareholder. [I.R.C. § 1361(b)(1)(B), (c)(3)]

(2) Grantor Trusts

A trust, all of the income of which is taxed to the grantor or to a third party who has control over the trust (the "deemed owner"), can be a shareholder. Such a trust can continue to be a shareholder for two years after the death of the deemed owner. [I.R.C. § 1361(c)(2)(A)(i), (ii)]

(3) Voting Trusts

A voting trust can be a shareholder. The beneficiaries of the voting trust are counted for purposes of complying with the 100 shareholder rule. [I.R.C. § 1361(c)(2)(A)(iv)]

(4) Testamentary Trusts

A testamentary trust can be a shareholder for a two-year period starting on the day the stock is transferred. [I.R.C. § 1361(c)(2)(A)(iii)]

(5) Qualifying Subchapter S Trusts

A "qualified subchapter S trust" ("QSST") can be a shareholder if the income beneficiary so elects (the election is irrevocable). The beneficiary will then be treated as the shareholder, and the trust will be ignored. Among other requirements, the trust instrument must provide that all trust income be distributable currently to one individual and that corpus be distributed only to that individual. [I.R.C. § 1361(d)]

(6) Electing Small Business Trusts

An electing small business trust ("ESBT") can hold stock in an S corporation. All of its beneficiaries must be individuals or estates that are eligible shareholders of an S corporation or certain charitable organizations. The beneficial interests in an ESBT must have been acquired by gift or bequest, not by purchase. Each potential current beneficiary is treated as a shareholder for purposes of the 100 shareholder limit. The ESBT's income is taxed to the trust, not to the individual shareholders, regardless of whether the income is distributed. [I.R.C. §§ 1361(e), 641(d)] An ESBT is a useful family financial planning device that can be used to "sprinkle" income among several beneficiaries in the trustee's discretion.

(7) Charitable Organizations, Pension Plans, or Profit Sharing Plans

A tax-exempt charitable organization or a qualified pension or profit sharing plan can hold stock in an S corporation. [I.R.C. § 1361(c)(7)]

c. One Class of Stock

An S corporation may have only one class of stock. However, differences in voting rights among the shares of common stock will not create a second class. Nor will a pooling agreement among shareholders create a second class. Similarly, a debt owed to shareholders will not be treated as a second class of stock if it is "straight debt" (meaning it is a written, unconditional promise to pay a sum certain; the interest rate is fixed; the debt is not convertible into stock; and the creditor is an individual, estate, or qualifying trust). [I.R.C. § 1361(b)(1)(D); (c)(4), (5)]

d. Ownership of Stock

An S corporation can own stock in a C corporation (including a controlling interest in a C corporation). An S corporation is also permitted to own stock in a second S corporation if the second S corporation is a "qualified subchapter S subsidiary" ("QSSS"). The parent S corporation must own 100% of the stock of the QSSS and must elect to treat it as a QSSS. The QSSS must be a domestic corporation and must be one that would qualify for S corporation status if it had individual shareholders. If the QSSS election is made, the subsidiary is ignored for tax purposes—its assets, liabilities, income, and deductions are treated as belonging to its parent. Transactions between the parent and the QSSS are ignored. [I.R.C. § 1361(b)(3)]

(1) Sale of Qualified Subchapter S Subsidiary Stock

A sale of QSSS stock to a non-S corporation results in the termination of the QSSS election. Under legislation enacted in 2007, the sale is treated as if it was a transfer of a portion of the assets of the QSSS equal to the proportion of stock sold to a new C corporation under section 351. [I.R.C. § 1361(b)(3)(C)(ii)]

2. Election Requirement

An S corporation must correctly elect to be taxed under subchapter S, and the election must not have terminated.

GILBERT
CHECKLIST OF ELIGIBILITY FOR SUBCHAPTER S STATUS
TO QUALIFY TO BE TAXED AS A PARTNERSHIP UNDER SUBCHAPTER S, A CORPORATION MUST:
☑ *Not have more than 100 shareholders*
☑ *Not have nonresident alien shareholders* (only individuals, decedents' estates, certain trusts, charitable organizations, pension plans, and profit sharing plans can be shareholders)
☑ *Not have more than one class of stock* (although rights can vary among the shares of the one class)
☑ *Make an election* to be treated as an S corporation

a. Making the Election

(1) Timing of Election

The corporation may make the election at any time during the preceding taxable year or at any time before the 15th day of the third month of the taxable year (for convenience, this is referred to as March 15, since most S corporations must use the calendar year). If made after March 15, the election is treated as made for the following year. [I.R.C. § 1362(b)]

(a) Exception

If an election is made late, or if no election at all is made, but the IRS determines that there was reasonable cause for the failure to timely make the election, the IRS may treat an election as timely made. [I.R.C. § 1362(b)(5)]

(2) Consent of the Shareholders

All persons who are shareholders on the date that the election is filed must consent to the election. If some shareholders consent after March 15, the election goes into effect the following year. [I.R.C. § 1362(a)(2), (b)(2)]

b. Termination of the Election

The election can be terminated either voluntarily or involuntarily.

(1) Voluntary Revocation

The election may be terminated by the corporation, but holders of *more than half of the shares must consent*. If a revocation is made before March 15, it is effective for the year in which it is made. If a revocation is made after March 15, it is effective for the following year or for any specified future year. [I.R.C. § 1362(d)(1)]

(2) Involuntary Termination—Ineligibility

The election is terminated on the date that the corporation *fails to meet the eligibility requirements* for S corporation status (for example, because it acquires a 101st shareholder). If this occurs during the middle of the taxable year, the year is split in two—the first part as an S corporation, the second part as a C corporation. [I.R.C. § 1362(d)(2), (e)]

(3) Involuntary Termination—Passive Income

The election is also terminated if the S corporation fails the *"passive income test."* The passive income test is quite narrowly stated. To fail this test, the corporation must have both (i) earnings and profits from prior years when it was a C corporation *and* (ii) excessive passive income.

(a) Definition of Passive Income

Passive income consists of gross receipts from royalties, rents, dividends, interest, annuities, or sales of stock or securities.

1) Exception—Dividends from Affiliated C Corporation

An S corporation is permitted to own and control a C corporation. (*See supra,* p. 167.) If the S corporation owns 80% of the stock of a C corporation and receives dividends from that corporation, the dividends are not counted as passive income of the S corporation. However, for this purpose, the dividends must be traceable to earnings and profits of the C corporation derived from the active conduct of a trade or business. [I.R.C. § 1362(d)(3)(F)]

(b) "Excessive" Passive Income

To flunk the passive income test, the gross receipts of an S corporation must consist of at least 25% passive income *for each of three consecutive taxable years*. [I.R.C. § 1362(d)(3)] The election is terminated at the beginning of the fourth year.

(c) Previous Earnings and Profits

Even though a corporation has more than 25% passive income for three years, its election will not be terminated if the corporation elected subchapter S status when it was *first formed* (it would not have any pre-subchapter S earnings and profits).

(4) Inadvertent Terminations

If the IRS finds that the circumstances resulting in a termination (either because of ineligibility or because of passive income) were inadvertent, and steps were taken to rectify the problem and make appropriate adjustments, the S election can be preserved. [I.R.C. § 1362(f)] The IRS has issued several Revenue Procedures to simplify the process for requesting relief for inadvertent terminations. [*See* Rev. Proc. 2003–43, 2003–1 C.B. 998—relief for late S corporation elections; Rev. Proc. 2004–48, 2004–2 C.B. 172—relief for late corporation classification election intended to be effective on the date of a filing of an S corporation election]

(5) New Election

If an election has been terminated voluntarily or involuntarily, a corporation cannot make a new election for five years without the IRS's consent. [I.R.C. § 1362(g)]

C. Taxation of S Corporations

1. General Rule

Generally, an S corporation pays *no tax*. [I.R.C. § 1363(a)]

a. Exception—Built-In Gain

An S corporation must pay tax on any recognized built-in gains occurring during the recognition period. [I.R.C. § 1374(a)]

(1) Built-In Gains

Built-in gains are the excess of the value of the assets of the S corporation at the beginning of the first year for which its S election is in effect over the adjusted basis of all such assets. [I.R.C. § 1374(d)(2)]

(2) Recognition Period

Recognition period means the first 10 years during which the S election is in effect. [I.R.C. § 1374(d)(7)]

(3) Exception

The tax does not apply if the corporation (and its predecessors) had an S election in effect for all of its taxable years. [I.R.C. § 1374(c)(1)]

Example: X Corp. was a C corporation for several years until it made an S election. Its only asset at the beginning of its first S corporation year was Blackacre. The value of Blackacre was $100,000 but its basis was only $2,000. Two years later, X Corp. sold Blackacre for $160,000. Because there was a net built-in gain at the time X's S election went into effect, it is liable for the tax under I.R.C. section 1374. It will be subject to corporate income tax on $98,000 of its gain. The remaining $60,000 of its gain is not subject to corporate tax. The entire $158,000 gain is taxed to the shareholders (but it is reduced by the amount of tax that X Corp. had to pay on the gain). [I.R.C. §§ 1366(f)(2), 1374]

b. Exception—Passive Income

If an S corporation has earnings and profits from its years as a C corporation, and its passive income exceeds 25% of its gross receipts, it must pay corporate income tax on the "excess net passive income." [I.R.C. § 1375] Passive income is defined for this purpose in the same manner as for the rule terminating an S election if the corporation has received excessive passive income for three years. (*See supra*, p. 169.)

(1) Computation

Compute the S corporation's gross passive investment income and its net passive investment income (*i.e.,* gross less applicable deductions). Excess net passive income equals net passive income times a fraction, the numerator of which is the amount by which gross passive investment income exceeds 25% of gross receipts, and the denominator of which is gross passive investment income.

Example: An S corporation (with subchapter C earnings and profits) has gross receipts of $10,000. Of this amount, $4,000 is passive investment income. After subtracting applicable deductions, net passive investment income is $3,000. Excess passive investment income equals:

$$\$3,000 \times \frac{\$4,000 - (\$10,000 \times 25\%)}{\$4,000} = \$1,125$$

The corporation must pay corporate income tax on $1,125. If the situation continues for three years, the S election is revoked (*supra,* p. 169).

2. Pass-Thru of Items to Shareholders

Generally, the various items of income, deduction, or credit of an S corporation "pass-thru" (so spelled in the Code) to the shareholders.

a. Separately Stated Items

Similar to partnership taxation (*see supra,* p. 11), items of income, deduction, or credit that might affect a shareholder specially are separately stated, and each shareholder takes a pro rata share of the item.

b. Remaining Items of Income, Deduction, Credit

The remaining nonseparately computed income or loss (*i.e.,* after removing the separate items) is also taken into account pro rata by the shareholders. [I.R.C. § 1366(a)]

c. Character of Items Unchanged

The character of each "passed-thru" item is preserved. Thus, an item of taxexempt income received by the corporation is tax-exempt to the shareholders; a long-term capital gain earned by the corporation is a long-term capital gain for the shareholders. [I.R.C. § 1366(b)]

d. Proration by Days

If a shareholder owns stock for less than the entire year, the items are prorated on a daily basis. [I.R.C. § 1377(a)]

(1) Exception

If a shareholder terminates his interest, and both the buying and selling shareholders agree, the S corporation can treat the taxable year as if it were two taxable years—the year up to the date of the sale and the rest of the year following the sale. However, this adjustment applies only to the buying and selling shareholders, not to other shareholders whose interests were not sold. [I.R.C. § 1377(a)(2)]

3. Basis of Stock and Debts

A shareholder must adjust the basis of her stock in an S corporation and the basis of the debts the corporation owes her.

a. Increases

The shareholder increases the basis of her stock by her pro rata share of corporate income (including tax-exempt income). [I.R.C. §§ 1366(a)(1)(A), 1367(a)(1)] Basis is increased for taxable income to be sure that it is taxed to the shareholder only once, when it is earned, and not again if it is retained and later distributed as a dividend. Basis is increased for tax-exempt income so that the shareholder will not ever have to pay tax on the income, either currently or if it is retained and later distributed as a dividend.

(1) Caution

The increase in basis for tax-exempt income has led to some odd results, which Congress has sought to foreclose. In a recent Supreme Court case [**Gitlitz v. Commissioner,** 531 U.S. 206 (2002)], the taxpayers were shareholders in an S corporation that realized discharge of indebtedness income. Because it was insolvent at the time, the corporation excluded the income under the insolvency exception in section 108. The taxpayers increased the basis in their S corporation stock to reflect their pro rata share of the "tax-exempt" discharge of indebtedness income. The Court upheld this treatment, despite the IRS's claim that it produced a double windfall to the taxpayers by allowing them to use the basis step-up to overcome the limits in section 1366(d) (*see infra,* p. 172) and take further loss deductions against income from other sources. Soon after the Court's decision in *Gitlitz* was announced, Congress amended section 108(d)(7)(A) to provide that for purposes of increasing a shareholder's basis in her S corporation shares, "tax-exempt income" would not include income excluded from income under section 108. [I.R.C. § 108(d)(7)(A)]

b. Decreases of Stock Basis

The shareholder decreases basis of her stock (but not below zero) by nontaxable distributions (*see infra,* p. 173) and by items of loss and deductions allocated to her. [I.R.C. § 1367(a)(2)]

c. Decreases of Debt Basis

If the items of loss and deduction reduce the basis of her stock to zero, the shareholder can continue to deduct these items and reduce the basis of any debts owed by the corporation to her. If she does so, and later increases her basis because income items are allocated to her, the basis of the debt will be increased back to its original level. [I.R.C. § 1367(b)(2)]

d. Limitation on Loss Deductions

If losses and deductions allocated to a shareholder have reduced the basis of both stock and debt to zero, she cannot deduct any further losses. However, disallowed losses can be deducted in a later year if the basis of the stock or debt rises above zero. [I.R.C. § 1366(d)]

(1) Effect of Guarantees

A shareholder often guarantees payment of corporate loans. When the corporation has losses that exhaust the basis of the shareholder's stock and direct loans to the corporation, the shareholder may assert that the guaranteed loan gives her additional basis against which corporate losses can be offset. However, the courts hold that the guarantee does not furnish the shareholder with any basis unless and until she actually makes payment on the guaranty (at which time that payment will be treated as a direct loan to the corporation). [**Harris v. United States,** 902 F.2d 439 (5th Cir. 1990); **Estate of Leavitt v. Commissioner,** 90 T.C. 206 (1988), *aff'd,* 875 F.2d 422 (4th Cir. 1989); *but see* **Selfe v. United States,** 778 F.2d 769 (11th Cir. 1985)— shareholder guaranty can be treated as loan to shareholder that is relent to corporation]

4. Rule for Family Groups

If a family member renders services to an S corporation, there must be *reasonable compensation* to that individual before allocation of the remaining income to stock held by other family members. *Rationale:* This provision prevents the use of an S corporation to split personal service income. [I.R.C. § 1366(e)]

5. Distributions

Most distributions of S corporations are *tax-free* to shareholders (because the amounts involved were taxed previously when the income was earned).

a. Exception—Distribution in Excess of Basis

Recall, however, that such distributions reduce the basis of corporate stock. If the distribution exceeds the basis of the stock, it is treated as capital gain. [I.R.C. § 1368(b)]

b. Exception—Accumulated Earnings and Profits

If an S corporation has accumulated earnings and profits (dating back to years in which it was a C corporation), its distributions may be taxable as dividends. Essentially, the S corporation is allowed to distribute tax-free an amount equal to the net income earned while it was an S corporation (this is referred to as the "accumulated adjustments account"). Distributions in excess of the accumulated adjustments account are taxed as dividends to the extent of earnings and profits. [I.R.C. § 1368(c), (e)]

(1) Dividend Election

An S corporation may elect to have its distributions taxed as dividends to the extent of earnings and profits even though there is an accumulated adjustments account. All shareholders must consent to this election. [I.R.C. § 1368(e)(3)]

(2) Purpose of Election

An S corporation might want to make this election in order to remove its earnings and profits, thus avoiding the problem of disqualification under the passive income rule.

(3) Losses in Year of Distribution

Suppose S Corp. has an accumulated adjustments account ("AAA") of $100 at the beginning of year 3. During year 3 it distributes $80 to its shareholders. During year 3, it also has a loss of $65. The distribution is entirely tax free because the AAA is reduced by distributions before being reduced by current losses. [I.R.C. § 1368(e)(1)(c)]

c. Post-Termination Distributions

After an S election terminates, the corporation can make tax-free *money* distributions to the extent of any previously undistributed accumulated adjustments account. [I.R.C. § 1371(e)] This privilege extends only during the *"post-termination transition period."* This period essentially consists of one year after the end of the year in which the S election terminates. [I.R.C. § 1377(b)]

6. Taxable Year of S Corporation

Generally, an S corporation must use the *calendar year*. If, however, it can persuade the IRS that there is a business purpose for use of a different period, the different period may be allowed. [I.R.C. § 1378]

7. Fringe Benefits

An S corporation is treated as a *partnership* for purposes of employee fringe benefits. Any 2% shareholder is considered a partner. [I.R.C. § 1372]

a. Comment

Some fringe benefits are much more favorable to taxpayers when the corporate form is employed. For example, a corporation can pay and deduct medical insurance premiums for its employees, yet these are not taxed as compensation or dividends to the employees. This is not possible in a partnership because the premiums are considered paid by partners directly (and thus can be deducted only within the limits of section 213). However, under the Code, the partnership (not corporation) fringe benefit rules apply to S corporations.

Review Questions and Answers

Review Questions

1. Alex and Becky form AB, a limited liability company ("LLC") under Madison state law. Alex and Becky are not liable for AB's debts. They have equal ownership interests in AB. The interests are freely transferable. Only Alex has management rights. Under Madison law, AB must be dissolved in the event that Alex or Becky dies. During its first year of operation, AB loses $100,000. Can Alex deduct his share of the loss?

2. Sally owns a camera store as a sole proprietorship. She gives a half interest to her daughter, Beth, and they form a partnership. During year 1, the partnership income is $40,000. Sally takes no salary, although she operates the store full-time. A reasonable salary would be $18,000.

   a. Is capital material in this partnership?

   b. What is Sally's income from the partnership in year 1?

   c. What is Beth's income in year 1?

3. Zipco is a partnership in which Alicia and Beryl are equal partners. In year 1, Zipco has taxable income of $16,000, not counting a short-term capital loss of $9,000. It has no other capital transactions. Does Zipco pay income tax?

4. In year 1, the Zipco partnership suffered a loss of $30,000. At the beginning of the year, Alicia's outside basis was $17,000 and Beryl's outside basis was $6,000.

   a. How much can Alicia deduct in year 1 by reason of the partnership loss?

   b. What is Alicia's outside basis for her partnership interest at the beginning of year 2?

   c. How much can Beryl deduct in year 1 by reason of the partnership loss?

   d. What is Beryl's outside basis at the beginning of year 2?

   e. Assume that Zipco earned a profit of $40,000 in year 2. How much should Beryl reflect as income from the partnership in year 2?

   f. Under the assumptions in "e.," what is Beryl's outside basis at the beginning of year 2?

5. Profits in the AB general partnership are divided 50–50 between Alma and Buford. However, losses are divided 90% to Alma, 10% to Buford. Will the special allocation of loss be honored if:

   a. The partnership agreement provides that on liquidation, after paying liabilities, all remaining partnership assets will be divided equally between Alma and Buford?

b. The partnership agreement calls for maintenance of capital accounts based on the tax basis of assets contributed rather than their fair market values? _____

c. The partnership agreement contains no deficit restoration provision, meaning that on liquidation Alma will not be required to restore to the partnership any negative capital account balance that Alma may have at that time. Nevertheless, the agreement permits allocation of loss to Alma that might cause Alma to have a negative capital account. _____

d. The partnership agreement does not contain a deficit restoration provision. However, it does provide that in no event should loss be allocated to Alma if the effect is to produce a negative capital account. Moreover, in the event that distributions produce a negative capital account, another provision requires that income be allocated to Alma to bring her capital account to zero. _____

6. AB is a limited partnership in which Alma is a general partner and Buford is a limited partner. Profits are divided 50–50. However, losses are divided 90% to Buford, 10% to Alma. Buford invests $200 in AB; Alma invests nothing but will be the manager. AB purchases a building for $1,000. It obtains an $800 nonrecourse loan from Chloe. Assume capital accounts will be maintained in accordance with the regulations. Buford will not be obligated to pay any additional amounts into the partnership, even if Buford has a negative capital account on liquidation. The agreement contains a minimum gain chargeback provision and a qualified income offset. Will the special allocation of loss be honored even if Buford's capital account becomes negative? _____

7. The taxable year of W Partnership ends on July 31 in Year 1. It was permitted by the IRS to use a fiscal year for valid business reasons. In that year it made a profit of $30,000, half of which is allocated to Ed, who uses the calendar year. In its year ending July 31 in Year 2, W had a loss of $66,000. Can Ed deduct any part of the loss on his Year 1 return? _____

8. Fred and Ginger (who use the calendar year) want to form a partnership in Year 1 and have its first taxable year end in January of Year 2, so that they can defer income for a year. Can they do so? _____

9. Dr. Ted buys a 25% limited partnership interest in the Goop Oil Co. Partnership on December 15 of Year 1. For all of Year 1, Goop has a $96,000 loss. The partnership agreement is amended to allocate 25% of this loss to Dr. Ted. Ted is not actively engaged in managing Goop. Can he deduct $24,000 on his Year 1 return? _____

10. X Partnership uses the calendar year. Up to October 1, it earned income of $50,000. During the balance of the year, it lost $8,000.

a. On October 1, Boris, who owned a 25% interest, sold it. What should Boris report on account of partnership operations for that year? _____

b. Suppose Boris sold only half of his interest. Now what should he report? _____

c. What result if Boris never sold his interest, but he died on October 1?

_____

11. In year 1, Q Partnership has income of $20,000 without considering the following: The agreement provides for a salary of $18,000 to Jock. The $18,000 is paid. No other payments are made to partners. Jock and Karen are equal partners. Assume the salary is a "guaranteed payment."

a. What is Jock's income in year 1 by reason of the above?

_____

b. If Jock's outside basis was $30,000 at the beginning of year 1, what is it at the beginning of year 2?

_____

c. What is Karen's income in year 1 by reason of the above?

_____

d. If Karen's outside basis was $30,000 at the beginning of year 1, what is it at the beginning of year 2?

_____

e. Suppose that the payment to Jock was treated as a distribution rather than as a "guaranteed payment." What is Jock's income in year 1?

_____

f. Under the assumption in "e.," and assuming Jock's outside basis was $30,000 at the beginning of year 1, what is it at the beginning of year 2?

_____

12. Frieda owns 85% of Q Partnership. In year 1, she makes the following sales to the partnership at the current value of the asset. What are the tax consequences to Frieda?

a. Stock in GM having a basis of $20,000 and a value of $8,000?

_____

b. Stock in IBM having a basis of $14,000 and a value of $42,000?

_____

c. Suppose instead that Frieda had contributed both the GM and IBM stock to the partnership in return for her 85% interest. Does she recognize gain or loss?

_____

d. Under the assumptions in "c.," what is Frieda's outside basis?

_____

13. Gloria became a 5% partner in the XY Law Firm. The value of her partnership interest is $60,000. She pays nothing for it.

a. Assume that the agreement provides that if the partnership was immediately liquidated, Gloria would get 5% of the assets. What are the consequences of her becoming a partner?

_____

b. Suppose that the agreement provides that Gloria gets no part of existing partnership assets if the firm was immediately liquidated. She will get 5% of the profits from now on, and 5% of any assets accumulated after she becomes a partner. Now what are the consequences of her becoming a partner?

_____

14. R Limited Partnership buys a building for $250,000; this is financed in part by a mortgage of $100,000 owed to the seller. Hal and Ione are equal partners. Hal is a general partner and Ione is a limited partner.

a. Assuming R is personally liable on the mortgage, does this transaction affect Ione's outside basis?

_____

b. Assume that Ione is subject to a minimum gain chargeback provision in the event that future deductions cause her capital account to become negative. Assuming R has no personal liability on the mortgage, does the transaction affect Ione's outside basis? _____

15. Ken is a 50% partner in Q Partnership. Ken sells his partnership interest for $12,000. The basis for his interest was $5,000, and he has held it for three years. What are the tax consequences of this sale in each of the following situations, considered as alternatives?

a. The partnership had accounts receivable in the amount of $2,000. The partnership is on the cash basis. _____

b. The partnership has trucks that have a basis of $2,000 and a value of $2,800. Depreciation claimed on the trucks has been $4,000. _____

16. Alim owns 60% of Z Partnership and Hosni owns 40%. The partnership taxable year ends on January 31. On October 15, 2011, Alim sells his interest in the partnership to Zahi. Does this have any effect on Hosni's income tax for 2011? _____

17. Paolo purchased for $20,000 a one-third interest in Z Partnership. At the time he did so, the basis of all of the assets of the partnership was $9,000. A year later, the partnership sold all of its assets for $66,000.

a. Assume that the partnership made the election under I.R.C. sections 743(b) and 754. What are the tax consequences of this sale to Paolo? _____

b. Suppose that no election under sections 743 and 754 was made. Now what are the consequences to Paolo? _____

18. Jamal's outside basis is $12,000 in X Partnership. What are the consequences to Jamal of the following distributions to him by the partnership? Assume these are not liquidating distributions.

a. Distribution of IBM stock worth $7,000. _____

b. Distribution of IBM stock worth $19,000. _____

c. The partnership distributes cash of $4,000 and shares of nonmarketable stock (purchased by the partnership five years ago) that have a basis of $1,000 and a value of $20,000. _____

d. The partnership distributes cash of $4,000 and nonmarketable stocks (purchased by the partnership five years ago) having a basis of $18,000 and value of $50,000. _____

19. P Partnership distributes $15,000 to Geraldo, a partner, in exchange for Geraldo's interest in P's substantially appreciated inventory, which had a basis of $6,000 in P's hands but was worth $15,000. Prior to the distribution, Geraldo's outside basis was $20,000. Is Geraldo taxed on this distribution? _____

20. Toni had an outside basis of $10,000 in Z Partnership. At the time of her retirement in year 1, the partnership agreement provided that she will receive $1,000 for her interest in the assets and 10% of the net income of the partnership for the next 10 years. Assume that $1,000 is the fair market value of Toni's interest in Z and that Z has no unrealized receivables or goodwill. Thereafter Toni will not be entitled to anything else from the partnership.

a. In year 1, Toni receives $14,000. What are the tax consequences to Toni?

_____

b. What are the tax consequences to the partnership of this payment?

_____

c. Suppose that instead of receiving 10% of profits, Toni is entitled to payments of $8,000 per year for the next 10 years. What are the consequences of the receipt of the first $8,000 payment?

_____

d. What are the consequences to the partnership of the $8,000 payment?

_____

21. Vic retires as a general partner. The agreement provides that he will receive an amount in exchange for his partnership interest equal to the fair market value of his share of the assets. His outside basis is $10,000. His share of the assets is appraised at $21,000, of which $4,000 is goodwill. In year 1, Vic receives $21,000. The partnership agreement contains no specific provision in respect to goodwill. Assume that capital is not a material income-producing factor in the partnership.

a. What are the consequences of Vic's receipt of $21,000?

_____

b. What are the consequences to the partnership of this payment?

_____

c. Suppose that the partnership agreement specifically provided for a payment of goodwill. What are the consequences to Vic now?

_____

22. Edwina has a $10,000 outside partnership basis. In liquidation, she receives cash of $6,000 and substantially appreciated inventory. The inventory has a basis to the partnership of $3,500 and a fair market value of $8,000. The inventory she receives is her pro rata share of the partnership inventory.

a. What are the tax consequences to Edwina?

_____

b. Assume the same facts but that IBM stock worth $8,000 was transferred instead of the substantially appreciated inventory. Now what are the consequences?

_____

23. Warren retires from a partnership. The basis for his interest is $10,000. The agreement provides for a payment based on the appraised value of partnership assets in exchange for the partnership interests. Warren's share is appraised at $12,000. Of this amount, $7,000 consists of accounts receivable. Assume Warren is a general partner and capital is not a material income-producing factor in the partnership. The partnership used the cash basis. What are the consequences of the $12,000 payment?

_____

24. Babette and Clarisse each own 50% of the stock of X Corp., which has taxable income of $120,000. They are planning to start a new Y Corp. in which Babette will own 40% and Clarisse will own 60% of the stock. Will Y Corp. be entitled to use the lower tax brackets for its first $75,000 of taxable income?

_____

25. X Corp. owns 55% of the stock of Y Corp. and renders services worth $100,000 to Y Corp. without charging for them. During the taxable year, X Corp. makes a large profit, but Y Corp. is operating at a loss. Can the Commissioner charge X Corp. with income?

_____

26. Splash Corp. (not an S corporation) was set up to operate a swimming pool and had no substantial capital contributed to it. It leased a swimming pool, which was closed down after a fatal accident. In the Michigan state courts, the corporate entity of Splash was ignored and its shareholders were held personally liable. Can the shareholders also include on their personal returns the losses incurred by the corporation? _____

27. Dee owns 30% of the stock of X Corp. The balance is owned by her son and daughter, who are 24 and 26 years old. Dee sells a building, which has a basis in her hands of $50,000 and a value of $90,000, to X Corp. The building is a capital asset. Assume the depreciation recapture rules are not applicable. Does Dee have capital gain on this sale? _____

28. The Commissioner has asserted that Delta Corp. (which makes bubble gum) is liable under the accumulated earnings tax.

    a. In analyzing the corporation's purpose for accumulating assets, the court concludes that tax avoidance was 25% of the motivation and other reasons were 75%. Can the tax be imposed? _____

    b. In considering whether the assets of Delta have been accumulated beyond reasonable business needs, it is discovered that IBM stocks having a basis of $100,000 and a value of $600,000 are among the corporation's assets. Is the appreciation in this asset a negative factor from the corporation's point of view in trying to show that it has not accumulated assets beyond its reasonable business needs? _____

    c. Delta Corp. seeks to show that it accumulated its assets for the purpose of buying out a large competitor. However, it will have to retain assets for about five years before this will be possible. Does this proof tend to show that it accumulated assets for reasonable business needs? _____

    d. Delta Corp. submits a statement to the Commissioner setting forth the facts mentioned in paragraph "c." The case is now before the Tax Court. Who has the burden of proof on the issue of reasonable business needs? _____

    e. It is shown that during the year the corporation paid no dividends and made a $100,000 loan to the shareholders. Is this a negative factor from Delta's point of view? _____

29. Oscar Worthy Corp. is engaged in screenwriting. One hundred percent of its stock is owned by Edna. The corporation earns a profit by making an agreement with film studios under which Edna will write screenplays for the studio. No other person can be substituted in Edna's place, and her services are uniquely valuable. Ninety percent of the corporation's income in the taxable year came from revenues produced by Edna's scripts. The remaining 10% came from revenues produced by scripts written by others. It paid income tax of $26,750 on taxable income of $100,000. Does it owe personal holding company tax? _____

30. Zeta Corp.'s shareholders are Fern and Gloria. Fern transfers $50,000 of cash in exchange for 50% of the voting stock and Gloria transfers a piece of land in exchange for the other 50%. In Gloria's hands, the land has a basis of $35,000 and a fair market value of $50,000. Does Gloria recognize gain on the exchange of her land for corporate stock? _____

31. Harold and Ida form H & I Corp. Harold contributes IBM stock in exchange for 75% of the stock of H & I. The IBM stock has a basis of $20,000 and a value of $75,000. The remaining 25% of the stock is issued to Ida in return for her personal services. The services involved are that Ida will manage the corporation, selling and reinvesting the IBM stock in real estate. What are the tax consequences to Ida? To Harold? _____

32. Hal forms Iota Corp. and transfers to it assets having a basis of $10,000 and a value of $14,000. These assets are subject to liabilities in the amount of $6,000. In exchange for these assets, subject to liabilities, Hal will receive 100% of the stock of Iota Corp.

   a. Does Hal recognize gain on this transfer? _____

   b. What is the basis of Hal's stock? _____

   c. What is the corporation's basis for the assets? _____

   d. Assume that the liabilities were $11,500. They are not accounts payable. What are the consequences to Hal? _____

   e. What is Hal's basis for his stock in the exchange described in "d."? _____

   f. What is the corporation's basis for the assets after the exchange described in "d."? _____

   g. What would the corporation's basis be if the property had been transferred with a basis of $14,000 and a value of $10,000 and had not been subject to any liabilities? _____

33. Jim contributes land to Kappa Corp. in return for 90% of its voting stock. Kappa also gives Jim $12,000 in cash. The land had a basis to Jim of $40,000 and a value of $78,000.

   a. What are the consequences to Jim of this transfer? _____

   b. Suppose instead that Kappa had given 90% of its stock and $50,000. What would be the consequences? _____

   c. Suppose again that Kappa gave 90% of its stock and $10,000. But assume that the basis of the land in Jim's hands was $100,000 and its value was $78,000. What are the consequences to Jim? _____

34. Keith transfers IBM stock to Lambda Corp. It has a basis of $10,000 and a value of $18,000. He receives in exchange 90% of the stock of Lambda and also Lambda's promissory note for $5,000, payable in 12 years. What are the consequences to Keith? _____

35. Leah forms Mu Corp. and, in exchange for $100,000 cash, receives 10,000 shares of common stock and Mu's promise to pay her $15,000 in five years. Assume that this debt is treated as debt for tax purposes. Mu goes bankrupt.

   a. Does Leah have capital loss on her $15,000 debt? _____

b. Assume that the stock was issued in accordance with the requirements of I.R.C. section 1244. Assume that Leah is single. What are the consequences of the worthlessness of the stock? _____

36. Ling and Mei each own 50% of the stock of X Corp. They contributed $10,000 each in exchange for the stock. X also issued each of them $60,000 in corporate debt. The debt resembled debt in all formal aspects. It was not likely that an outside creditor would have made such large loans to X. In year 1, X pays Ling interest on her debt of $60,000. Can X deduct the interest? _____

37. How much are the current earnings and profits of the Z Corp. under these assumptions: It has taxable income of $100,000. It also received $15,000 in interest on state of Illinois bonds. It paid income taxes of $40,000, paid a $6,000 dividend, and paid salaries to shareholders, which exceeded the reasonable value of the services of the shareholders by $10,000. _____

38. During the years prior to this year, Y Corp. accumulated $100,000 (this was the total of its income, minus income taxes and dividends). This year, its deductions exceeded its income by $10,000, and it paid a $5,000 dividend to its shareholders.

a. Is this dividend taxable? _____

b. What is the amount of tax due from Alvin shareholder on the dividend, assuming that Alvin is in the top marginal rate bracket and owns 50% of the stock of Y Corp.? _____

c. Suppose that in all the years prior to three years ago the corporation had lost a total of $100,000 and in this year it lost an additional $50,000. It pays a $5,000 dividend this year. Is it taxable? _____

39. P Corp. owns 25% of the stock of S Corp. At a time when S Corp.'s earnings and profits are $500,000, it pays a dividend to its shareholders. P Corp. receives land with a value of $40,000 and a basis to S Corp. of $10,000. What are the tax consequences to P Corp.? _____

40. C Corp. goes through a complete liquidation at a time when its earnings and profits are $200,000. Pedro is the sole shareholder. His basis for his stock is $1,000. He receives $300,000 in the liquidations. What are the tax consequences to Pedro? _____

41. C Corp. owns Blackacre, which it sells for nothing down, the balance of $300,000 payable in five years with 10% interest. It distributes this installment obligation, which is worth $300,000, to Pedro in complete liquidation. Pedro's basis for his stock is $1,000. Does Pedro have a $299,000 capital gain? _____

42. Last year, A Corp. bought all of the stock of B Corp. for $40,000 in cash. B Corp.'s assets had a basis of $18,000, and B Corp. had $2,600 of liabilities. This year, A Corp. completely liquidates B Corp. At the time of the liquidation, the assets of B Corp. have a fair market value of $48,000, but their basis remains $18,000.

a. What are the tax consequences of this liquidation to A Corp.? _____

b. What is the basis of the acquired assets in the hands of A Corp.? _____

c. What is the basis of assets to A Corp. if a section 338 election was made?   _____

43.   P Corp. owns 90% of the assets of Sub Corp. Joey owns the other 10%. Sub Corp. is completely liquidated. In the course of the liquidation, Sub Corp. distributes Blackacre to P Corp. and Whiteacre to Joey. The basis of both Blackacre and Whiteacre in Sub Corp.'s hands is zero. Blackacre is worth $9,000 and Whiteacre is worth $1,000.

a. Does Sub Corp. have gain on the distribution of Blackacre?   _____

b. Does Sub Corp. have gain on the distribution of Whiteacre?   _____

44.   Al owns 70% of the stock of X Corp. and Bob owns 30%. They are brothers. The basis for Al's stock is $1,000 and the value is $20,000.

a. The corporation purchases all of Al's stock. Does Al have a $19,000 capital gain?   _____

b. Suppose instead that Al is Bob's father. After the redemption, Al continues to work as an employee of the corporation. Does Al have a $19,000 capital gain?   _____

c. Suppose the same facts as in "b." except that Al stops working in the business. He files an agreement with the IRS to the effect that if he acquires any interest in the corporation within the next 10 years, he will notify the IRS. Assume that Al and Bob have each held their stock for 25 years. Does Al have capital gain?   _____

d. Suppose the same facts as in "c." but assume further that Al has died and the redemption is from Al's estate. Assume that Bob is the sole beneficiary of the estate. What are the tax consequences?   _____

e. Assume that Al and Bob are not related and that X Corp. purchases the stock from Al's estate. However, assume that the beneficiary of the estate is Gladys, who is Al's daughter and is Bob's wife. What are the tax consequences to the estate?   _____

45.   The stock of Sigma Corp. is held as follows: Carol has 40 shares, Adele has 30 shares, and Ed has 30 shares. The shareholders are not related. The corporation purchases 10 of Carol's shares. Redemption or dividend?   _____

46.   Rec Corp. built swimming pools and resurfaced tennis courts. As a consequence of losing a number of breach of warranty actions resulting from cracked tennis courts, it decided to go out of the tennis court business and redistributed all of the assets used in building tennis courts to its sole shareholder, Ida. Is this distribution taxed as a dividend to Ida?   _____

47.   Flo owned all 100 shares of X Corp. stock before her death. The value of these shares was more than 50% of her gross estate for estate tax purposes. After her death, the corporation purchased nine shares from her estate for $10,000. The total of the estate's death taxes and administration expenses is $10,000. Is the repurchase from the estate taxed as a dividend?   _____

48.   Georgia owns all 100 shares of Y Corp. stock. She sells 70 shares to Vasilios for $70,000. The corporation then redeems Georgia's remaining 30 shares. Is this redemption taxed as a dividend?   _____

49. Ned owns 60% of Alpha Corp. (60 shares), and 100% of Beta Corp. He sells 10 shares of Alpha Corp. having a basis of $1,000 and a value of $10,000 to Beta Corp. for cash. Does Ned have a $9,000 capital gain? (Assume Beta has no earnings and profits but Alpha has earnings and profits of $50,000.) _____

50. X Corp. pays a dividend to its sole shareholder, Jackson. It distributes to him IBM stock having a basis of $10,000 and a value of $16,000.

   a. Does the corporation recognize gain on this distribution? _____

   b. Suppose instead that the stock was distributed in connection with a complete liquidation of the corporation. Now does the corporation recognize gain? _____

51. Charlene has owned 40% of the stock of X Corp. for five years. The corporation redeems her shares by distributing to her IBM stock having a basis of $63,000 and a value of $16,000. Because the remainder of the stock is owned by a close relative of Charlene, the distribution was taxed as a dividend to her under I.R.C. section 302. Can the corporation recognize loss on the distribution of the IBM stock? _____

52. Marta is the sole shareholder of X Corp. X Corp. owns IBM stock with a basis of $16,000 and a value of $80,000. As part of the complete liquidation of X Corp., it sells this stock. Is X Corp. taxable on this sale? _____

53. Ann owns 10 shares of common stock of Q Corp. Is she taxed on any of the following stock dividends in the alternative?

   a. A stock dividend of 20 additional shares of common. _____

   b. A distribution of 10 shares of preferred stock. _____

   c. Ann gets a dividend of 20 shares of common stock but could have elected instead to receive $15,000. _____

   d. Ann receives 20 shares of common stock but some other shareholders receive cash with respect to their common stock. _____

54. Zeb owned half of the common stock in X Corp. His basis on this stock was $10,000. He received a stock dividend of preferred stock worth $20,000. After the stock dividend, Zeb's common stock was also worth $20,000.

   a. Is the stock taxable when received? _____

   b. What is the basis of the preferred stock? _____

   c. Assume that at the time of the stock dividend, the corporation had earnings and profits of $60,000. This year, Zeb sold his preferred stock for $26,000. What are the tax consequences? _____

   d. Suppose that instead of selling his stock to outsiders, Zeb sold it back to the corporation for $26,000. At the time of the sale, the corporation had no earnings and profits. What are the consequences of the sale? _____

e. Suppose the same facts as in problem "c." in which Zeb sold his preferred stock to outsiders, and at the same time, he sold his common stock. What are the consequences of the sale of the preferred stock?

_____

55. For many years, P Corp. has owned 20% of the stock of A Corp. Its basis for those shares was $10,000. On March 1, P Corp. purchases for $300,000 an additional 75% of the stock of A Corp. The remaining 5% of A Corp.'s stock is owned by Xavier. On that day, the assets of A Corp. were worth $500,000. These assets consisted of undeveloped raw land; A Corp.'s basis for this land was $60,000. A Corp.'s liabilities were $100,000. On April 9, P Corp. makes an election under section 338 (but makes no other election).

a. What are the consequences to P Corp. of making this election?

_____

b. What are the consequences to Xavier?

_____

c. Does A Corp. recognize gain?

_____

d. What is the basis of the assets of A Corp. after the election is made?

_____

56. Rec Corp. is engaged both in the swimming pool and tennis court construction businesses, and has carried on both these businesses for eight years. It has two equal shareholders, Al and Bob, who are not getting along. Al is in charge of the swimming pool part of the business, and Bob is in charge of the tennis court part. To settle their disputes, Rec Corp. forms a new corporation, Nets Corp., and puts the tennis court business into Nets Corp. The stock of Nets Corp. is distributed to Bob in exchange for all of his interest in Rec Corp.

a. What are the tax consequences of this distribution to Bob and Rec?

_____

b. Suppose that the swimming pool business had been conducted for only two years and the tennis court business for six years. Now what are the consequences to Bob and Rec?

_____

57. X Corp. owns, among other assets, a very valuable parcel of land that has appreciated greatly. The sole shareholder, Alice, wanted to extract the land and sell it while keeping the corporation going. Therefore, a spin-off was performed. This was done by having X Corp. form a new corporation, Y Corp., and placing the land into Y Corp. X Corp. then distributed the Y stock to Alice. Two months later, Alice sold the Y stock to Bob. Bob completely liquidated Y Corp. so as to obtain the land. Assume that X Corp. had owned the land for 25 years. How should the spin-off be taxed to Alice and to X Corp.?

_____

58. Lincoln & Douglas Corp. is a professional corporation that practices law. It has been extremely successful and has accumulated earnings and profits of about $100,000. The shareholders would like to get this money out, but do not want to have it taxed as a dividend. On the other hand they would like to continue practicing law in corporate form. Therefore Lincoln & Douglas Corp. is completely liquidated and all the assets are transferred to the shareholders.

a. The law practice is contributed to a newly formed Grant & Lee Corp. The shareholders of Grant & Lee are the same as those of Lincoln & Douglas. Would the complete liquidation be taxed as a capital gain? _____

b. Assume that in connection with the formation of Grant & Lee, new lawyers are added to the firm and become shareholders. The new shareholders will have 60% of the stock of Grant & Lee. Is the complete liquidation of Lincoln & Douglas taxed as a capital gain? _____

59. Local Corp. is merged under state law into International Corp. The Local shareholders (who have a zero basis for their Local stock) receive nonvoting preferred stock of International.

a. Should the Local shareholders recognize gain or loss? _____

b. Suppose that International used a mixture of bonds and stock in its acquisition. Eighty percent of the value of Local was paid by bonds and 20% by stock. Should the Local shareholders recognize gain or loss? _____

c. Suppose instead that 80% of the value of Local was represented by International stock and 20% by International bonds. Should the Local shareholders recognize their entire gain? _____

d. Under the facts given in "c.," above, should Local recognize gain on the transfer of its assets to International? _____

60. Local Corp. transferred its assets, subject to liabilities, to International Corp. in exchange for International voting preferred stock. Then Local was completely liquidated, distributing the International stock to its shareholders.

a. Assume that the assets of Local are worth $80,000 and that the liabilities are $16,000. Would it satisfy the IRS if International acquires (in exchange for voting stock) only $60,000 worth of the assets? _____

b. Would the transaction qualify as a "C" reorganization if International acquired all of the assets, subject to liabilities, in exchange for $62,000 worth of voting stock and $2,000 in cash? _____

c. Would the transaction qualify if International used nonvoting preferred stock? _____

d. Suppose that the acquisition is done through the transfer of Local's assets to a subsidiary of International. However, International (the parent of the acquiring corporation) issues International voting stock in exchange for the assets. Does this qualify as a "C" reorganization? _____

e. Suppose that International acquires Local's assets, subject to liabilities, in exchange for $60,000 of its voting stock plus the promise to issue up to an additional $20,000 more stock if a particular lawsuit, now being litigated by Local, is decided favorably to Local in the future. Is this permissible in a "C" reorganization? _____

61. International decides to acquire Local by acquiring its stock in exchange for International's stock.

    a. International acquires 75% of the Local voting stock in exchange for its own stock. Would this be tax free to Local shareholders? _____

    b. International acquires $100,000 worth of Local stock (which is 100% of it) in exchange for $60,000 of International stock and $40,000 in cash. As to the shareholders receiving both stock and cash, is their entire gain recognized? _____

    c. Suppose 50% of the Local shareholders immediately sell their newly acquired shares of International stock on the open market? Would the original transaction still qualify as a tax-free reorganization? _____

62. Assume that International acquires Local in a tax-free "A" reorganization. Assume further that Local has a net operating loss carryforward of $100,000.

    a. Does the loss carryforward survive the merger? _____

    b. Assume that the Local shareholders end up with 5% of the stock of International. Is the loss carryforward fully usable? _____

    c. Assuming the same facts as in paragraph "b.," suppose that International's primary purpose for acquiring Local was to use the loss carryforward. Can it do so? _____

63. A Corp. has 99 shareholders. They have an existing election under subchapter S, which has been in effect for two years. Will any of the following events require termination of election?

    a. Joe sells his shares to two people. _____

    b. Terry dies and her stock is transferred to an estate. _____

    c. Bill gives his stock to an irrevocable inter vivos trust for his five children. _____

    d. Shareholders enter into a pooling agreement valid under corporate law. Under this agreement, they agree to vote their shares in elections for directorships as Abdul and Ernesta (who are two of the shareholders) decide. _____

    e. The corporation has outstanding bonds owned by many of the shareholders. It has been determined that this debt should be reclassified as equity for tax purposes. _____

64. Beta Corp. was formed in 1972. On February 21 of this year, it filed its election to be taxed under subchapter S for this year. Is this election valid for this year? _____

65. Zeta Corp. was a C corporation formed in 1984. It had accumulated earnings and profits of $200,000. In 2014, Zeta became an S corporation. All of its income comes from rents.

    a. Is Zeta liable for any tax in 2014? _____

    b. Assume the same situation holds true in 2015 and 2016. Is Zeta's S election terminated in 2016? _____

66. When Lambda Corp. was formed last year, one of its assets was Blackacre, which had a zero basis and a value of $50,000. This year, Blackacre was sold for $60,000. Lambda was an S corporation for both last year and this year. Is Lambda liable to pay tax on any part of its gain on the sale of Blackacre? _____

67. Gamma Corp. is an S corporation, and this year it pays cash dividends of $18,000. Its taxable income this year is $100,000.

   a. The corporation has only one shareholder, Debra. How much income does Debra have this year? _____

   b. What is the effect on the basis of Debra's stock? _____

68. Last year, Fiesta Corp. (an S corporation) had a $100,000 net operating loss. The sole shareholder is Juanita. The basis for her stock is $50,000. Juanita has also loaned $75,000 to the corporation. Can Juanita deduct Fiesta's net operating loss? _____

Answers to Review Questions

1.	**YES**	Under the check-the-box regulations, an LLC is taxed as a partnership unless the members elect to have it taxed as a corporation. Because no election was made, AB is a partnership and Alex can deduct his share of the loss. The four-factor test formerly applied might well have classified AB as a corporation (since three of the four factors pointed toward corporate status), but this approach has been abandoned. [**p. 4** ***et seq.***]
2.a.	**YES**	The store buys and sells cameras; because it makes a profit from the sale of goods, capital is material. Thus, the family partnership rules of section 704(e) are applicable. [**p. 9**]
b.	**$29,000**	Sally must be taxed on a reasonable salary from the family partnership. Thus she is taxed on the $18,000 salary plus one-half of the remaining $22,000 of income. [**p. 10**]
c.	**$11,000**	She is entitled to half the income after deducting a reasonable salary for Sally. *See* previous answer.
3.	**NO**	Partnerships are not taxpaying entities. [**p. 10**]
4.a.	**$15,000**	Alicia can deduct her full one-half of the loss. If it exceeds her other income for the year, it will create a loss carryback (back two years) or carry-over (forward 20 years). [**p. 12**]
b.	**$2,000**	Partnership losses reduce basis. [**p. 12**]
c.	**$6,000**	Deduction of partnership losses is limited to outside basis. [**p. 12**]
d.	**ZERO**	Taking $6,000 of the loss reduced her basis to zero. [p. **12**]
e.	**$11,000**	Beryl takes in her half of partnership income ($20,000) and that increased her basis to $20,000. Now her outside basis has gone above zero, and she can deduct the $9,000 of the year 1 loss that she could not deduct in year 1. [**p. 12**]
f.	**$11,000**	Basis went up to $20,000 and then down to $11,000 because she deducted the $9,000 remainder of the year 1 loss. [**p. 12**]
5.a.	**NO**	Distributions on liquidation must be in accordance with capital accounts; Alma's capital accounts would be diminished by the special allocation of loss. [**p. 14**]
b.	**NO**	Capital accounts must be maintained in accordance with fair market value of the assets at the time they are contributed, not their tax basis. [**p. 14**]
c.	**NO**	Partners with negative capital accounts must be required to restore the negative balance at the time of liquidation. [**p. 14**]
d.	**YES**	This special allocation will be respected even though there is no deficit restoration provision. The provision allocating gain to an unexpectedly negative capital account is called a qualified income offset. Note that the allocation must also meet the

"substantiality" test as well as the "economic effect" test. **[p. 13]**

6.   **YES**   Under the minimum gain chargeback, if Buford has a negative capital account arising out of the allocation of nonrecourse deductions, the minimum gain chargeback provision requires that gain be allocated to Buford to bring a negative capital account up to zero. The regulations allow special allocation of losses arising from nonrecourse loans if a chargeback provision is present. Of course, the allocation must meet the "substantiality" test as well as the "economic effect" test. **[pp. 13, 14]**

7.   **NO**   Partners take income or loss items into account on the last day of the partnership taxable year. That means that no part of the operations for the year ending July of Year 2 can be reflected on Ed's Year 1 return. **[p. 15]**

8.   **NO**   The partnership cannot have a year different from that of its principal partners unless the IRS finds there was a business purpose for doing so. Under these facts, IRS approval is extremely unlikely. **[pp. 15–16]**

9.   **NO**   Retroactive allocations are forbidden. He can deduct only $1,000. Although 25% of the loss for the year is $24,000, he owned an interest for only about 1/24 of the year and so can deduct only 1/24 of the loss. Moreover, under the passive loss rules, he can deduct the $1,000 only against passive income (if he has any). **[pp. 17, 31]**

10.a.   **$12,500**   The partnership year closes with respect to a partner who sells his entire interest. Twenty-five percent of $50,000 is $12,500. **[p. 17]**

b.   **$11,500**   The year does not close if a partner sells less than his entire interest. So Boris has 25% of operations up to October 1 and 12.5% after that. Twenty-five percent of $50,000 is $12,500; 12.5% of the $8,000 loss is $1,000. **[p. 16]**

c.   **$12,500 GAIN TO BORIS; $2,000 LOSS TO ESTATE**   The taxable year of a partner terminates when the partner dies. Profits and losses of the partnership before death are reported on the decedent's final return; profits and losses after death are reported on the estate's return. **[p. 17]**

11.a.   **$19,000**   The guaranteed payment is taxable in full. It is deductible by the partnership, which leaves $2,000 as the partnership income. $1,000 of it is taxed to Jock. **[p. 19]**

b.   **$31,000**   The guaranteed payment does not affect basis. Basis is increased by Jock's distributive share—$1,000. **[p. 19]**

c.   **$1,000**   Karen is entitled only to one-half of income after deduction of the guaranteed payment. **[p. 19]**

d.   **$31,000**   Basis is increased by her distributive share. **[p. 12]**

e.   **$10,000**   He is simply taxed on one-half of income; there is no deduction for the cash distribution, and he is not taxed on it either. **[p. 20]**

f.   **$22,000**   Basis is increased by his distributive share ($10,000) and reduced by the cash distribution ($18,000). **[p. 38]**

12.a.	**NONE**	Loss is nondeductible under I.R.C. section 707(b)(1)(A). **[p. 21]**
b.	**CAPITAL GAIN OF $28,000**	The stock will be a capital asset in the hands of the partnership, as well as the partner; thus the rule of I.R.C. section 707(b)(2) will not apply to turn capital gain into ordinary income. **[p. 21]**
c.	**NO**	I.R.C. section 721 so provides. **[p. 21]**
d.	**$34,000**	The basis of the assets determines the basis of the partnership interest under I.R.C. section 722. **[p. 27]**
13.a.	**$60,000 ORDINARY INCOME**	She has received an interest in partnership capital, and it is taxed as ordinary income on its fair market value. **[p. 24]**
b.	**NO INCOME**	Under Rev. Proc. 93–27, the IRS will not contend that the profits interest is taxable, assuming that Gloria does not dispose of it within two years of receiving it. **[p. 26]**
14.a.	**NO**	A partner's outside basis increases when partnership liabilities increase—but a limited partner gets no basis increase from debts on which the general partner is personally liable. **[p. 29]**
b.	**YES**	Now both partners share the basis increase in accordance with profit-sharing ratios. Ione's basis rises $50,000. Note that if depreciation deductions cause the basis of the building to fall below the amount of the mortgage, the minimum gain chargeback provision will be actuated. In that situation, liabilities equal to the amount of minimum gain will be allocated to Ione. However, in the year in question, there is no minimum gain because the basis of the building is more than the debt. Consequently, the nonrecourse obligation is allocated in accordance with profit shares. **[pp. 14–15, 30]**
15.a.	**$1,000 ORDINARY INCOME, $6,000 CAPITAL GAIN**	The accounts receivable give rise to ordinary income, the basis is zero, and Ken's share is $1,000. This leaves $11,000 of the purchase price allocated to the sale of partnership interest, which is a capital asset. **[p. 33]**
b.	**$400 ORDINARY INCOME, $6,600 CAPITAL GAIN**	Depreciation recapturable under I.R.C. section 1245 is treated as an unrealized receivable and thus ordinary income when a partnership interest is sold. Ken's share of the recapturable depreciation is $400 under I.R.C. section 1245(a)(1)(B). This leaves $6,600 to be capital gain. **[p. 34]**
16.	**YES**	The sale of 50% or more of the partnership interest has the effect of terminating the partnership. The effect of termination is that the income to the date of termination is taxed to all the partners. Therefore Hosni (as well as Alim) is taxed both on the partnership income for the year ending January 31, and also for the income in the period ending October 15 of the same year. **[p. 37]**
17.a.	**$2,000 GAIN**	The effect of the election as to Paolo was that the basis of his share of the assets was stepped up to his purchase price of $20,000. Because one-third of the sale price of $66,000 is $22,000, Paolo has only $2,000 of gain. **[p. 35]**

b.	**$19,000 GAIN**	In the absence of an election, the basis of Paolo's share of the assets would be $3,000, and therefore he would have a gain of $19,000, because his share of the assets was sold for $22,000. **[p. 35]**
18.a.	**NO INCOME, BASIS REDUCED TO $5,000**	Under I.R.C. section 731(a)(1), gain is not recognized on a partnership distribution of money or marketable securities as long as it does not exceed the partner's basis. **[p. 38]** However, basis is reduced by the amount of the money or the value of the securities. **[p. 38]**
b.	**GAIN OF $7,000**	When cash or marketable securities that exceed the partner's outside basis are distributed, the partner recognizes gain. Outside basis would be reduced to zero. Ordinarily, this would be a capital gain, as long as there are no I.R.C. section 751 items. **[p. 38]**
c.	**NO INCOME**	His basis is reduced by $5,000 ($4,000 cash plus $1,000, the partnership's basis in the stocks). The nonmarketable stocks take a basis of $1,000 in Jamal's hands. **[pp. 38, 40]**
d.	**NO GAIN, REDUCED BASIS TO ZERO**	In this situation, the nonmarketable shares will have a basis of only $8,000 in Jamal's hands. The rule is that the basis to the distributee cannot exceed the outside basis ($12,000), reduced by any money distributed in the same transaction ($4,000). Therefore, $10,000 of basis would be wasted. This problem can be cured, however, if an election is made under I.R.C. sections 734 and 754. This will permit the partnership to increase the basis of its remaining assets by $10,000. **[pp. 40, 49]**
19.	**YES**	Under section 751(b), Geraldo is treated as having sold his interest in the substantially appreciated inventory to the other partners. Mechanically, this is treated as if Partnership first distributed the inventory to Geraldo (a transaction producing no gain, reducing the basis for Geraldo's interest from $20,000 to $14,000, and giving him a basis of $6,000 for the inventory). He is then treated as having sold the inventory back to the partnership. This sale produces $9,000 in ordinary income (the inventory was sold for $15,000 and had a $6,000 basis). **[pp. 40–41]**
20.a.	**$9,000 CAPITAL LOSS AND $13,000 ORDINARY INCOME**	Toni received $1,000 for her interest in the assets; because her basis was $10,000, she has a $9,000 capital loss. The remaining $13,000 is treated as a distributive share of partnership income and therefore is taxable to her on the last day of the partnership's taxable year. Her basis is increased $13,000 and is then decreased $13,000 by the cash distribution. **[p. 44]**
b.	**$13,000 DEDUCTIBLE**	Because $13,000 of the payment is treated as a distributive share, it reduces the distributive shares taxed to the other partners; the effect of this is the same as a deduction. The $1,000 is not deductible. **[p. 44]**
c.	**ORDINARY INCOME**	This is treated as a guaranteed payment and is taxed in full. **[pp. 19, 44]**
d.	**DEDUCTIBLE**	Guaranteed payments are deductible by the partnership. **[p. 19]**

21.a.	**$4,000 ORDINARY INCOME, $7,000 CAPITAL GAIN**	Under I.R.C. section 736(b), payments made in exchange for the partnership interest are treated as distributions; if made in cash, they give rise to capital gain or loss. However, payments for goodwill are treated under I.R.C. section 736(a) instead of I.R.C. section 736(b) unless the partnership agreement specifically provides for a payment of goodwill, which it does not here. However, payments for goodwill are section 736(a) payments only if the partner is a general partner and capital is not a material income-producing factor in the partnership. Therefore, the $4,000 paid for goodwill is a guaranteed payment under I.R.C. section 736(a). The balance of the payment—$17,000—is in exchange for the partnership interest, which has a basis of $10,000. Therefore, Vic has a $7,000 capital gain. **[pp. 45, 45]**
b.	**$4,000 DEDUCTION**	Payments under I.R.C. section 736(a) are deductible by the partnership; payments under I.R.C. section 736(b) are not. **[pp. 44–46]**
c.	**$11,000 CAPITAL GAIN**	Now that the partnership agreement makes this specific provision, the payment for goodwill is treated under I.R.C. section 736(b) and the entire payment gives rise to capital gain or loss. **[p. 45]**
22.a.	**$500 CAPITAL LOSS**	When substantially appreciated inventory or unrealized receivables are distributed to a partner in liquidation of her interest, they will have the same basis in her hands as they had in the partnership's hands, or $3,500. This is a situation in which loss can be recognized. Note that if the distribution had not been of Edwina's pro rata interest in the inventory, the partnership would have realized gain on the distribution of the inventory under I.R.C. section 751(b). However, this occurs only if the partner receives the receivables or inventory in exchange for her interest in other partnership assets. **[p. 47]**
b.	**$4,000 CAPITAL GAIN**	The IBM stock is a marketable security and is thus treated like cash at the time of the liquidating distribution. **[p. 38]**
23.	**$7,000 ORDINARY INCOME, $5,000 CAPITAL LOSS**	Payments for unrealized receivables must be taxed under I.R.C. section 736(a); therefore the $7,000 payment is a guaranteed payment and is ordinary income. This leaves only $5,000 of the payment to be allocated against Warren's basis; therefore, he has a $5,000 capital loss. Note that the treatment of payments for unrealized receivables under section 736(a) occurs only if the partner is a general partner and capital is not a material income-producing factor in the partnership. **[p. 44]**
24.	**NO**	X and Y Corps. are brother-sister corporations within the meaning of I.R.C. sections 1561 through 1563 and must share the low brackets. Brother-sister corporations fall within these rules if more than 50% of the stock is owned by the same five or fewer persons, taking into account their interests only to the extent they are identical. Babette has at least 40% of both X and Y, and Clarisse has at least 50% of both X and Y. Thus, their ownership is 90% identical and they meet the test. **[p. 55]**

25.	**YES**	X Corp. can be charged with income under I.R.C. section 482. Y Corp. is given a deduction. **[p. 56]**
26.	**NO**	The standards for ignoring the corporate entity are different in tax cases than in corporate law cases. Because the corporation actually carried on business, it will be recognized as a taxable entity. This means that the shareholders cannot deduct the losses on their returns. Assuming that Splash Corp. never does any other business, these losses will not give rise to a tax benefit to anyone. **[p. 58]**
27.	**NO**	Section 1239 applies if the individual owns more than 50% of the stock. The stock owned by Dee's children would be attributed to her. Therefore, Dee has 100% of the stock, and thus she has ordinary income. **[p. 60]**
28.a.	**YES**	Under *Donruss*, if the tax avoidance is one of the purposes for accumulation, the tax is applicable. **[p. 62]**
b.	**YES**	Under the *Ivan Allen* case, marketable assets have to be valued at current value, not book value, in deciding whether assets have been retained beyond reasonable needs. **[p. 63]**
c.	**YES**	Reasonable needs of the business include reasonably anticipated needs. If the court decides that this really was the purpose for the accumulation, the amount accumulated for this purpose is deductible from accumulated taxable income. **[pp. 63, 64]**
d.	**COMMISSIONER**	If taxpayer submits a sufficiently specific statement of the reasons for its accumulation, the burden shifts to the Commissioner in Tax Court to prove that the assets were accumulated beyond reasonable business needs. **[p. 64]**
e.	**YES**	A nonpayment of dividends and the making of loans to shareholders tend to indicate that the corporation accumulated assets beyond its reasonable business needs. **[p. 63]**
29.	**YES**	Oscar Worthy is owned by one individual and 90% of its income is personal holding company income. This is so because Oscar Worthy's contract with the studios names the individual who will perform the services. Because more than 60% of the adjusted ordinary gross income is personal holding company income, the corporation is liable for the tax. It subtracts the income tax paid for the year ($26,750); the balance of its income ($73,250) is subject to the 50% personal holding company tax. **[pp. 65–68]**
30.	**NO**	This is covered by I.R.C. section 351. Fern and Gloria are in the control group and together they own 100% of the stock of the corporation. Consequently, neither recognizes any gain or loss on the exchange. The corporation's basis for the land is $35,000. Gloria's basis for her stock is $35,000. **[p. 68]**
31.	**$25,000 ORDINARY INCOME; $55,000 CAPITAL GAIN**	Assuming that the corporation is worth $100,000, Ida's 25% interest is worth $25,000. Stock received for services is ordinary income. (Obviously the valuation here is questionable because the only tangible asset is the IBM stock worth $75,000. Consequently, Ida's 25% interest might be worth less than

$25,000.) Harold must recognize his gain because the transferors of property did not receive 80% control. **[pp. 68, 71–72]**

32.a.	**NO**	Hal is within I.R.C. section 351. The assumption of liabilities is not treated as boot (I.R.C. section 357(a)). **[pp. 68, 74–75]**
b.	**$4,000**	The basis of the stock is the same as the basis of the assets transferred, minus liabilities assumed. **[p. 79]**
c.	**$10,000**	The basis of the assets is the same as in Hal's hands. **[p. 78]**
d.	**$1,500 GAIN**	When liabilities exceed basis, gain is recognized (I.R.C. section 357(c)). **[pp. 75–76]**
e.	**ZERO**	The basis for the stock is the basis for the assets transferred ($10,000), plus gain recognized ($1,500), minus liabilities assumed ($11,500). **[p. 79]**
f.	**$11,500**	Corporation's basis is the same as the transferor's basis ($10,000), plus gain recognized to him ($1,500). **[p. 78]**
g.	**$10,000 (PROBABLY)**	Under section 362(e)(2), property transferred to a corporation in a section 351 transaction with a built-in loss is held by the corporation with a fair market value basis, absent an election to limit the transferor's basis in the stock to fair market value. **[p. 79]**
33.a.	**$12,000 GAIN**	I.R.C. section 351 is applicable, but gain is recognized to the extent of the boot. Basis of the stock is $40,000. **[p. 73]**
b.	**$38,000 GAIN**	In an I.R.C. section 351 transfer, gain is recognized up to the amount of boot, but never more than the total realized gain. Basis of the stock is $28,000. **[p. 74]**
c.	**NO GAIN OR LOSS**	Loss is never recognized in an I.R.C. section 351 transfer, even though boot is paid. Basis of the stock is $90,000. **[p. 73]**
34.	**$5,000 GAIN (PROBABLY)**	A promissory note is probably treated as boot, and gain is recognized up to the amount of the boot. However, if debt is classified as "equity" no gain would be recognized. **[p. 73]**
35.a.	**YES**	Under the *Whipple* case, the debt is a nonbusiness bad debt and its worthlessness gives rise to a capital loss. **[p. 83]**
b.	**$50,000 ORDINARY LOSS; $35,000 CAPITAL LOSS**	The stock is I.R.C. section 1244 stock. This entitles Leah to $50,000 (as a single person) of ordinary loss. The remainder of the basis allocated to the stock is capital loss. **[p. 84]**
36.	**PROBABLY NOT**	Whether debt will be treated as equity depends on an analysis of all factors. Negative factors here: stock and debt are held proportionately; outside lender would not have made the loan; debt to equity ratio (6:1) is fairly high. Thus the debt is likely to be treated as equity. **[pp. 85–86]**
37.	**$59,000**	The earnings and profits are increased by nontaxable items, such as interest on state and municipal bonds. It is decreased by income taxes, dividends, and such nondeductible items as unreasonable compensation. **[p. 92]**

38.a.	**YES**	Although there are no current earnings and profits, the dividend is less than the accumulated earnings and profits of $100,000 and is therefore taxable. **[pp. 92–94]**
b.	**$500**	Dividends are subject to tax according to the capital gains rate. Therefore, Alvin's 50% share of the $5,000 dividend is subject to a 20% rate.
c.	**NO**	The corporation has neither current nor accumulated earnings and profits. Therefore the dividend is not taxable. Instead it would reduce the basis of the stock of the shareholder and, if it exceeds basis, it would be capital gain. **[p. 96]**
39.	**$8,000 ORDINARY INCOME**	Under I.R.C. section 243(c), a corporation may deduct 80% of the dividends received from a more than 20% owned corporation. Because P Corp. owns 25% of S Corp., P Corp. must include only 20%, or $8,000, of the $40,000 value of the land distributed. **[pp. 94–96]**
40.	**$299,000 CAPITAL GAIN**	Under I.R.C. section 331, a complete liquidation produces capital gain or loss. The earnings and profits are irrelevant. **[pp. 99, 100]**
41.	**NO**	Pedro is entitled to use the installment method to collect on the note. Therefore, he is not immediately taxed on the value of the note. **[p. 100]**
42.a.	**NO GAIN OR LOSS**	Under I.R.C. section 332, the liquidation of a subsidiary (of which the parent owns more than 80%) is a nontaxable transaction. **[p. 101]**
b.	**$18,000**	In a section 332 liquidation, the parent corporation acquires the same basis as the basis of the assets in the hands of the subsidiary. **[p. 102]**
c.	**$42,600**	A section 338 election steps up the basis of B's assets to A's purchase price plus liabilities. **[p. 125]**
43.a.	**NO**	Sub Corp. does not recognize gain on distribution of assets to an 80% or more shareholder in a section 332 liquidation. **[p. 102]**
b.	**YES**	Sub Corp. recognizes gain on distribution of assets to minority shareholder in a section 332 liquidation. **[p. 102]**
44.a.	**YES**	This redemption is covered by I.R.C. section 302(b)(3) as a complete termination. There is no attribution between brothers. **[p. 103]**
b.	**NO**	The distribution is taxed as a dividend (assuming there are earnings and profits equal to at least $20,000). Bob's stock is now attributed to Al, so that Al is treated as owner of 100% of the stock in the corporation before and after the redemption. Because Al continues to work for X, the waiver of attribution provision of I.R.C. section 302(c)(2) is not applicable. **[pp. 103–105,]**
c.	**YES**	The waiver of attribution provision of I.R.C. section 302(c)(2) is now applicable. This provision waives family attribution provided that the distributee has no continuing interest in the

corporation and files the agreement to notify the IRS if he acquires an interest in the next 10 years. **[pp. 105–106]**

d. **PROBABLY $20,000 DIVIDEND**

Stock is attributed from the beneficiary of the estate to the estate. So the estate is treated as owning 100% of the stock before and after the redemption. The waiver of family attribution does not apply because it waives only family attribution, not attribution to estates. **[pp. 104, 106]**

e. **NO GAIN OR LOSS**

Now the waiver of attribution provision of I.R.C. section 302(c)(2) is applicable and it breaks the chain of family attribution between Bob and Gladys. **[p. 106]**

45. **PROBABLY REDEMPTION**

To qualify as a redemption under I.R.C. section 302(b)(2), the shareholder must have less than 80% of the ratio that she had before. Previously, Carol had 40% of the stock. After the redemption, she has one-third (30 shares out of 90), or 33 1/3%. However, she would have to have less than 32% (80% of 40) to qualify under I.R.C. section 302(b)(2). Nevertheless, under IRS ruling policies, there is an excellent possibility that the transaction would be treated as a redemption under I.R.C. section 302(b)(1) as a "meaningful reduction" in Carol's interest. **[pp. 106–108]**

46. **NO**

This appears to be a partial liquidation under I.R.C. section 302(b)(4), resulting from a bona fide contraction of the corporate business. Therefore, Ida is entitled to be treated as if she received capital gain or loss from the sale or exchange of a capital asset rather than the less favorable treatment of net capital gain from the receipt of qualified dividend income. **[pp. 108–109]**

47. **NO**

Under I.R.C. section 303, the corporation can repurchase shares and not have them taxed as a dividend to the extent of the estate's death taxes and administration expenses. The shares must total more than 35% of her gross estate (less certain deductions). **[p. 110]**

48. **NO**

Under the *Zenz* case, it is treated as a complete termination. **[p. 111]**

49. **NO**

Under the rules of I.R.C. section 304(a)(1), this sale is treated as if Ned contributed the Alpha shares to Beta. Following this contribution, Ned still owns 60% of Alpha Corp. shares—50% directly, 10% because of attribution from Beta Corp. (Because he owns 100% of the stock of Beta, Beta's stock in Alpha is all attributed to Ned.) Because Ned's interest in Alpha did not go down at all, he cannot meet the standards of I.R.C. section 302. Consequently, the "sale" is treated as a dividend from Beta. Because Alpha and Beta combined have more than enough earnings and profits, the entire $10,000 is a dividend. Beta has a basis of $1,000 for its Alpha stock. Ned's basis for his Beta shares rises by $1,000. **[p. 113]**

50.a. **YES**

A corporation recognizes gain when it distributes appreciated assets to pay a dividend. **[p. 114]**

b.	**YES**	A corporation recognizes gain in connection with distribution of its appreciated assets in partial or complete liquidation. **[p. 114]**
51.	**NO**	X Corp. cannot recognize loss on property distributed as a dividend or redemption. **[p. 114]**
52.	**YES**	X Corp. is taxed on gain or loss on sale of its assets even though the sale occurs as part of complete liquidation. Thus, there is double tax—on the corporation and again on the shareholders. **[p. 115]**
53.a.	**NO**	This is tax free under I.R.C. section 305. **[p. 118]**
b.	**NO**	A dividend of preferred stock on common stock is not taxable. **[p. 118]**
c.	**YES**	If a shareholder has the right to choose either stock or property, the stock dividend is taxable. **[p. 118]**
d.	**YES**	If the distribution gives property to some shareholders and increases the interest of others, the stock dividend is taxable. **[p. 118]**
54.a.	**NO**	Stock dividends of preferred on common stock are not taxable. **[pp. 118, 119]**
b.	**$5,000**	The basis of the old common stock is divided among the common and preferred shares in proportion to their respective fair market values. Because the two blocks of stock have the same value, the basis is divided equally between them. **[p. 118]**
c.	**$20,000 NET CAPITAL GAIN, $5,000 BASIS RECOVERY, $1,000 CAPITAL GAIN**	I.R.C. section 306 is applicable to this sale. When the preferred stock was first distributed, there would have been $20,000 of net capital gain (gain that was fully includible in income and that could not be offset against capital losses) if cash had been distributed instead. **[p. 119]** Therefore, the preferred stock has a $20,000 "taint" that is fully includible as net capital gain when the stock is sold. After $20,000, basis can be recovered ($5,000) and the balance after recovery is capital gain. **[pp. 119–120]**
d.	**$21,000 CAPITAL GAIN**	When section 306 stock is redeemed, the "taint" that was originally on the stock is ignored; instead, the earnings and profits at the time of the redemption are the relevant measure. Because there are no earnings and profits, I.R.C. section 306 is not applicable. There cannot be a dividend if there are no earnings and profits, so the amount received is offset against basis, and the balance is capital gain. **[pp. 119–120]**
e.	**$21,000 CAPITAL GAIN**	Now there has been a complete termination of Zeb's interest in the corporation, so I.R.C. section 306 is not applicable. Therefore the sale of the preferred stock gives rise to capital gain. **[p. 120]**
55.a.	**NONE**	The consequences of a section 338 election occur at the level of the controlled corporation—not at the shareholder level. **[pp. 125–127]**

b.	**NONE**	Although the election is treated as if A Corp. sold its assets and repurchased them, there is no actual liquidation of A Corp., and thus Xavier is not affected. **[p. 126]**
c.	**YES, $440,000**	Gain is fully recognized in connection with a section 338 election. **[p. 126]**
d.	**$430,000**	The gross-up fraction is 80/75. The numerator (80) is 100 less the percentage of nonrecently purchased stock (20). The denominator is the percentage of recently purchased stock (75). 80/75 × $300,000 = $320,000. Then add the liabilities ($100,000) and the basis of the nonrecently purchased stock ($10,000). Here, if P Corp. had elected to recognize the gain on its nonrecently purchased stock, it would have used a gross-up fraction of 100/95 instead of 80/75. **[p. 126]**
56.a.	**NO GAIN OR LOSS**	This appears to be a tax-free corporate division under I.R.C. section 355. Both of the businesses have been conducted more than five years, there is a valid business purpose, and there does not appear to be any indication of a device to distribute earnings and profits. This transaction is called a "split-off." Because it meets the requirements of section 355, it is a tax-free reorganization. Bob recognizes no gain or loss, and Rec Corp. recognizes no gain or loss on distributions of Nets. **[p. 132]**
b.	**PROBABLY TAXABLE AS CAPITAL GAIN**	Assuming that Rec Corp. had two separate businesses, one of them has not been conducted for five years, and this disqualifies the transaction under I.R.C. section 355. Therefore, the transaction is taxed as a redemption or as a partial liquidation to Bob, either of which produces capital gain. Rec recognizes gain or loss on the distribution of Nets. However, the taxpayers would argue that there has been only a single construction business, which has been divided in half. Because part of the construction business had been carried on more than five years, it may well be that the entire transaction qualifies under section 355 and the *Coady* case. *Coady* permitted a single business that had been conducted more than five years to be divided in parts; the fact that one of the parts had been conducted less than five years would not matter. **[pp. 135–136]**
57.	**DIVIDEND**	This does not qualify under I.R.C. section 355. It is quite similar to the famous *Gregory* case. There was no "business purpose" for the spin-off; instead, it was a tax avoidance device. It appears to be a device for the distribution of earnings and profits under section 355. Moreover, land ownership is not a separate active business. For all these reasons, section 355 is not applicable. Therefore, the spin-off should be treated as a dividend (assuming that the corporation had earnings and profits equal to or greater than the value of Y stock). X Corp. recognizes gain or loss on distributions of Y stock. **[pp. 132–133]**
58.a.	**NO**	This is a "D" reorganization qualifying under I.R.C. section 354(b), which applies if "substantially all" the assets have been

transferred. Here, all the liquid assets were removed from Lincoln & Douglas, but the essential part necessary to conduct the law practice was all reincorporated in Grant & Lee. Therefore Grant & Lee has acquired substantially all the assets of Lincoln & Douglas. Because this transaction was a reorganization, all the property distributed to the shareholders is taxed as a dividend (although it will be taxed at capital gains rates). [pp. 141–142]

b. **YES**

If there is not 50% continuity of interest between the old and new corporations, the transaction cannot be considered a reorganization. Therefore the liquidation of Lincoln & Douglas Corp. is entitled to capital gains treatment. The IRS might argue that the whole transaction was a sham, but has not had too much success with this theory. [p. 141]

59.a. **NO**

This is an "A" reorganization, and gain or loss is not recognized. The fact that nonvoting stock of International was used is irrelevant. [p. 142]

b. **PROBABLY YES**

This is no longer a reorganization because there is insufficient continuity of interest. The fact that only 20% of the value of Local is represented by stock in International would probably disqualify the transaction. Therefore, it is entirely taxable. [p. 146]

c. **NO**

This transaction qualifies as a reorganization because there is sufficient continuity of interest. However, the bonds are treated as boot, and gain will be recognized to the extent of the boot. [p. 157]

d. **NO**

Because the transaction qualified as a reorganization and because Local distributed all of the International stock to its shareholders, it does not recognize gain on the transfer of its assets even though International paid partly with boot. [p. 157]

60.a. **YES**

While the Commissioner no longer gives rulings on most reorganization issues, this meets what used to be the Commissioner's ruling policy for a "C" reorganization. Seventy percent of the gross assets is $56,000. The net assets are $64,000 and 90% of them would be $57,600. Therefore, acquiring $60,000 of the assets qualifies under the Commissioner's ruling policy as being "substantially all." [p. 153]

b. **NO**

A "C" reorganization must involve a transfer of assets "solely" for voting stock. There is a narrow exception in which boot equal to not more than 20% of the value of the assets can be given; however, the liabilities assumed count as boot. In this case, boot ($2,000) plus the liabilities ($16,000) would total $18,000, which is more than 20% of the assets. [p. 150]

c. **NO**

A "C" reorganization can involve only voting stock. [p. 150]

d. **YES**

It is permissible to use voting stock of a parent of the acquired corporation. [p. 151]

e. **YES**

As long as the promise is to issue voting stock, it is permissible. The additional stock can be issued without recognition of any gain. To obtain a favorable ruling, the promise can extend for not more than five years and at least 50% of the total stock that can ever be issued must be issued immediately. **[p. 153]**

61.a.	**NO**	It is necessary to obtain at least 80% of the voting stock in order for the transaction to qualify as a "B" reorganization. **[p. 144]**
b.	**YES**	In a "B" reorganization, the acquiring corporation can use only voting stock as the medium of exchange. The transaction here is entirely disqualified from reorganization treatment. Even if International had acquired 80% of Local's stock in exchange for stock and the shareholder had received only stock, reorganization treatment would be denied. **[pp. 149–150]**
c.	**YES**	Under the continuity of interest regulations, a post-reorganization sale of stock, even if it is prearranged, will not defeat continuity unless the sale was to International Corp. or a related party. **[p. 146]**
62.a.	**YES**	Under I.R.C. section 381, a loss carryforward (along with other tax attributes) will survive an "A" or "C" reorganization. **[p. 159]**
b.	**NO**	In case of an equity shift of more than 50%, the loss can be used only against International's earnings equal to the value of Local at the time of the shift times the tax exempt bond interest rate. **[p. 160]**
c.	**NO**	Under I.R.C. section 269(a)(2), if the primary purpose of the acquisition was to obtain the loss carryforward, it is wiped out. **[p. 159]**
63.a.	**YES**	There are now 101 shareholders, assuming the two new shareholders are not family members and neither are members of the same family as an existing shareholder, and the election is terminated. **[pp. 166, 169]**
b.	**NO**	An estate can be a shareholder of an S corporation. **[p. 166]**
c.	**YES**	If it so elects, the trust qualifies as an electing small business trust ("ESBT"), which can hold stock in an S corporation. **[p. 167]**
d.	**NO**	A pooling agreement does not create a second class of stock, which would disqualify the corporation. **[p. 167]**
e.	**NO**	Debt classified as equity will not be treated as a second class of stock if it is "straight debt," meaning that it is a written, unconditional promise to pay a sum certain, the interest rate is fixed, the debt is not convertible into stock, and the creditor is an individual, estate, or qualifying trust. **[p. 167]**
64.	**YES**	An election must be filed by March 15 of the taxable year, or at any time during the preceding taxable year. **[p. 168]**
65.a.	**YES**	Zeta has passive income and subchapter C earnings and profits. It must pay tax on 75% of its net passive income. **[p. 170]**
b.	**YES**	If an S corporation has gross receipts consisting of passive income for three consecutive years and it has subchapter C

earnings and profits, its election is terminated at the beginning of the fourth year. [p. 169]

66. **NO** Lambda is not liable for the built-in gains tax under section 1374 because it had an S election in effect for all of its taxable years. [p. 170]

67.a. **$100,000** The entire $100,000 of corporate income is taxed to her. The distribution is not taxable. [pp. 171, 173]

b. **INCREASES $82,000** The basis of stock is increased by $100,000 and reduced by $18,000. [pp. 171–172]

68. **YES** Juanita is entitled to offset the loss against both the basis of the stock and corporate debts. Because she had more than $100,000 of basis available, she can deduct the entire loss. The basis of her stock is now zero and the basis of her debt has been reduced to $25,000. [pp. 171–172]

Exam Questions
and Answers

QUESTION I

Cam Shaft was the sole proprietor of Greasepit Garage, an unincorporated automobile repair business. For a number of years, Mike Rometer had been his foreman. Rometer's salary was $1,000 per month.

Rometer announced he was thinking about quitting in order to start his own garage. To induce him to stay, Shaft said, "Look—I just can't spare you. Would you stay if I gave you a one-third interest in the business?" Rometer nodded. Shaft shook Rometer's hand and said, "Welcome, partner." This occurred as both men were in a festive mood on January 1 of Year 5.

On January 3 of Year 6, things were quite different. Sullen with a hangover, Shaft became incensed at Rometer's spitting tobacco juice. Shaft said, "I can't stand you anymore. I want you out now. I'll pay you $20,000 for your interest in the business." Rometer accepted gladly. Shaft immediately wrote out a check for $20,000 drawn on Greasepit's account.

During Year 5, Greasepit continued to pay Rometer $1,000 per month. Rometer made no other cash withdrawals from the business.

During the calendar year of Year 5, Greasepit made a profit of $27,000 (*after subtracting* the payment of $1,000 per month to Rometer). Greasepit was worth $36,000 on January 1 of Year 5; it was worth $60,000 on January 1 of Year 6.

On January 1 of Year 6, the assets were:

		Basis	Value
Cash		$25,000	$25,000
Machinery & Equipment			
Original Cost	$30,000		
Depreciation	-16,000	14,000	26,000
Goodwill		-0-	9,000
	Total:		$60,000

There were no liabilities.

What are the *income tax* consequences to *Rometer* in Year 5 and Year 6? (Ignore the consequences to Shaft and Greasepit.)

Assume: Rometer uses the cash method of accounting. All machinery and equipment were purchased in Year 1. No documents were executed to evidence any of the transactions. No partnership tax elections were made.

QUESTION II

Speculation Land Corporation has been engaged since Year 1 in the real estate development business. Its sole shareholders are Arnold and Clyde (who are unrelated). Prior to the transaction set forth in this problem, Arnold owned 1,200 shares of stock having a basis of $200 per share ($240,000 total basis). Clyde owned 600 shares having a basis of $200 per share ($120,000 total basis). The stock is section 1244 stock. Speculation is not an S corporation.

Speculation operated profitably for several years but has had some losses since Year 4. Nevertheless, it has accumulated earnings and profits of $250,000. Starting in Year 5, Speculation developed a large tract of land in Ventura County, California. It sold almost all of the homesites, but it retained a shopping center site in hopes that it could later build and operate a shopping center. However, its cash difficulties were such that it had to sell the shopping center site, and in Year 7, it began to make vigorous selling efforts. The basis to Speculation for its shopping center site was

$160,000. There was a $110,000 mortgage on the shopping center site. It may be assumed that the land is not a capital asset or a section 1231 asset in the hands of either Speculation or its shareholders.

In Year 8, a possible buyer—Blight, Inc.—was found. After several months of negotiation, it was agreed that the property (if unmortgaged) was worth $150,000, so that Speculation's equity was $40,000. A rough oral agreement was worked out that Blight would pay $40,000 cash and take subject to the mortgage. On April 1 of Year 8, Clyde asked the attorney for Blight if there would be any objection to his selling the site as an individual rather than through the corporation. There being no objection, on April 10 of Year 8, Speculation conveyed the property (subject to the mortgage) to Clyde in exchange for 300 shares of stock (which had a basis of $60,000).

On April 18 of Year 8, Clyde sold the property to Blight for $40,000 cash, subject to the mortgage.

Clyde reported on his income tax return that he had a $20,000 long-term capital loss on the exchange of his shares for the property (computed on a fair market value of $40,000 for the property and a $60,000 basis for the stock). Only $3,000 of this loss was deducted on his return, as he had no capital gains against which he could offset the balance of the loss. He reported no gain or loss on the sale of the property to Blight. Speculation Land Corp. reported no gain or loss on this transaction. Did Clyde and Speculation correctly report these transactions? Discuss. (Ignore the effect of sections 341, 482, and 1237 on this transaction; ignore the tax consequences to Arnold and to Blight, Inc.; assume that all taxpayers are on the cash basis.)

QUESTION III

Glen and Barbara were 50–50 partners in Treacle Co., a general partnership. Treacle is engaged in conceiving ideas for a television series, producing pilot films for the proposed series (a pilot film is a single filmed episode), and actually producing the series if it is accepted by a network.

Production of TV pilots is very expensive and risky. Glen and Barbara try to avoid using their own funds; instead, they try to interest investors in putting up the money to produce pilots. When a series is accepted by a network, Treacle often produces the TV series itself; on several occasions, however, Treacle has sold its rights in an accepted series to outside investors. When the series has been sold to outside investors, Glen or Barbara will produce the series as an employee of the purchaser.

In Year 5, all of Treacle's former series had been canceled. It was having difficulty producing any new pilots or selling the few it did produce. Barbara wrote a script for a pilot film for a series based on the life of first-year law students. The series would be called *Halls of Brick*. In April of Year 5, Barbara and Glen asked Kenny, a wealthy investor, to help finance a pilot for *Halls of Brick*. They needed about $100,000 to make the pilot.

Kenny did not have the cash available, but he had a piece of vacant land in Oxnard. The land had a basis of $5,000 in his hands, was subject to a first mortgage of $10,000, and was worth $150,000. Kenny suggested that the necessary funds could be raised by borrowing on the land. Accordingly, he suggested that there be a corporation ("Brick, Inc.") formed to produce a pilot and, hopefully, future episodes of *Halls of Brick*. Kenny would receive 50% of the stock of Brick, Inc. in exchange for the Oxnard land; he would also receive Brick, Inc.'s promissory note in the amount of $100,000, payable with 8% interest in two years. The note could be prepaid at any time. Treacle Co. would receive the remaining 50% of the stock in exchange for the script of *Halls of Brick* and Treacle's promise to devote itself full-time to producing a pilot and, if it is accepted, the subsequent series. The parties valued the idea and script for *Halls of Brick* at $10,000 (although it had a zero basis for tax purposes). Barbara told Kenny that there was a good chance that Brick, Inc. could sell *Halls of*

Brick to an outside investor, once it was accepted by a network; in that case, Kenny could get a quicker return on his investment.

Brick, Inc. was formed in June of Year 5, in accordance with Kenny's suggestions. He conveyed the Oxnard land, subject to the first mortgage, in exchange for the Brick, Inc. stock and note. In July of Year 5, Brick, Inc. borrowed an additional $100,000 on security of the Oxnard property, but it had no personal liability to repay the loan (*i.e.,* it was a nonrecourse loan). By December of Year 5, Barbara had completed the pilot. Because it cost only $88,000 to produce, the unneeded $12,000 was paid to Kenny in December in Year 5, in order to reduce the balance owing on his promissory note.

In January of Year 6, the pilot was shown to NBC executives. They were ecstatic and agreed to take one year's worth of *Halls of Brick* with an option to take three additional years. As a result, the stock of Brick, Inc. was worth $1 million in January of Year 6.

In February of Year 6, Glen and Barbara had a furious argument over the future of Treacle. As a result, Barbara purchased Glen's interest in Treacle in exchange for $400,000 in cash. Glen had held his interest for 10 years, and it had an outside basis in his hands of $150,000.

In February of Year 6, the parties had made no decision about whether to produce *Halls of Brick* themselves or sell it to outside investors. However, in April of Year 6, they decided not to sell it. Instead, Brick, Inc. began producing the series itself. Brick, Inc. made no cash distributions in Year 6.

The *fair market value* of Treacle's assets (it had no liabilities) in February of Year 1 was as follows:

Cash	$250,000
TV production equipment*	50,000
Stock in Brick, Inc.	500,000
Total:	$800,000

* The basis for income tax purposes of the TV production equipment was $10,000. Straight-line depreciation of $80,000 had been claimed on the equipment.

What are the federal income tax consequences of the Year 5 and Year 6 events to **Kenny** and to **Glen**? Ignore consequences to Brick, Inc., Barbara, or NBC. Assume that the script, pilot film, and completed episodes of *Halls of Brick* are assets described in sections 1221(3) and 1231(b)(1)(C), and that Brick, Inc. did not elect subchapter S.

QUESTION IV

Argon Corp. has 300 shares outstanding. They are owned by Max Smith (25 shares), Smith Family Trust (100 shares), Taurus Corp. (100 shares), and Paul Smith (75 shares). Max is 70 years old and has been the chief executive officer of Argon for many years. He wishes to retire; in conjunction with his retirement, Argon plans to purchase his shares at their market value of $220,000.

Argon plans to pay for Max's stock with cash ($50,000), an interest-bearing promissory note ($100,000), and a piece of investment real estate (value $70,000, basis $200,000).

Argon's earnings and profits are $100,000. Max inherited his shares in 1982 from his mother, Gilda. The shares were worth $55,000 when Gilda died. Gilda had originally purchased the shares for $1,000 in 1960. Max's father, Lloyd, is still alive but has never owned any stock in Argon.

The Smith Family Trust is a testamentary trust set up by Gilda when she died. Max is the trustee of this trust. The beneficiaries consist of Dorothy (Max's daughter) and Earl (Paul's son). Paul is Max's younger brother who will take over Max's job when Max retires. Unfortunately, Paul is in ill health, and it is possible that Max might have to take over management of Argon if anything happens to Paul.

Taurus Corp. is also controlled by the Smith family. Dorothy owns 50% of the stock of Taurus; Earl owns the other 50%. Taurus acquired its shares in Argon in 1987 by converting into stock a loan it had previously made to Argon.

Advise Argon and Max of the tax consequences of the proposed purchase of his shares. Make suggestions for improving the tax consequences.

QUESTION V

RaceCo, Inc. has operated a drag strip for many years in Albuquerque. Although once profitable, the value of the business has plummeted because nobody wants to watch drag races any more. The shareholders of RaceCo are quite unhappy and want to sell out.

Cement, Inc., which operates a cement factory on land adjacent to RaceCo's drag strip, is interested in acquiring RaceCo's real property. Cement's stock is traded on the American Stock Exchange. Cement would like to tear down the bleachers and use the land for employee parking.

Cement, Inc. hopes to sell the real property someday to the city for a trash dump. Consequently, the Cement, Inc. management wants the real property to have as high a basis as possible. The shareholders of RaceCo are not interested in holding Cement, Inc. stock and plan to dispose of any Cement, Inc. stock as quickly as possible.

On June 30 of Year 1, Cement, Inc. exchanged two shares of its voting preferred stock for each share of RaceCo stock. The aggregate value of both the RaceCo stock and the Cement, Inc. preferred stock was $240,000. On July 10, RaceCo (now a subsidiary of Cement) sold all of its drag racing equipment and supplies to unrelated buyers for $40,000—an amount exactly equal to the adjusted basis of those assets. On July 11, Cement, Inc. completely liquidated RaceCo, acquiring its $80,000 in cash and the drag strip. On July 20, Cement, Inc. converted the drag strip into a parking lot. The RaceCo shareholders began selling their Cement, Inc. stock immediately and, by July 15, all of it had been sold.

On July 1, the adjusted basis of RaceCo's real property was $600,000. Its market value was $160,000. RaceCo had no net operating loss carryforward.

Stan Stock, an unmarried RaceCo shareholder, owned 5% of RaceCo's stock, which had a basis of $80,000 and was worth $12,000 on June 30. It was not section 1244 stock. He had owned it since 1976. He received Cement, Inc. stock worth $12,000. He sold the Cement, Inc. stock on July 7 for $13,200.

What are the tax consequences of the foregoing to RaceCo, to Cement, Inc., and to Stan Stock?

QUESTION VI

Prior to Year 1, Jane was a lawyer in solo practice. In Year 1, she formed Law, Inc., a professional law corporation. Law, Inc. does not make a subchapter S election. Law, Inc. issued one share to Jane, in exchange for one dollar. Jane transferred no other assets to Law, Inc., and made no contracts with it. Jane's office did not display the name of the corporation. A client knew nothing about the corporation until she received a bill from Law, Inc.

During Years 3 to 13, Law, Inc. received $300,000 per year attributable to Jane's services. It paid Jane a salary of $100,000 in each year. The corporation adopted a qualified pension plan and contributed $15,000 to it each year on Jane's behalf (the pension plan met all Code requirements). With its remaining funds, Law, Inc. invested in publicly traded stocks.

At the beginning of Year 13, the accumulated earnings and profits of Law, Inc. were $160,000. In Year 13, Law, Inc.'s gross income from legal services was $300,000 and its gross income from dividends was $125,000. What are the tax consequences to Jane and Law, Inc. in Year 13?

QUESTION VII

Peachco, Inc. has owned and operated peach orchards in California since Year 1 when it was formed by Jay. Jay contributed orchards having an adjusted basis in his hands of $95,000 in exchange for 100 shares of Peachco stock. This was the only stock ever issued. It was issued pursuant to a validly adopted plan under I.R.C. section 1244. The orchards were worth $140,000 in Year 1.

In Year 13, Jay gave 20 shares to his daughter Abby and 20 shares to his daughter Brenda. Both daughters were active in Peachco's management. Jay correctly paid no gift tax on the transfer. The main purpose of the gift was to give an equity interest to his daughters in recognition of their managerial skills. However, Jay also wanted to have part of his income from corporate dividends taxed to his daughters instead of himself. At the time of the gift, Brenda's 20 shares were worth $27,000.

In April of Year 26, Brenda and Jay had a major dispute about whether to diversify into growing kiwis (an exotic Australian fruit). A great deal of animosity resulted, and all parties decided that Brenda should be bought out. Consequently, in May of Year 26, Peachco repurchased Brenda's 20 shares in exchange for one of Peachco's peach orchards, which Brenda continued to manage on her own. Brenda withdrew entirely from Peachco's management and intends to stay out.

The orchard distributed to Brenda had been purchased by Peachco in 2000 for $10,000. (Assume that the entire cost was correctly allocated to the trees.) Straight-line depreciation of $6,000 had been claimed on the trees in the orchard. The present value of the trees in the orchard is $12,000 (assume that is the entire value of the orchard). Brenda's 20 shares were also worth $12,000 at the time they were repurchased. Peachco's accumulated earnings and profits were $80,000 in Year 26.

What are the consequences of the repurchase of Brenda's shares in Year 26 to Brenda and to Peachco?

QUESTION VIII

Prior to Year 1, Violet operated a tanning parlor as a cash basis sole proprietor. She had promised her faithful employee Burns that he would soon receive an interest in the business in return for his loyal services. Violet also wanted to involve Ray in the business because he could contribute much needed cash and could also contribute Wasteland, a potentially valuable piece of vacant real property. Besides, Violet wanted to give part of the business to her son Sonny, in order to interest him in business rather than in professional skateboarding. To achieve all these objectives, Tanbod, Inc. was incorporated on January 2 of Year 1.

On January 3 of Year 1, Violet transferred the assets of her proprietorship subject to liabilities to Tanbod, Inc. in exchange for 250 shares of stock and a Tanbod, Inc. unsecured $10,000 promissory note, payable in five years, with interest at 14% payable quarterly. Tanbod issued an additional 100 shares directly to Sonny. Violet filed a gift tax return to reflect this transfer but correctly paid no gift tax.

The following assets were transferred by Violet to Tanbod:

	Basis	Value
Cash	$20,000	
Accounts receivable	-0-	
Tanning machines (net of depreciation)*	12,000	14,000
Goodwill	-0-	58,000
Total:	$32,000	$100,000

* The tanning machines were purchased two years before for $16,000. They had an eight-year useful life. Straight-line depreciation of $4,000 has been claimed on the machines.

The proprietorship owed $40,000 in accounts payable. None of these payables had been deducted by Violet, nor had any of them been added to the basis of any asset.

On February 19 of Year 1, Tanbod issued 150 shares to Burns in consideration of his past and future services. The reasonable value of these shares was $15,000.

On March 13 of Year 1, Tanbod issued an additional 300 shares to Ray in exchange for cash of $20,000 and Wasteland. Wasteland had a basis of $35,000 in Ray's hands and a present value of $10,000. Thus, after the issuance of stock to Ray, there were 800 shares of stock outstanding: Violet (250), Sonny (100), Burns (150), and Ray (300).

Although Tanbod made a profit in Year 1, a brutal recession struck early in Year 2 and consumers cut back their purchases of nonessentials like artificial suntans. Business shriveled up, and in November of Year 2, Tanbod ceased operations and declared bankruptcy.

What are the federal *income tax* (not gift tax) consequences of the Year 1 transactions to Violet, Sonny, Burns, and Ray? What is the basis of the stock and debt instruments each received?

What was the basis of each asset Tanbod, Inc. received?

What are the consequences to Violet, Sonny, Burns, and Ray when Tanbod, Inc. declared bankruptcy and their various stock or debt instruments became worthless? (Assume that none of them is married.)

QUESTION IX

Art and Fab Corp. formed a limited partnership (Stretchco) on December 31 of Year 1, to run an aerobic dancing studio. Art agreed to be a general partner and run the studio. Fab Corp. agreed to be a limited partner and contribute a building suitable for the purpose. Fab Corp. manufactures trash compactors. It is closely held and not an S corporation. Art is not a shareholder of Fab Corp. They agreed to share 50–50 in any profits or losses.

a.   If both Art and Fab Corp. use the calendar year for tax purposes, can Stretchco adopt a fiscal year ending February 28?

b.   Art pays nothing for his partnership interest, which is estimated to have a fair market value of approximately $10,000. It is an interest solely in future profits, not in any of the assets contributed to Stretchco at its formation. Is Art taxable on receipt of his partnership interest?

c.   The building had an adjusted basis in Fab Corp.'s hands of $40,000 and a market value of $70,000. Fab Corp. claimed straight-line depreciation on the building totaling $12,000. The building is subject to a nonrecourse loan to Coast Savings in the amount of $30,000. What is Stretchco's basis for the building? What is Fab Corp.'s basis for its partnership interest? What is Art's basis for his partnership interest?

d. Pursuant to the partnership agreement, Stretchco paid Art a salary of $21,000 for his services in Year 2, the first year of operation. Not counting the salary, Stretchco had an operating loss of $12,000 in Year 2. How should Art and Fab Corp. have reflected the foregoing on their Year 2 tax returns?

e. Early in Year 3, Art died. The fair market value of his interest at the date of death was $17,000 (of which $4,000 is attributable to partnership goodwill). The moment before death, assume that Art's outside basis was $7,000. Stretchco had no unrealized receivables or substantially appreciated inventory. Fab Corp. paid Art's estate $17,000 for his interest. What are the tax consequences to Art's estate? Does Stretchco's taxable year close on Art's death? Does it close on the sale of the estate's interest in Fab Corp.?

ANSWER TO QUESTION I

Formation of Partnership: Although informal, the Year 5 events clearly should be treated as the formation of a partnership. Rometer has received a one-third interest for services. If it is a capital interest, he is immediately taxed on its value ($12,000—one-third of $36,000). This is a bargained-for business transaction, not a gift (despite the use of the word "give"). Thus, the income cannot be excluded under section 102.

If the interest received by Rometer is a profits interest, it is probably not taxable under *Campbell*, although *Diamond* would suggest that it is taxable. No ruling from the IRS could be obtained because Rometer sold the interest within one year. [Rev. Proc. 93–27] However, under the facts, it would seem that he received a capital interest. This is borne out by the fact that Shaft paid Rometer one-third the full fair market value of the assets only one year later. He would not have paid Rometer anything for the assets in the partnership if Rometer had only an interest in future profits.

Thus, Rometer has $12,000 of ordinary income. It could be argued that the partnership would have a deduction of $12,000 for compensation for services (which would reduce Rometer's distributive share of Year 5 profits), but this is unlikely. The partnership has, in effect, paid Rometer for future services for an indefinite period and should not receive any deduction for the same.

Rometer's basis for his interest is $12,000.

Year 5 Operations: Rometer's $12,000 salary is a guaranteed payment. It appears to be reasonable compensation for services. It is taxed as ordinary income to Rometer and does not affect his basis.

It was correct to subtract the $12,000 in salary from the Year 5 profits, as a guaranteed payment is ordinarily deductible. Thus, Rometer's distributive share of profit is $9,000 (one-third of the $27,000 Year 5 profit), which is taxed to him as ordinary income. It increases his basis for his interest from $12,000 to $21,000.

Year 6 Sale: The facts are not clear as to whether Rometer sold his interest to Shaft or Greasepit. There is no economic difference, but there is often a tax difference. Because Greasepit made the payment with its check, it is likely that it was the purchaser. However, in his "negotiations," Shaft said, "I'll pay you . . . " which suggests that he was the purchaser. This could go either way, but the fact that Greasepit actually paid for the interest would probably be decisive.

Note that the problem contains recapturable depreciation of $12,000, which is treated as an unrealized receivable. Rometer's share of this item is $4,000.

If the transaction is treated as a liquidation, the results differ depending on whether capital is a material income-producing factor. Probably, capital is material in an auto repair garage because of the substantial investment required in machinery and equipment.

If capital is *not* material, the payments for both goodwill and unrealized receivables are taxed as ordinary income to Rometer under section 736(a). Goodwill falls under section 736(a) because there is no written partnership agreement. Under this approach, there is ordinary income of $7,000 ($4,000 from the unrealized receivable, $3,000 from goodwill). The balance of the transaction is the receipt of $13,000 in exchange for Rometer's interest in other assets. This produces capital loss of $8,000 (outside basis of $21,000 less amount realized of $13,000).

If capital *is* material, the payments for all assets (including receivables and goodwill) are taxed under section 736(b). The amount allocable to the receivables, however, produces ordinary income of $4,000. Thus there is a capital loss of $5,000.

If Shaft is the purchaser instead of Greasepit, it is a sale under section 741. The results are the same as in the previous paragraph: $4,000 ordinary income, $5,000 capital loss.

ANSWER TO QUESTION II

Speculation: The sale should probably be attributed to Speculation under the *Court Holding Co.* doctrine. The deal had been pre-negotiated before the distribution, and Clyde's sale was immediate and at the same price as that negotiated by the corporation. Consequently, Speculation should be entitled to deduct its $10,000 ordinary loss.

If, however, the sale is not attributed to Speculation under *Court Holding Co.,* section 311(b) would prevent Speculation from deducting its loss.

It is possible from the facts that the transaction would be considered a partial liquidation. If so, and if *Court Holding Co.* is not applied, section 311(b) would still be applicable and Speculation still could not deduct its loss. A corporation can deduct loss on a distribution only in a complete liquidation. Because the property was being held for sale to customers in the ordinary course of business (this is known because it is neither a capital asset nor a section 1231 asset), it seems unlikely that it was a partial liquidation. It was just a disposition of inventory-type assets, not a disposition of part of the business.

Clyde: Clyde has sold 300 of his 600 shares. Prior to the deal, he owned one-third of the shares. After the deal, he has 300 of 1,500 (20%). Thus, he qualifies under section 302(b)(2) (he has less than 80% of his previous holdings and also less than 50%). Thus, the transaction is treated as a redemption, rather than a dividend, and there is a $20,000 loss.

The loss is an ordinary loss under section 1244 and is fully deductible by Clyde.

The land has a basis of $150,000 in his hands, and his sale of it to Blight produces no gain or loss.

If *Court Holding Co.* is applied, Clyde would be treated as receiving $40,000 in cash rather than the land. The consequences would be the same.

If the transaction was a partial liquidation, the result would again be the same to Clyde.

ANSWER TO QUESTION III

A. Formation of Brick, Inc.

1. **Kenny, Year 5:** Kenny's transfer of land qualifies under I.R.C. section 351 because the transferors of property to Brick have control of Brick. Although Treacle transferred property and services (*see infra*), it nevertheless qualifies as a transferor of property for section 351 control group purposes.

   Kenny must recognize capital gain of $25,000 under section 357(c) because the mortgage exceeded the basis of the property.

   The note for $100,000 should be treated as debt, not equity. The favorable relevant factors are the nonproportional holdings of stock and debt, and the reasonable debt-to-equity ratio of approximately two to one (assets are worth about $160,000, liabilities are $110,000, and thus equity is about $50,000). In addition, the debt calls for reasonable interest payments, confers no management rights, and is not subordinated. On the other hand, Brick's ability to pay the note in two years is questionable, so it might be argued that Kenny assumed greater risks than are normal for a creditor. Under the case law approach, the note should probably be recognized as debt.

   Thus, Kenny has received boot of $100,000. His $145,000 gain must be recognized to the extent of $100,000 (plus the $5,000 under section 357(c) already mentioned). The recognized gain is capital gain.

Kenny's basis for the debt is $100,000. His basis for the stock is zero (old basis of $5,000, plus gain of $105,000, less boot received of $100,000, less liability assumed of $10,000). Brick's basis for the land is $110,000 (old basis of $5,000 plus gain recognized of $105,000).

2. **Glen, Year 6:** Treacle has received stock for services, which is taxable despite section 351. However, the script can be transferred without recognition of gain under section 351. One way to value the stock received for service is to ask what would happen if Brick were dissolved the day after it was formed. After payment of debts ($10,000 mortgage, $100,000 to Kenny), there would be assets of $50,000 remaining (*i.e.,* assets are now worth $160,000, liabilities are $110,000). That would leave $25,000 for Treacle. Because it contributed property worth $10,000, the service element must have been $15,000. Thus, Glen's share of Treacle's income would be $7,500.

Treacle would have a basis of $15,000 for its stock. Brick would have a zero basis for the script. It probably could not deduct the amount paid for future services because this would have to be capitalized.

B. Corporate Borrowing

The corporation's borrowing produces no tax consequences to anyone. Section 465 would inhibit Brick from deducting losses, if it had any, because the $100,000 borrowed on security of the Oxnard property was not at risk. However, none of this is relevant to the problem, and clearly Kenny and Glen have no consequence.

C. Repayment of Kenny's Note

The note has a $100,000 basis. Repayment of the $12,000 is recovery of basis and is not taxed. If the debt had been considered as equity, the $12,000 payment would be a distribution taxed under I.R.C. section 301. However, because Brick had no earnings and profit in Year 5, it would not be a dividend. Instead it would be taxed as capital gain to the extent that it exceeded the basis of the "note."

D. Glen's Sale of His Interest in Treacle

On the surface, Glen would have a $250,000 long-term capital gain under section 741 on the sale of his interest. However, there is recapturable depreciation on the TV equipment. The recapturable depreciation is $40,000. Glen's share is $20,000; this is an unrealized receivable. Thus, $20,000 of the amount realized must be ordinary income.

ANSWER TO QUESTION IV

A. Tax Consequences

In considering a redemption of stock, it is necessary to first apply the section 318 attribution rules. In addition to his own 25 shares, Max is treated as owning 50 shares from the trust. Stock held by a trust is proportionately attributed to its beneficiaries; thus, 50 shares are attributed to Dorothy and, by family attribution, to Max. [I.R.C. § 318(a)(2)(B), (a)(1)(A)(ii)] In addition, Max owns 50 shares owned by Taurus for the same reason—Taurus's stock is attributed proportionately to Dorothy and then to Max. [I.R.C. § 318(a)(2)(C)]

However, the stock held by Paul and Earl is not attributed to Max. Although Paul's and Earl's stock can be attributed to Lloyd (Paul's father and Earl's grandfather), it cannot be reattributed to Max. Double family attributions are prohibited by section 318(a)(5)(B).

Max is treated as owning 125 shares of Argon before the redemption (*i.e.,* 41.7%) and 100 out of 275 shares after the redemption (36.4%). The issue is whether this qualifies as a redemption under section 302.

It does not qualify under section 302(b)(3) because it is not a complete termination. It does not qualify under section 302(b)(2) because Max's interest is not reduced to less than 80% of his former interest (it is only 87%). It is very possible, however, that Max qualified under section 302(b)(1) because there is a material reduction in his interest and he owns less than 50% of the stock by attribution.

If the purchase of shares qualifies as a redemption, Max would realize a gain of $165,000 (amount realized $220,000, basis of $55,000). He could account for it on the installment method, and the immediate gain recognized on the sale would be $90,000. (The fraction is 165/220 or 75%; thus, 75% of $120,000 would be immediately taxable.)

If the redemption is treated as a dividend, $100,000 would be net capital gain, $55,000 would be tax free as a recovery of basis, and the balance of $65,000 would be capital gain. Presumably, the net capital gain and capital gain could be taxed by using the installment method of taxation, probably with the net capital gain taxed first, the capital gain later.

Argon cannot recognize its loss on the transfer of the real property. Section 311(b) provides that loss shall not be recognized on property transferred to redeem stock.

B. Suggestions for Improving the Tax Consequences of the Transaction

1. Max should consider not having his stock redeemed. Perhaps, if the other family members want him to give up voting stock, a recapitalization could convert his stock into nonvoting preferred. If he holds his stock until death, he can pass it on to his daughter without any income tax because it will receive a stepped-up basis. If he needs cash, perhaps he might borrow against the stock rather than sell it.

2. If Max insists on selling, he should apply for a private ruling that the redemption qualifies under section 302(b)(1). It is risky to use this section without a ruling, but it seems quite likely that a ruling could be obtained. [*See* Rev. Rul. 75–502]

3. Max should file the agreement described in section 302(c)(2). He qualifies for waiver of family attribution spelled out in section 302(c)(2) because he is giving up all of his interest as an employee and shareholder (he is permitted to retain his interest as a creditor). In the agreement, he promises to notify the IRS if he acquires any such interest for 10 years. Note that section 302(c)(2) waives only family attribution under section 318(a)(1), but all of the stock of the trust and of Taurus Corp. is attributed to Max by family attribution through his daughter; therefore, the chain of attribution can be broken by filing the agreement. The only problem is that Max might have to take over management of Argon if Paul is unable to continue; if he does so, he must notify the IRS and the benefit of section 302(c)(2) would be lost. That is why it is important for Max to qualify under section 302(b)(1). If he does, it would not matter if he had to take over management again.

4. Argon should not use the investment real estate to redeem Max's stock because it cannot recognize the loss on the real estate. It should sell the real estate instead so as to recognize its loss.

ANSWER TO QUESTION V

If the transaction is characterized as a reorganization, the following results occur: Cement, Inc.'s basis for the real property is the same as RaceCo's ($600,000) because of sections 332 and 334(b)(1). RaceCo does not recognize its loss on the transfer of the property. [I.R.C. § 337(a)] Cement, Inc. recognizes no gain or loss on the liquidation of RaceCo. [I.R.C. § 332]

Stan recognizes no loss on the exchange of his stock for stock. When Stan sells his Cement, Inc. stock for $13,200, he has a realized and recognized capital loss of $66,800.

If the transaction is not a reorganization, but instead is a taxable sale, Cement, Inc.'s basis for the land remains $600,000 unless Cement, Inc. foolishly made a section 338 election, in which case the basis of the asset would be reduced to $160,000. Again, RaceCo does not recognize its loss on the real estate. [I.R.C. § 337(a)]

If the sale is taxable, Stan realizes and recognizes his capital loss of $68,000 when he receives the Cement, Inc. stock. The stock has a basis in his hands of its value—$12,000. He has a $1,200 capital gain on the sale of his Cement, Inc. stock for $13,200.

Thus, the key question: Is the transaction a "B" reorganization or a taxable sale? The transaction may qualify as a "B" reorganization. Cement, Inc. acquired control of RaceCo by exchanging solely voting stock for RaceCo stock. However, there are two remaining issues: continuity of interest and continuity of business enterprise.

The continuity of interest requirement is met despite the fact that RaceCo shareholders planned to, and in fact did, unload their stock as rapidly as possible. Under the new continuity of interest regulations, a post-reorganization sale of the newly acquired stock to anyone other than the acquiring corporation or a related party will not defeat continuity. [Treas. Reg. § 1.368–1(e)(1)]

The regulations also require continuity of business enterprise. Treasury Regulation section 1.368–1(d) provides that the acquiring corporation must either continue the acquired corporation's historical business or use a significant portion of its historic business assets. Clearly, Cement, Inc. abandoned the racing business, but it did use the land (without its bleachers) in Cement, Inc.'s business. The contrary argument is that tearing down the bleachers so changed the land that it should not be treated as the same asset. This seems unnecessarily strict, however; it should be sufficient that the land continued to be used for business.

ANSWER TO QUESTION VI

A. Consequences to Jane

Jane has ordinary income of $100,000 in salary. Contributions to the pension plan are not currently taxable. The IRS will argue on four grounds that Law, Inc. should be ignored so that Jane is taxed on Law, Inc.'s entire income.

1. **Ignoring the corporate entity:** It is very difficult for either the IRS or the taxpayer to argue successfully that a corporate entity should be ignored. If a corporation conducts any business activities, its entity will be respected. Because Law, Inc. performs billing services and adopted a pension plan in corporate form, its entity should be respected. The IRS's attempt to treat professional corporations differently from other corporations has long since been abandoned.

2. **Form-substance approach:** Jane should be treated as the earner of the income. It can be argued that, in substance, Jane is working for herself, even though in form she is working for Law, Inc. It is very significant that there is no employment agreement between Law, Inc. and Jane, nor is Jane bound to work exclusively for Law, Inc. Clients are not told in advance that they have hired Law, Inc. to perform services for them. Law, Inc. appears to hold no property other than cash and stocks and does not even have an office. No formal documents evidence the transfer of the legal practice to the corporation. Aside from sending bills, Law, Inc. is insufficiently involved in the relationship between Jane and her customers, and the IRS will probably succeed in this argument.

3. **Assignment of income:** If the argument in the previous paragraph is not accepted, the IRS might argue that traditional income-splitting principles apply. Under *Lucas v. Earl,* service income is taxed to the person who does the work, not to an assignee of that income. However, the IRS has not been successful in pushing this argument in the personal service corporation context, because it produces a result identical to ignoring the corporate entity. Because there is a more precise tool for coping with the problem (*see* the next paragraph), the assignment of income approach has been rejected.

4. **Section 482:** The IRS has had mixed success in using section 482 in this situation. The theory is that Jane and Law, Inc. are treated as commonly controlled businesses; the IRS can allocate income between them in order to clearly reflect income. Because Law, Inc. contributed nothing to the earning of income and Jane contributed everything to the earning of income, she should be allocated as income the entire amount of income generated by her services. Note that *Fogelsong* rejected this theory, but *Haag* accepted it.

5. **Pension plan:** It follows that Jane should be taxed on all of the $300,000 her efforts produced under either section 482 or the form-substance approach. It is not clear whether the corporate contributions to the pension plan could be treated as if made by Jane personally. If so, the pension plan could be treated as a Keogh plan. The limit on the amount deductible is the same as for a corporate profit-sharing plan.

B. **Tax Consequences to Law, Inc.**

1. **Jane as income earner:** A number of tax consequences have already been spelled out. If Jane is treated as the earner of the income, either under a form-substance approach or under section 482, Law, Inc. will not be taxed on the income earned by Jane and will have no deductions attributable to her. Also, the corporation is entitled to deduct 70% of the dividends received by it. [I.R.C. § 243]

2. **Accumulated earnings tax:** If its income is taxed to it rather than to Jane, Law, Inc. is subject to the accumulated earnings tax. It indicates no reason for the substantial accumulation of assets that it has invested in publicly traded stocks. These amounts could readily have been paid out as dividends. Thus Law, Inc. seems to fail the test of sections 532 and 533: it has allowed its earnings to accumulate beyond its reasonable needs and therefore has been formed or availed of for the purpose of tax avoidance. Its taxable income ($125,000 from interest, plus whatever amounts of Jane's earnings are taxed to it) would be reduced only by its taxes paid and its compensation deductions.

   It is not entitled to any "minimum credit" under section 535(c)(2). This credit is usually $250,000 but is only $150,000 in the case of corporations that provide professional services. Because its accumulated earnings and profits of $160,000 at the beginning of Year 1 are more than $150,000, it gets no minimum credit. It might be argued that if section 482 is applied to previous years, Law, Inc.'s earnings and profits should be reduced to reflect the fact that it is not taxed on Jane's previous earnings. In that case, it might well be entitled to a minimum credit. The accumulated earnings tax is 15% on accumulated taxable income.

3. **Personal holding company:** Even worse, Law, Inc. may be a personal holding company ("PHC"), in which case it is excused from the accumulated earnings tax. More than 50% of its stock is owned by five or fewer individuals. The dividend income is PHC income. The service income (assuming it is taxed to Law, Inc.) is probably not PHC income. Under section 543(a)(7), amounts received under contracts to furnish personal services are PHC income if an outsider has the right to designate the individual who is to perform the services and that individual holds 25% of the outstanding stock. Therefore, amounts generated by Jane are potentially PHC income. However, in the case of one-person

professional corporations, the IRS has essentially ruled that the PHC tax is inapplicable. It held the income is not PHC income unless the client can prevent the substitution of another individual in place of the shareholder-employee of the corporation or that person is so unique that there are no substitutes. [Rev. Rul. 75–67] Because there is no contractual prohibition on the substitution of anyone else for Jane, the IRS will probably not argue that the service income is PHC income. If all the service income is taxed to Law, Inc., it is not a PHC because the dividend income (the only PHC income) is not 60% of its adjusted ordinary gross income. But if all the service income is taxed to Jane, Law. Inc. is a PHC and is subject to the 50% PHC tax (but not the accumulated earnings tax).

ANSWER TO QUESTION VII

The original incorporation clearly qualified as a nonrecognition exchange under section 351 because Jay transferred property in exchange for shares giving him control of Peachco. Consequently, the basis of Jay's shares was $95,000. The basis of Brenda's shares would be 20% of Jay's basis ($19,000).

A. Consequences to Brenda—Redemption vs. Dividend

1. **Consequences of alternative treatments of transaction:** If the transaction with Brenda is a redemption, not qualified dividend income (from a domestic corporation), she has a realized loss of $7,000 ($19,000 basis less $12,000 value of orchard). This is not ordinary loss by virtue of section 1244 because that section applies only to original issues of stock. [Treas. Reg. § 1.1244(a)–1(b)] Instead, Brenda has a long-term capital loss of $7,000 (unless it is treated as a dividend).

   If the transaction is treated as a dividend, not a redemption, Brenda has a $12,000 dividend, taxable as net capital gain (no basis recovery and it cannot be offset with capital losses). The basis of her shares would be used to increase Jay's basis for his shares.

   Either way, Brenda's basis for the orchard is $12,000.

2. **Treatment under section 302(b)(3):** Jay's shares, but not Abby's, are attributed to Brenda under section 318(a)(1), and so the termination is not complete. However, the waiver of attribution provision of section 302(c)(2) may be applicable. If it is, it removes family attribution so the redemption is treated as a complete termination.

   The requirement under section 302(c)(2) that Brenda entirely withdraw from management is met; she must also file an agreement to notify the IRS if she does get involved in the corporation during the next 10 years. Section 302(c)(2) is inapplicable, however, if the distributee has acquired shares from someone from whom stock is attributed during the 10-year period immediately preceding the redemption. Brenda has done so. But this requirement is waived if the acquisition did not have tax avoidance as a principal purpose. Here two purposes are given—diversification of management and income splitting. As the latter is income tax avoidance, it would appear that the section 302(c)(2) waiver provision is inapplicable. Thus, this is not a section 302(b)(3) complete termination.

3. **Treatment under section 302(b)(2):** Immediately before the redemption, Brenda owned 80% of the stock. Afterwards, she owns 75% (60 of 80 shares). Thus, she meets neither the 80% nor the 50% test of section 302(b)(2).

4. **Treatment under section 302(b)(1):** Under *Davis,* the test of "essentially equivalent to a dividend" focuses on "meaningful reduction" in interest. In all likelihood, a reduction from 80% to 75% is not meaningful because it continues to represent corporate control.

Under *Haft Trust,* attribution is not mandatory under section 302(b)(1) if it is belied by the facts. Here, Brenda and Jay are quarreling, and so attribution is contrary to realities. However, the *Metzger* decision disagrees with *Haft Trust.* If *Haft Trust* is applied, attribution is improper for purposes of section 302(b) (1), and the redemption is not essentially equivalent to a dividend.

5. **Treatment under section 302(b)(4):** Brenda has exchange treatment under section 302(b)(4) as a partial liquidation if the distribution represents a "corporate contraction," which arguably it does. It could be argued that Peachco is scaling down its orchard operations by this distribution. Moreover, the orchard meets the mechanical test of section 302(e)(2)—it was actively conducted for five years and the corporation continues to carry on an active trade or business. Thus, the distribution is a partial liquidation.

B. Consequences to Peachco—Repurchase Transaction

Distributions in redemption or partial liquidation are treated as realizing transactions to the corporation. [I.R.C. § 311(b)]

Depreciation must be recaptured by Peachco under section 1245 on the distribution. Here, the amount recaptured as ordinary income would be $6,000. The remaining $2,000 of gain is taxed under I.R.C. section 1231.

ANSWER TO QUESTION VIII

A. Consequences of Year 1 Incorporation to Shareholders

1. **Consequences to Violet:** Violet's exchange of assets for the note plus the stock will be fully taxable unless she qualifies under section 351, which requires that the transferors of property have 80% of the voting stock. The stock issued to Sonny counts as stock issued to Violet. However, the stock issued to Burns purely for services was 30% of the total. If the transfer to Burns is considered part of the same transaction in which Violet and Sonny got their stock, Violet is disqualified, because the transferors of property would have received only 70% of the stock. On the other hand, if Ray's transfer is included with that of Violet and Burns, Burns would have received only 150 of 800 shares and the transferors of property (Violet and Ray) would have received more than 80% of the total. The general rule is that all transfers will be treated as a single transaction if they are interdependent. In other words, if none would have been made unless all were made, all should be viewed together even though split up by several months. In light of the explanation of Violet's activities in the first paragraph of the problem, it is likely that all three transfers will be viewed together so that the transferors of the property did receive control of the corporation.

Violet's gain is recognized in part because she received a $10,000 note, which is treated as boot. The boot must be allocated between the assets—20% to cash (no gain), 8% to receivables ($800 ordinary income), 14% to machines ($1,400 of ordinary income because of section 1245), and 58% to goodwill ($5,800 of capital gain). Thus she recognized $2,200 of ordinary income and $5,800 of capital gain. [*See* Rev. Rul. 68–55]

If the debt is treated as equity, Violet recognized no gain. However, the note would probably be treated as debt, not equity, because the holdings of stock and debt are not proportional and the debt-equity ratio is low.

Under section 357(c), the accounts payable are ignored, both as boot and as a reduction of Violet's basis because it is a cash basis partnership and the debts were accounts payable, not used to increase the basis of any asset.

Violet's basis for her debt is $10,000. The basis for her stock (ignoring the transfer to Sonny for a moment) is $30,000; her old basis ($32,000), plus gain recognized ($8,000), less boot received ($10,000). Then the basis is allocated proportionately between Violet's stock and Sonny's (70% or $21,000 to Violet, 30% or $9,000 to Sonny).

2. **Consequences to Sonny:** Sonny received his shares as a gift, and they are excluded from income under section 102. Since no gift tax was paid, he cannot increase his basis above $9,000 by reason of section 1015(d).

3. **Consequences to Burns:** Stock for services is taxable as ordinary income. Burns has $15,000 of ordinary income. The basis of his shares is $15,000.

4. **Consequences to Ray:** As discussed, Ray's transaction is probably counted as part of the single integrated incorporation transaction. Consequently, he cannot recognize his realized loss of $25,000. The basis of his stock is $55,000.

B. Tanbod, Inc.'s Basis

Tanbod's basis for Wasteland is $35,000 because the transaction was covered by section 351. Tanbod's basis for assets received from Violet must be increased by gain recognized: receivables $8,800, machines $13,400, and goodwill $5,800.

C. Year 2 Bankruptcy

1. **Violet's debt:** Because the $10,000 debt has a $10,000 basis, Violet has a nonbusiness bad debt (short-term capital loss) of $10,000. No showing of any facts suggests it is other than an investment under *Whipple* and *Generes*.

2. **Violet's stock:** This stock qualifies as 1244 stock. Thus, Violet has ordinary loss of $21,000.

3. **Sonny's stock:** Section 1244 applies only to an original issue of stock, and it is likely this stock would be treated as going to Violet and not directly to Sonny. Even if it did go directly to Sonny, section 1244 requires a contribution of money or property, and this stock was issued gratuitously. Thus, Sonny does not qualify under section 1244 and has a $9,000 long-term capital loss.

4. **Burns's stock:** Burns did not contribute money or other property for his stock; thus, it is not 1244 stock. He also has a $15,000 long-term capital loss.

5. **Ray's stock:** Ray has $35,000 in ordinary loss because of section 1244.

ANSWER TO QUESTION IX

a. No. A partnership must use the taxable years of all of its principal partners unless it obtains the Commissioner's permission to use a different year. [I.R.C. § 706(b)(1)(B)]

b. No. Under *Campbell* and Rev. Proc. 93–27, the profits interest is not taxed when received.

c. A partnership takes over the contributing partner's basis for the asset ($40,000) when the asset is contributed for a partnership interest. [I.R.C. § 723]

A partner's basis is increased by his share of partnership liabilities. However, when a partnership takes over a partner's liability, this is treated the same as a distribution of cash. [I.R.C. § 752(a), (b)] Thus Fab Corp.'s basis for its interest is $25,000. This is computed by taking the basis for the building ($40,000) plus $15,000 (Fab Corp.'s one-half share of the partnership liability) less $30,000 (the liability of which Fab Corp. was relieved).

Art's basis is zero (assuming, under paragraph b., above, that he is not taxed on receipt of his interest) plus one-half of his share of the liability, or $15,000. [I.R.C. § 752(a)] In the case of a nonrecourse loan in a limited partnership, both limited and general partners share the liability in accordance with their profit sharing ratio for purposes of increasing basis (until such time as there is minimum gain).

d. The salary is a guaranteed payment, which is ordinary income to Art and deductible by Stretchco. [I.R.C. § 707(c)] This makes Stretchco's operating loss $33,000 in 2010. Fab Corp. can deduct its one-half of this loss ($16,500), which reduces its basis from $25,000 to $8,500. [I.R.C. § 705(b)(2)] Under the passive loss rules, Fab Corp. can deduct Stretchco's loss against its net active income but not its investment income. [I.R.C. § 469(a)(2)(B), (e)(2)] Art cannot deduct the entire loss. His basis is only $15,000. He can deduct $15,000, reducing his basis to zero. The remaining $1,500 of the loss is not currently deductible. [I.R.C. § 704(d)] Art materially participated in operating Stretchco and so is not limited by the passive loss rules. [I.R.C. § 469(c)]

e. The estate's basis for the stock is stepped up to $17,000—its value at the date of death. [I.R.C. § 1014(a)] Consequently, the estate has no gain or loss on the sale. The partnership taxable year does not close on Art's death, but it does close on the sale of his interest to Fab Corp. [I.R.C. §§ 708(b), 706(c)(1)]

Table of Cases

Tables

Table of Code Sections

Table of Revenue Rulings